Inventing
BE

BE ALINK

CONTENTS

I reside, as an uninvited visitor on the unceded (stolen) Traditional Coast Salish Lands including the Squamish (Sḵwx̱wú7mesh Úxwumixw), Tsleil-Waututh (səlilwəta?ɬ) and Musqueam (xʷməθkʷəy̓əm) Nations currently called Vancouver, Canada, and it is my work to become a welcome visitor on these lands. We cannot undo the past, but it is our collective responsibility to acknowledge our collective conditioning, decolonize ourselves so we can be present to and build a future together, anchored in values of reciprocity, regeneration, respect and love. Leaving our mother earth and our collective community livable and hopeful, built with love and respect for all living beings, for many generations to come.

ADVANCE PRAISE FOR
INVENTING BE

"I met BE through her invention, the Alinker. And to meet BE is to
love BE, as that is what you feel in her presence. Unfailingly human,
the best of the best, BE invites us all into this book, the memoir of an
incredible life told in adventures of world travel. And with compassion
and truth, we see the greatest creation of her life so far, living in
the freedom of being BE. I love this human, and I think you will too.
Gorgeous writing pulled me in straight away, the perfect companion."

—Selma Blair, Actress and Author

"I've had the pleasure of reading a chapter of *Inventing BE* during
her time in Afghanistan. I first met BE in Jalalabad, Afghanistan,
during a consulting stint I was doing on Afghan craft, embroidery
and the importance of women's education. I took a shine to her bold
and unapologetically authentic personality and the ease that she
navigated Afghan society wearing men's clothes working with locals
in a manner that gained my trust immediately. She was there to work
with and for the people. She treated locals as equal and with genuine
love and kindness and I was thrilled to read that the love and respect
was reciprocated by people she encountered in Afghanistan during
some of the most challenging times in Afghan society. For people that
live on the periphery of society standards and having a nomadic soul
that fits in everywhere yet always stands out shockingly in the binary
frame of Western existence, it was refreshing to see her navigate
at ease in a way that wasn't so simple for any expats living in a war
zone. I cannot wait to read the book at its entirety and savor every
experience vicariously through BE's amazing storytelling. A life that
has found its purpose and has realized that we are here to service our

fellow humans should be celebrated and recognized, and I'm looking forward to seeing this book become a staple in everyone's reading lists and libraries."

—Matin Maulawizada, Makeup Artist

"The only thing more important than reinvention—and sometimes radical reinvention—is invention. BE Alink has mastered it. She rises above traditional definitions of diversity and inclusion, spreading her colorful wings into true belonging and helping others get there. As she says, invention is for the brave, not faint, of heart!"

—Maureen Lippe, Media Powerhouse/Entrepreneur, former *Vogue* and *Harper's Bazaar* Editor, and Author of *Radical Reinvention*

"BE is a really remarkable person, who has demonstrated from Amsterdam to Afghanistan, extraordinary ingenuity, resilience creatively and generosity of spirit."

 —Rory Stewart, Author and Founder of Turquoise Mountain Foundation, Afghanistan

"I worked with BE (then Babs) during her international career and often wondered how she was able to achieve all she did in such difficult places at such difficult times. More than once, I found myself asking, 'Who is this person?' This book allowed me to better answer that question by reading how she developed the strong will and mental attitude, which she applied to the difficulties she faced. Her writing gave me a better understanding of not only who she is but also, how she became that fearless humanitarian who, when faced with overwhelming challenges and frustrations, persevered. I was also able to see how she developed and then maintained the amazing level of empathy for those most marginalized, to whom she dedicated her life's work, and which came to define her. I enjoyed the flow of the book and while there was a seriousness to the message, I still found it funny and entertaining along the way. Her book also reminded me of times when I was faced with a risky activity in a dangerous place but that really needed to be done, and I had just two options. I could try and find a team of 'battle hardened, fearless, tough-as-nails, ex-military special forces SOB types…or…I could send in Babs."

—Gary Helseth, former UNOPS Country Director, Afghanistan

"BE Alink has remarkable gifts: storytelling in the most natural, evocative way that comes with a blanket and fireplace, so you stay till the end, altruism that took her all over the world to help in crisis, design skills that led to the storied Alinker, and the courage of a warrior to align her body with her soul. She is a remarkable invention we can all learn from."

—Marcia-Elizabeth C. Favale, Tech Entrepreneur and Inventor, and Author of *Leading Innovation and Inclusion* and *Risk, Recovery, and Empowerment: The Kazakhstan Bank Recovery Case Study*

"*Inventing BE* is a story a person finding their oneness in community with others. Yet, it is a deeper story of how to (re)create ways of being with/as each other that can heal us, while dismantling social structures that seek to separate us from our authentic selves and from each other. *Inventing BE* shows us the joy in connecting and it is only through connection that we can be free."

—Dr. Elizabeth (Dori) Tunstall, author of *Decolonizing Design: a Cultural Justice Guidebook*, and Lead Executive Officer, Dori Tunstall, Inc.

"It's possible to love a book and not know much about the person behind it. When you love a book and the person who wrote it, you've got a double bonus. When you love a book, the person who wrote it, *and* you know the impact it is going to have on countless people, you have a perfect trifecta. I've known BE for more than ten years. I've watched as she has *Invented BE*—discovering peace and power in the being she was created to BE. She is, quite simply, an extraordinary human being with a heart focused on making life better for people and the planet. It is a privilege to be her friend. This book is a beacon of light and truth for people who have walked the same path, who are walking the path now, or those who desire to understand the path others walk. The world needs this book!"

—Ginny Dye, Bestselling Author of *The Bregdan Chronicles*

"*Inventing BE* invites us on a journey of empathy sharing helplessness, hopefulness, honesty and heart. Alink confronts the harsh realities of societal expectations while encouraging readers to embrace their authentic selves, no matter how far that journey takes them. This book will resonate with anyone who wants to be inspired to disrupt the status quo."

—Melanie Mark, HLI HAYKWHL W̓II XSGAAK- Retired MLA Vancouver- Mount Pleasant| BC Cabinet Minister| CEO and Founder, HLI HAYKWHL W̓II X SGAAK Consulting & Remarkable First Nations Regenerative Industries

"I just started reading *Inventing BE*, and it immediately offers a powerful and introspective look at identity, resilience, and the process of reinventing oneself. BE Alink's story is inspiring and thought-provoking, especially for those on a path of self-discovery. As someone who uses the Alinker, I find her reflections on living authentically deeply resonant. The Alinker has empowered me to embrace my disability and stay connected with my surroundings in ways I hadn't imagined. This book invites readers to challenge conventional ideas of being, pushing toward a fuller understanding of how we connect with ourselves and the world."

—Frances "Franco" Stevens, Founder of *Curve* magazine

"BE's unique perspective takes us on a fascinating journey to distant cultures and has us experience humanity at the edges. From that vantage point BE crafts her way into inventions that address how people want to live; with dignity, with care and with hope."

—Vicki Saunders, Founder of Coralus

"I was completely transfixed by this book. BE has a story that takes my breath away and a way of telling it that made me feel like I was sitting around a fire listening to a storyteller of the ages."

—Lorna Davis, former Corporate CEO and TED speaker

"*Inventing BE* is a deeply moving and unforgettable story of finding the courage to embrace who you truly are. BE Alink's journey is one of resilience, love, and discovery, reminding us that even in the hardest moments, there is light waiting to be found. Her memoir and manifesto speak straight to the heart, offering comfort to anyone who has ever felt out of place or misunderstood. BE's story reminds us that we are never truly alone, and sometimes, the most unexpected paths lead us to where we're meant to be—home within ourselves."

—Melina Guglielmo, Director of the Board, Alinker Inventions

"BE embodies the energy of compassion, love, and respect for all humanity. Over the nearly ten years since we met, we have had many conversations about what it means to live authentically, to thrive outside the boxes that are woven into societal norms—in other words how to just BE—be anything and all that you are, to be limitless. BE exemplifies growth and the expansion of what it means to be human and has given me the courage to be fearless, to explore my own reinvention. I can't wait to read *Inventing BE* for the wisdom on steroids that I have come to rely on from one of the most profoundly original people I have ever known."

—MaryAnne Howland, Founder, Ibis Communications & Global Diversity Leadership Exchange

"This is the best possible invitation to be curious about what can happen when we all release the attachments and just BE."

—Amanda Upson, Producer, Tuck and Roll Productions, Attorney, Advocate, Polymath

"Inventing BE stirs the soul. Be ready to be taken on a journey of deep adventure, reflection, courage and love. BE takes us on an exhilarating adventure behind many closed doors that you only get invited through when you fully see the potential in everyone around you including yourself. This book should come with a warning. Beware: You may finally get to see who you are in this world."

—Tania Lo, Founder, Tandem Innovations, and Business Partner, The Alinker

ACKNOWLEDGMENTS

Twenty-five years ago, I discovered that I like writing. I was in Kenya, in the School for the Deaf in Rongo, on my first laptop, a 'brick', no Internet and barely electricity. I wrote many newsletters from foreign countries to my friends at home to keep them abreast with views from another world. While in Argentina in 2006, I wrote to get things out of my system after ten years of international work, and I learned that writing has healing capacities. Over the years, writing happened in waves; it changed from writing for me, to writing with a purpose, for others to read.

Last year, I gathered all my writings from the last twenty-five years. I had dreams about publishing this book, but it seemed an insurmountable task to select and structure all these writings, of all the experiences grown into philosophies and life's practices into a book that would have purpose and is interesting for you to read. I had nearly given up on ever publishing, but thanks to Jen Grace of Publish Your Purpose, who introduced me to my brilliant editor, Candi S. Cross, we were able to find the storylines, the red threads and the purpose of sharing it with you. By no means is this book a full account of all the experiences that now live inside of me as memories, as ingredients and nutrients for how I view the world and my role in it; rather, we have selected stories that give background and illustrate my perspective on the importance of us being alive, right now, this moment in time, on this planet. Let me take you on an unusual journey, I hope an experience that will change you, as it has shaped me.

I have been so lucky to have met so many incredible people in all the places around the world where I had the privilege to live and work. Places that taught me deeply what it is to be an uninvited visitor on lands that are not my native lands, cultures so different than how I was

1

raised. I have always made it my work, my responsibility to become a welcome visitor, wherever I was. The more I lived with people of all cultures, the more I learned that we are far more similar than different.

Many of these people have been my teachers who generously shared their heart and soul with me, their food and homes, shared grief, anger and sorrow, and shared joy and love. Many people I would like to thank have passed into other realms, though very present in my life always. My deep gratitude for your teachings, wisdom and love, ongoingly from the beyond, I can feel you.

I am deeply grateful to all my teachers and you for reading this. I hope this book is a window into a greater collective awareness about who we are in this time here on this planet. This is the time, we have a collective responsibility for who we are, shaping the present, to have a future that is based on respect for all living beings.

I am hoping that this book in an active read that leads to conversations, a connector that brings us together in our shared experiences of being human, to see what we have been taught, remember who we truly are, and liberate our deep knowing. Let me take you on this unusual journey and enjoy. After you read it, let's connect.

—With all my love, BE

FOREWORD

It is with deep admiration and joy that I write this foreword
for *Inventing BE*. I first met BE Alink at the B Corp Champion's
Retreat, where a chance moment of shared frustration led to an
unexpected connection. We had just gotten off a shuttle bus only
to find ourselves at an old monument building in Philadelphia that
was completely inaccessible. As I stood there, upset at the lack of
proper accommodations, I noticed BE, who, without missing a beat,
was carrying her Alinker mobility device up the stairs. The image of
BE handling that situation with such resilience and grace struck me
deeply, and it sparked a conversation that not only introduced me to
her extraordinary invention but also, to the incredible person behind it.

This moment embodies so much of what BE and this book are
about—facing barriers with ingenuity, pushing against systems that
exclude, and creating something new where there are gaps. BE's
journey is not just about solving problems but about reshaping the
very way we approach inclusivity and accessibility, themes that
resonate deeply within the B Corp community, where a shared
passion of ours lies. In the B Corp community, we often speak about
"Business as a Force for Good". This shared commitment binds us,
but within this collective, there are individuals like BE who elevate this
mission to a higher level. BE's journey, as recounted in these pages,
is not just a personal story; it is a call to action, an invitation to rethink
how we design our lives, our work, and our society. BE has crafted
an extraordinary example of how business and personal integrity can
align to create a profound sense of belonging and inclusion for those
who often feel unseen.

BE's Alinker is much more than a mobility device. It is a reflection
of BE's heart and soul, designed for people to feel empowered, to

move through life with dignity, and to be fully seen for who she is, rather than defined by her limitations. The creation of the Alinker, much like this book, stems from a philosophy that insists on reimagining the systems around us—systems that have long failed to accommodate or include everyone. This book takes us on a deeply personal and philosophical journey, one where the concept of "fitting in" is rightfully discarded in favor of simply being, as BE so eloquently conveys.

The title, *Inventing BE*, is both literal and symbolic. BE's life and work have been about invention, not only in the traditional sense of creating something new but also, in the more profound sense of creating space for oneself in a world that doesn't always make it easy. BE's path is one of constant reinvention, of finding ways to live fully and authentically in a society that often resists that kind of honesty. And in that, BE's journey is one that so many of us in the B Corp community resonate with—a journey toward purpose, authenticity, and impact. It is impossible to talk about *Inventing BE* without acknowledging the importance of community. BE's story is not a solo venture but a collective one, shaped by the many people, experiences, and places that have been an influence along the way. This mirrors much of what we value within the B Corp movement—the belief that we are stronger, more impactful, and more resilient when we work together. BE's story reminds us that even when the world seems vast and isolating, community, empathy, and shared purpose are the threads that tie us back to one another.

BE and I have found common ground in our shared passion for pushing boundaries, for asking difficult questions, and for standing firmly in the belief that business can, and must, be a force for good. BE's work is a reflection of the best parts of this community: innovation, empathy, and a relentless drive to improve the systems that govern our lives. But what stands out most about BE is the spirit in which she approaches every challenge with an open heart and a determined spirit.

4

As a leader in the B Corp community, I have witnessed firsthand how BE's work has inspired others. The Alinker has transformed lives—not just through its functionality but through the sense of belonging it provides to those who use it. It is a reminder that true innovation lies in the ability to see and solve problems that others overlook. BE sees people, truly sees them, in a way that is rare and invaluable.*Inventing BE* is much like its author—bold, unfiltered, and deeply connected to the truth of our shared humanity. It invites readers to explore the boundaries of identity, purpose, and belonging, while also serving as a guide for anyone who has ever felt out of place in a world that demands conformity. BE's journey is not just one of personal discovery, but a call for all of us to reexamine how we see and support one another in our own journeys. In these pages, BE takes us from the personal to the universal, showing us how the lessons she has learned—through loss, triumph, struggle, and love—apply to all of us, whether we are leaders, creators, or simply fellow travelers on this path of life. This book is a gift, not only because of the wisdom it contains but because of the heart behind it. It is a work of love, courage, and deep empathy, and it will undoubtedly inspire anyone who reads it to live more authentically and to connect more deeply with those around them.

I am honored to be part of BE's community and to share this journey. I encourage you, dear reader, to not just read *Inventing BE*, but to allow it to transform the way you see the world and your place in it. Let BE's story inspire you to be more compassionate, more curious, and more willing to invent yourself anew.

With deep respect and gratitude,

Jenn T. Grace (she/her)
Founder and CEO, Publish Your Purpose
Co-Founder & Board Chair, B Local Connecticut

Introduction
SENSING AND FEELING

I was five, maybe six years old, rushing into the house with a skinned knee. "Mum, I hurt myself, my knee is bleeding, feel how much it hurts."

My mother said, "Come here, I'll pick you up." As I got up, I felt tricked; it wasn't what I needed, but more strongly, I wanted her to feel what I felt. Since I was a little me, I've always wanted others to actually feel what I felt and got frustrated when I couldn't ensure this.

My grandma taught me a practice, sitting at her kitchen table with an old newspaper spread out, snapping the peas we picked from her garden. She said, "Every day, choose a person who is not like you—choose them based on how different they are from you—then borrow their shoes. Walk in their shoes for a bit, imagine what they see, what they feel."

Through metaphors and parallels, imagination, storytelling, and empathy, she taught me that I could come close to sharing what I felt and to feel what someone else was experiencing. I learned that feelings were universal. I learned that emotions were feelings with attachments, the feelings pure, the attachments what causes suffering.

Growing up, I felt often lonely. I did not fit in, I was different, there was no one like me, no examples or people as role models, so over the years, I invented myself and had to define who I am in this binary world. Because I did not fit, the conditioning for a boy or girl did not rub off on me. *N/A.* Not applicable! My perspective on systems, and who people are within these systems, is from an external place.

People often say, "BE, you really think outside of the box," and I think, *what box?*

I am on a continued quest to invent me, BE, in this evolving world. This is not an easy time to be alive, yet we are here for a reason. Who am I in a world that has no space or interest for people who are different and therefore, uncomfortable for the establishment?

I incorporated the Alinker, my company, in 2012, and find myself in the role of CEO, with a product that is designed for the experience of the user, to support wellness, quality of life and the sense of belonging in a world where disability is seen as a burden, and people with disabilities are discarded. Who am I as a leader of what is becoming a movement, a place where people feel seen and acknowledged? How is the company a reflection of all that I have learned, and how has the Alinker, in turn, become a teacher for me to further evolve in this world where everything is focused on solving problems? Though these are not problems to fix—none of them—I have learned through the teachings of my father and grandmother, to see them as symptoms of a system that is designed to make money, that even has healthcare turned into an industry of needing sick people to make profits.

I want to take you on this journey, an unusual story, through many countries. I want to introduce you to characters who are all me, me through different phases of my life when I responded to different names, through various explorations to piece together my existence in this Western world that is not welcoming people who don't fit the mould. This is a story for all of us who have questioned our worthiness as we struggled to fit in, trying to fit in a construct that excludes you by design. The feeling of being dismissed is mutual. *Enough.* Let's create new language and tools, to understand ourselves better, and flip things around to become aware of the conditioning and how deeply the system is ingrained in us, as we endeavor to re-member who we are, what our souls resonate with. Become aware that there is nothing wrong with us as diverse people despite previous notions that difference is a threat and needs to be isolated and eradicated.

Not for the faint of, but for the brave of, heart, in these pages, I am challenging the sense of reality, including experiences in this realm, dreams, visions during plant medicine excursions, and other experiences of altered states. One is not more real than the other. These are a diverse selection of my life experiences, teachers on a path to wholeness.

As a white person, female-assigned at birth, born and raised in the Netherlands, I left everything that was familiar, to find my purpose for being on this planet, Mother Earth, at this incredible moment in time. My journey to *Inventing BE, a true awakening,* started in Afghanistan mid-2001. September 11th had just happened and the whole world was suddenly aware of Afghanistan, the Taliban, and the state of women's rights in the Islamic nation.

At first blush, this may sound like an uncanny place for you, along with others I've tread, but they allowed BE to form and flourish. In my story, I invite you to be curious and open. Come with me...

—BE Alink

PART I.
WHO AM I?

Chapter I

CLOSE YOUR EYES

It is summer and excruciatingly hot, well over 50 degrees Celsius in Jalalabad, a city of 300,000 in eastern Afghanistan. I am apprehensive about the huge job ahead of me. To top it off, I have barely set up my office, and I am recovering from a hysterectomy. Despite this, I find myself filled with anticipation and wonder—the thrill of being in a country where everything is different from what I've previously known.

We jump out of the cars just outside the village. You cannot get any further by car. People walk. I am wearing the androgynous *salwar kameez*, or traditional dress, that the local tailor made for me. This is the first meeting I have with the women in the village, and we are supposed to make a list of the "most deserving" people of our resources to rebuild their homes. Scanning the village as we enter, I surmise that everyone would qualify. I wonder, *who the hell am I, to just walk as a complete stranger into a village, with the expectation to compile a list of most deserving families, a list of beneficiaries for my fancy project, designed from behind a desk in Europe? Who am I to be here?* What a concept, a Western idea for a project to benefit locals—I feel the arrogance.

As we proceed toward the village, a woman with a beautiful, weathered face approaches me. Her mesmerizing eyes, green blueish like others in this region, distinguish her as a *Chinoo*. I acquired the same nickname soon after I arrived.

The woman wears a scarf lightly wrapped around her hair, as I have noticed older women wear them more loosely, sometimes even just over their shoulders. She walks barefoot, walks slowly, and has not taken her eyes of me. My eyes are locked with hers. There is

13

something. I am wondering. I halt and she stands in front of me, a wee bit closer than I expect any stranger to be at a first encounter. She looks at me, I look at her. There is a kindness permeating the space. The pause, before she starts speaking, is also a wee bit longer than in any first encounter with a stranger.

She looks down as she reaches for my hand. Our hands connect, she holds my hand, I feel the years of life on her skin, and she puts her other hand on top of the back of my hand. Her head tilts back up and she looks me back in my eyes. I am not sure what is happening but feel myself completely surrendering to the moment. I could be blindfolded and fall back into the arms of this enigmatic being Noorzia translates, "She says, I see you are wondering." The woman continues. Noorzia translates, "I see you are wondering who you are, as you walk into my village. You think you're this *kharidji* (foreigner) who comes to do a project here, and you think I am this poor, old woman who has never left her village." The translations are crappy; Noorzia's English is what she learned from her brother during the Taliban years when she was locked up at home. But I comprehend the gist of what she says. Yes! I am wondering, for sure! She says, 'I would like to invite you to my house, and then we meet again."

In Afghanistan, I quickly learn that the plans we make, always change. We follow her to her house; she is still holding my hand. The village has a lot of ruins, mud walls eroded, damaged, and between the ruins are little houses with small courtyards. A nan (flatbread) oven in the corner, some chickens, and goats here and there.

She moves the cloth in the doorway aside and we enter her eroded mudbrick house that has no roof; the aroma of green tea and cardamom welcomes us. She waves her hand down, gesturing us to sit down. We are in a small living room, with *toshaks* (flat mattresses) against all the walls, between the toshaks a vinyl cloth with cups and little bowls with nuts and dried mulberries. We sit down and she retrieves a pot of tea from behind a wall. It feels like she had expected

14

us. We had announced our visit to Samarkhyel to meet with the women shura, so maybe she had planned to invite us?

She sits down and pours the green tea, not looking at us, not saying anything.

She sits back, takes a sip of her tea, and says, "I would like to invite you to close your eyes, and keep them closed until I ask you to open them." We look at each other and somehow, I feel completely at ease, surrendered to whatever is going to happen now.

I close my eyes.

She coos, "I am closing my eyes as well." I am assuming Noorzia has too.

"Now we meet again," she invokes. I am just feeling all the sensations in my body, catching thoughts, and abandoning them again, just trying to be present in this unusual place, with a stranger, and my eyes closed. Her gentle voice continues, "When we have our eyes closed, we can see better, when we see with our eyes, we are distracted from who we are."

I want tea. My mouth fizzes with desire for the sacred taste. I feel the challenge to keep my eyes closed. I feel into the sensory world and open up to all that I can see without my eyes. My hand is finding my teacup in front of me. I find it without knocking it over, rotating it to pick it up by the ear. Slowly, I bring it to my mouth not to spill it and I take a sip. I put it back in front of me, safely.

As she talks, I notice that I pay less attention to the bare translations of Noorzia but start hearing what she says. Not literally, but it is strange, I somehow understand what she says.

She asks, "Now, are you the kharidji who is here to do a project, and am I the old woman who has never left her village?" A long pause, a silence, as the question is suspended in a vast universe behind my eyes. "Who are you now... who am I now..." interspersed with long pauses between her suspended questions.

We sit for minutes without words. Minutes, hours, days, who knows, I feel timeless and expanded. She breaks the silence and asserts in a stronger tone, "Who you think you are, is not who you are. Who you think I am is not who I am."

And back into a long-suspended silence. I hear some kids playing outside, a goat bleating, trucks in the far distance. I want to take another sip from my tea, but refrain from it, as it seems to interrupt the non-material world I have entered. I sit cross-legged and change up my position to not have my leg go numb. Deeper relaxation takes hold.

Random thoughts come up about the meeting we were supposed to have, and I dismiss them as pesky intrusions. Some words start forming in my head, small sentences, nearly like a mantra. It repeats and I am taken aback by feeling so overwhelmed. Tears escape the corners of my eyes as the voice in my head repeats, "We are all one, we are all one, we are all…"

I sink deeper and deeper into the world where I feel I have access to a huge expansion. The top of my eyeballs tingle. I have never felt this weird sensation because it is in my head. My breathing is shallow. Oxygen seems irrelevant on this plane.

After some time, she says, "I am glad we met, keep your eyes closed." Her voice is stern as she continues, "When I was a little girl, I remember sitting with my grandmother who was blind. She knew so much, but she could not read. She knew things that no one else knew, and she was wiser and more connected to Allah than any of us. She taught me to see with my eyes closed. When she died, it was like the light went out, but every time I close my eyes, I am in the light."

Pure silence again. I have no thoughts that distract me, just the light. This time the silence is longer than before, and I feel altered.

She says, "You can open your eyes when you are ready."

We stare at each other. She smiles and says, "I see that you see that too. The light." She gets up and sits down on her knees in front of me, grabbing my head with both her hands and kisses my forehead, the kind of kissing that elder Pashtun women do. *Mwahmwahmwahmwah.* Her lips keep touching my forehead as she plants a series of kisses there, her hands firmly on my cheeks and ears.

She gets back up and I stand up with her. I give her a hug and whisper, "Dera manana" ("thank you" in Pashto). "Sit," she gestures, and I sit back.

In a raised voice, she says, "Rasha rasha" (come come), and the women I was supposed to be meeting that day, all rush in. I glance at my watch, and we have been here for nearly four hours by the time she calls the women. Sensing the time too, Noorzia studies me and smiles.

I now understand the peace that is within people here. A peace, a deep surrendering to a higher power, that I accredited to their faith in Allah, but maybe it is my limited western idea about how we define God, a man in the sky with all the limitations of that idea, the separation of man and God, an idea I have rejected. I lived opposing a God presence, because of the Western controlling idea of a God, through religious institutions manipulating people with guilt and shame.

What I experienced this afternoon has blown my world open. I did not feel any separation—only union, oneness, and peace. This afternoon, I feel closer to God than what I have ever felt before. More precisely, this is the first time I experience God. In the expansion of self, reaching far beyond my body, we are all one, we are God. The God for people here, has no face, is not a man in the sky. Allah has many names and there are no images of Allah. I have arrived in Afghanistan, and my soul feels home like never before.

Chapter 2

NATURE WILL TAKE YOU THERE

2023—Twenty-Two Years Later

Tania, my friend and business partner, lives upstairs, or better said, I live underneath Tania, her husband and two children, in the basement suite of their house in Vancouver.

During one of our daily walks, I share with Tania this story of the woman asking me to close my eyes. She takes it in, then asks me if I ever met the woman again. I answer her without a thought, "I have not, and thinking about her," I playfully add, "I don't even know if I could have. Was she an actual person in this realm? Maybe I was just ready to have that experience, to be introduced to the world where we are all one, and she came as an angel to this realm?" This is a comment I can only make to Tania without getting a weird, questioning-my-sanity stare-down.

Tania and I were introduced to each other by a woman who considered investing in my early start-up in 2016, but my finances were a mess, like with every other entrepreneur in the early stages of a company. She introduced me to Tania to clean up my books as part of her due diligence for a potential investment. The investment never happened, but Tania and I stuck. She has been my partner in the company that started with a comment my mum made when we walked to the market in Lochem, the village where she lived. You know how some people sit together in a public space and share the last gossip with each other? They were a small group on the benches under a large tree in front of one of the café terraces. Their walkers and electric scooters positioned as useful family members beside them. My mum points at them, and out of the blue, says: "Over my dead body will I ever use one of those", meaning their mobility devices. Two things happened in that moment. One was that my mum caught herself on her own judgments about these people with their devices. The second thing that happened is that I realized that their mobility devices emphasize their disabilities, creating a social divide between people with and people without disabilities. That became an instant justice issue for me, and I decided that I was going to design a device that even my stubborn, opinionated mum would want to use. Tania equally gravitated to the mission and me.

We look in the same direction, can hold a lot of chaos and envision a future that comes through us. Tania and I can time travel through the different realities and realms, seeing this consensus reality, this temporary expression of who we are, for what it is. We live in it, but it controls us and the businesses we manage, less and less. Experiencing psychedelic journeys is like opening doors to different realms, to places where fear and scarcity do not control us, where we can connect with our full potential and live into the energy of why we are here.

I have been curious and wanting to do a plant medicine journey since the woman in Afghanistan asked me to close my eyes, but it needed to be right. Ayahuasca retreats in the Amazon with large groups of searching travelers did not appeal to me, nor did trying mushrooms by myself. Plant medicine is sacred, and the setting needs to be able to hold a journey of healing.

When my dear friend, Nicolette, invites me to a healing weekend on Vancouver Island hosted by a trusted couple she has already done plant medicine journeys with, it feels right. I decide to trust and surrender to this invitation, relieved that Tania is in too.

We are taking the ferry over to Vancouver island. Tania and I are joining twelve women in a four-day ceremony weekend, held by two healers, a couple who were chosen by the sacred plants. I have a strange sense of excitement in anticipation of my first journey with plant medicine. I do not quite know what to expect but am surrendering to whatever I am entering. I am so ready!

We are in the large room upstairs of the house of Lisa and Devon, everyone on their own mattress. They open the sacred space with music, while burning sandalwood and cedar, fanning feathers to cleanse our energetic bodies, drumming, singing, and prayers to bless our journeys, opening realms beyond.

We share our individual intentions for our journey. I feel rather apprehensive being part of a group experience. I am not much of a group person, but I am here and surrender to whatever this group experience is, whilst protective of the reason I am here and this journey I have longed for, for over twenty years since closing my eyes to wondrous expansion and oneness in Afghanistan.

My intention relates to the realm of unity, the realm where we are all one. To convey to the group the realm above, I put my hand underneath my eyes, looking up to the world above, where we are connected. The realm I am in when I close my eyes, but then I have to switch to the consensus reality where my body needs food and shelter. I move my hand up to above my eyes, the material world, the consensus reality, which we are conditioned to accept as the only reality. I live in either, or I can switch, but it feels separated and not integrated.

My intention for this journey is to be able to move my hand away from my face, to be connected in where we are one, whilst managing the material world in which we live here, without being in the grip of the scarcity and fear mindset that keeps us small.

We lay down. We drink our medicine, psilocybin, and we are each on our own journeys.

The medicine kicks in quite immediately. I pull the blanket over me. I have my eye mask on, and it is pitch dark as the visions start. I realize that I'm taken back to the beginning of time. I see protons, neutrons, particles, muons, atoms, like all the building blocks of the universe. I get initiated into the wisdom of it all. This is the essence. This is what's there. Protons don't change. Neutrons and muons don't change over millions of years. They do not change. One initiation ceremony after the other, each time I am taken to a temple and a ceremony takes place. I get initiated and information is downloaded into me.

Everything is covered in the colors of the rainbow, it is radiant. I move through space and time. The temples where I am initiated have organic shapes, futuristic arcs, cellular structures. I feel spacious, expansive, and so eager to take everything in. My mouth moves and I am aware that I say, "yes" all the time, "yes, take me further," "yes, show me more". There are zeros and ones. Aliens. Spaceships. There's movement, a lot of space. In every initiation, there's an old, majestic, indigenous matriarch with a lived, weathered face, deeply kind but piercing eyes, living wisdom, a complete sense of ease and peace in her face.

I'm initiated in the laws of the universe. There's no nature in those first hours.

Nature is much later. Spaceships and futuristic looking temples and aliens, life forms, and no humans, except for the matriarchs.

I die many times and with each initiation I am reborn, but not in the shape of a human. The visions are so intense, and I am aware of my body barely breathing, like I don't need oxygen. I get born and I die, I rebirth all the time, and every initiation feels like a rebirth, knowing more and more, feeling more and more, expanding more and more.

At a certain time, towards the end, nature appears. Before the trees, it's just colors and particles and mathematical calculations and temples, mostly temples and spaceships and space and time, and I experience an endless sensation of floating covered in all the colours of the rainbow.

Just before nature appears, there is one last initiation. An Indigenous woman, this matriarch holding a massive staff, stands next to me, close. She tells me, "Just hold out your hand. Put out your hand," as she puts her hand forward, showing me what to do. The moment I hold out my hand, my palm facing forward, everything wrinkles like in triangles, I am amazed, and like a whole sheet, it wrinkles, and I am in a completely different dimension. I have an overwhelming joy while I wrinkle the veils between universes. I travel time and between dimensions. In each dimension, I recognize the essences, I can see through everything that seems transparent, and through the veils I see that everything is constructed from the same building blocks. Every dimension is just one expression of how the building blocks come together and how they express themselves; how we express ourselves. Our first expressions in this life, in the womb, then out into the world.

Chapter 3
HAIL THE QUEEN OF HENGELO

1964

My mum faints while she is on the toilet and scrapes her face open against the rough plasterwork on the wall. She often recalls that event later, when she told me how she instantly knew that she was pregnant. The day before was my father's birthday, the 1st of May, and I was created on that day. His birthday, my inception day.

My parents lived in an uninsulated house with one gas stove downstairs in the living room. It was late January, and this year was a particularly cold winter. My mum's labor started, and the doctor had arrived. He checked her crowning and said he would go to the living room and read a book; the opening was only a few centimeters. Before he had finished the first page, my mum yelled, "Doctor, now!" When he arrived, I was already born. I came out in one contraction and with stretched legs as if I had launched myself out. It was 4:20 p.m. on the 28th of January 1964.

I am my father's daughter and barely acknowledge my mum, who my older brother is most fond of. I am my father's window to the world.

I love my grandma and grandpa and before pre-school, my mum and I go visit them every morning. Grandpa has a shed with tools, grandma a vegetable garden behind their home.

My mum was the baby born after a still birth that devastated my grandma. This is all just years before World War II started, industrialization ramping up, factory workers treated as disposable, working conditions that were far below health standards, and wages not enough to support the large Catholic families, forced to grow by frequent visits of the pastor making sure the women bread more souls to sign up in the registers of the church. The pastor did his rounds to tell women to get pregnant every year, right after they gave birth. So, the pastor came by after my grandma's stillborn, and commanded her to get pregnant again as soon as possible, so she would forget the grief over her stillborn baby, as if he had any idea. Nothing of what this guy said had any appreciation for a grieving woman who managed a whole household without resources, but with children she would have never had, given a choice.

She got pregnant with my mum, who, once born, was not as quiet as the dead baby, who had demands for clean diapers and food. Who cried and threw tantrums as she did not get her needs met, like babies do. My grandma, a dirt-poor woman, though only by the absence of money, had a lot on her plate. Her husband, my beloved grandpa, was a steel worker, working hard, long hours in a filthy factory that filled his lungs with metal dust, destroying his lungs, and ultimately, he suffocated to death when he was barely fifty. He disappeared sometimes to volunteer for the Red Cross, especially during the war, leaving my grandma to host his mum, her mother-in-law, and my mum was the fourth child already. Having a noisy, demanding baby take the place of the beautiful, quiet baby, the loss she was still grieving, was picked up by my mum as not being wanted. Of course, she was not wanted, but it was not personal. My grandma did not choose anything of her life—she was a poor woman of her time, breeding children because as a Catholic, birth control existed only in the so-called, "leave the church before the singing starts" way (Dutch expression meaning, *the man has to withdraw before he ejaculates*).

My grandma escaped in imagining different realities, was an amazing storyteller and tapped into her unbridled fantasy. All she ever wanted was to be an actress, be on stage, be seen, be in a play, someone else's story. No one else would see that though. My grandma somehow managed to graciously accept her life and made magic, lived in her fantasy, made up stories for her grandchildren, sat on her throne and ruled her family. Using her imagination as an escape out of a very harsh life.

After my mum, she gave birth to two more children, adopted a French child during the war and took in a young German soldier who lived with them till the war ended. My grandma did not judge people on what they were, as taking in a German soldier during the war, living close to the border with Germany in the Netherlands, was deeply frowned upon. Neighbors gave her shit because wasn't he the enemy?

The doorbell rung one evening, you know one of these pull bells, nested in the door frame. You pull the knob towards you, connected inside the house to a rope, which was attached to a spring blade close to the ceiling. When pulled, the bell at the end of the spring moved. My grandpa was in Germany for the Red Cross at that time. My grandma opened the front door and saw a confused and lost sixteen-year-old German soldier. He was crying. My grandma invited him in. Effectively he deserted the army the moment he moved in. He ended up staying with her till the war was over.

With an extended household in a tiny laborers' house, she managed to be the matriarch and keep her head high. I knew my grandma, of course, as my grandma, so I did not have the tensions and complicated feelings daughters have with their mums. That unique dynamic was my own to discover in my own life, with my own mum. Like mum-daughter relations are woven through generations and are as fascinating as annoying, and as happy as damaging.

My mum grew up in the unique neighborhood called Tuindorp 't Lansink, or "Garden Village". Stork was the factory where my grandpa worked, and in a time the steel factory, making turbines, flourished, they bought fifteen hectares of ground to build a village for all their staff. The essence of the architectural design of the whole neighborhood was inspired by an English model for neighborhoods, where different classes lived together. The unschooled laborers lived alongside the engineers, doctors, and factory barons in the same neighborhood. A social and revolutionary concept that was based on the idea that when you give people quality housing with lots of garden spaces and playgrounds in a neighborhood with a variety of people throughout the classes, it would be a good environment and outcome for the whole factory. Poor people would have examples, a different outlook, gardens to grow their own food, children playing with all children of different classes. Conversely, rich people would be able to connect and show up for the poor people, relate to their lives instead of being separated in shanty laborers' neighborhoods, and wealthy rich areas in a town. The fact that my mum grew up in this Garden Village has marked the whole trajectory of our family.

All the family stories from my mum's side of the family were coloured by the setting of the neighborhood. While raising her children, my grandma worked as the maid for a textile baron, the De Monchy family, just one block over, with a view at the central pond where all the kids from the neighborhood learned to swim. De Monchys owned the spinnery, the factory where cotton was twined into threads and textiles were woven. De Monchy was a rich family, and my grandma loved working for Madam, the grandma, and her children. She imagined being part of their family, an escape out of her own poverty. My grandma was of the one branch of her family that became impoverished through circumstances, but the family line up the tree was a good middle-class family. In the time that widow pensions, medical care, and social security did not exist, a family could fall into poverty as soon as the breadwinner died, leaving the family without income or a safety net. My grandma somehow had that lineage in her; she never settled to be the poor woman without a voice. She had her inside knowing of her life in her imagination, juxtaposed to the harshness of her consensus reality.

Madam De Monchy was very fond of Manna, short for "Hermanna", my grandma's name, and passed on the dresses to her that she would not wear anymore. The illusion and dreaming of being part of De Monchy family was supported by Manna wearing Madam's old clothes that were well above her class as a laborer's wife. My grandma prancing around in Madams' dresses through the neighborhood, was frowned upon by people. She was not behaving according to the social constructs of her class. *Who did she think she was!*

Madam asked my grandma to bring her daughters to work for them too, now that my grandma had her hands full with her own family. The oldest sister of my mum, Auntie Dieneke, and my mum, followed in my grandma's footsteps and worked as maids at De Monchys too, adding some income to the sober salary of my grandpa. Working for De Monchy had a lot more perks than just having some extra income. They cooked their meals and got to eat their share in the kitchen, they learned about classical music from the endless records Madam played, they hung out with her children who played the piano and brought interesting friends home, they heard French being spoken, and Madam had walls filled with bookshelves. My mum read hundreds of books there, books she would not have had access to otherwise. Madam noticed it, and enjoyed sharing her house, their wealth.

My grandma was a proud woman, living in parallel realities. She always told me that whatever people do to you, whatever they take from you, you always have your own pride and thoughts. No one, whatever they do to you, can take that away from you. She would say, "Hold your head up high, chin up, you decide who you want to be."

Her nickname in town was the Queen of Hengelo; she did not behave as the typical laborer's wife, obedient and keeping her head low. She would stride through town in the couture dresses of Madam De Monchy and speak her truths. Growing up, my mum would often share the stories of how my grandma would defy the laws of the classes and speak up against injustice.

One day, the Baron of Stork came to their tiny, humble home. My grandpa previously got his weekly salary in a little brown bag; most factory workers would take that brown bag at the end of the week into the bar and drink it away, escaping their poverty, their reality. The contents of the brown bag would never arrive to the family, adding to a cycle of poverty. My grandma, however, was the matriarch, and my grandpa, besides the fact that he was himself not your typical factory worker, brought the brown bag home and my grandma managed the family budget, to the cent.

She had to turn every nickel and decide what the spending priority was. New shoes for one of the kids, or eggs to supplement the nutrition value. One day, my grandpa came home and shared what the Baron had announced to the factory workers. Each family had to open a bank account, so the weekly cash would no longer be handed out. Bank accounts in that time, a completely new phenomenon, were in the name of the husband; women did not have that right yet, they had barely gotten the right to vote. The Baron had also announced that part of the salaries would be held in reserve to secure childcare expenses, before the men would drink it away.

My grandma objected on a fundamental justice issue, as well as her pride. She did not need to be patronized by the Baron, holding back pay because of the mismanagement of funds by the men in other families. She managed my grandpa's salary and would take the interest herself, thank you very much. She sent my grandpa back with a message for the Baron, that she did not agree with the Baron collecting all the interest of the accumulative salary portions he would withhold in the name of creating childcare funds for the families. My grandpa, averse to conflict or confrontations, especially with his employer, passed on the message, knowing that he could not come back home without passing the message. The Baron was adamant, and so was my grandma to the point that one day, the Baron stood at their door. He rang the bell, and my grandma opened the door.

He asked to see the boss, and my grandma said the historic words: "Speaking. My husband's name is on the outside of the house," she quipped, pointing at the name sign. "Inside the house is where I'm the boss." Not long after that epic visit, my grandpa received his full salary in his bank account.

Somehow my grandma managed to be respected, not necessarily liked, but respected by people of all walks of life. She received many visitors throughout the day, her door was always open. Behind the house she had created a pea patch where she grew vegetables to feed her family more than potatoes and behind the house was a paved area where she did the laundry every Wednesday. Of course, there were no washing machines yet, so she had a series of galvanized tin tubs outside where first the laundry went through. Then the children went for their weekly bath after the laundry, so she used the water that was heated up for the linens, efficiently.

She always offered coffee to everybody who came to the house. She did not make a difference between the family doctor on the corner, the factory workers next door, the textile baron of the spinning factory or the guy with mental challenges who roamed around the neighborhood. She said that "we are all born as naked, little creatures that just want to be happy". Some are born with money, wealth, family, love, a certain skin colour, access to education and some are not, but it does not make us different in who we are in our essence.

Before I go to pre-school, my mother first takes my brother to school and then we stroll to see Grandma and Granddad, along the big pond in the Garden Village, where we learned to skate in winter and swam in summer. I always was a bit apprehensive about swimming because I imagined how a fish would bump into me one day or slide against me with slimy fins or worse, that a pike would bite my toes. I am too young for coffee, but my grandma gives me a small cup and spoon with an enameled tile from Cologne, which she fills with coffee milk and sugar. I stir it and enjoy it spoon by spoon. We sit around the table in the living room, my fingers playing with the hairs of the plush tablecloth. My granddad is sitting opposite, with the portrait of Jesus behind him on the wall, steaming stamps of envelopes.

Sometimes a sentence someone says, lands. Some sentences my grandma said have impregnated me one way or the other and remain a guiding line in my life. One has become part of my soul: "Possession is the end of fun."

My grandma probably often said it to herself as a higher reason not to buy things. After all, she simply did not have the money. Besides that, my grandma truly had a higher insight in these things—she was a wise woman. When I visited her and said, "Gran, that really is a pretty painting," she said, "Take it, girl, if you like it that much, you can have it." She did not care about possessions but had suffered from and learned from the steel and textile industry bosses who exploited their workers and used their powers to oppress the workers because they had the power. She had suffered under that injustice but at the same time, she had not let one chance pass to fight injustice and do what was right.

The deep sense of justice my grandma instilled in me has become a red thread throughout my life, and a driving force for the start of the design of the Alinker mobility bike. With the comment of my mum ("Over my dead body…"), I start diving in the world of mobility devices and soon identify, that most of them are a technical solution for a "body-with-a-problem". But we are not a body with a problem that just needs the logistical solution of moving it from A to B, we are whole human beings who want to be active and engaged in life, regardless of how we move. With these insights, I set out to design something so cool that people would love to use it and be the one on that cool thing.

I am five years old, and my grandma tells me something that deeply captures my imagination. It impacts me and shapes the rest of my life and ultimately my philosophy of design. Designing objects, structures and life itself. While in her fifties, her hands are showing deep lines and coloured skin as a testament to hard labour.

We are squatting in the shallow ditches between the bamboo stick-constructions my grandma had so perfectly tied together to facilitate the beans to grow high up. Her vegetable garden was filled with vegetables and herbs, growing to perfection supported by the wealth of her invisible knowledge. She taught me how to look at what you see, and truly see what you are looking at.

She planted shallots between the rows of carrots, put parsley around the rose bushes, kale to surround the beds of lettuce. She asks me what I see. As we are surveying the plants, she explains the relation between them and that they are neighbors for a reason. The shallots keep the worms out of the carrots, the parsley makes for more fragrant blossoms and the kale adds more nutrients to the lettuce.

There in her garden, my grandma says, "If ever you have a problem or you feel stuck, turn it around and see if it is still a problem." My puzzled face triggers her to explain a bit more, so she continues, "Say from where you sit, you see me, and everything behind me, but when you were to borrow my shoes, and take my perspective, you see everything behind you, all the things you do not see while being in your own shoes." She looks at me, now with a wisewoman's face who is passing on life's knowledge to a young one. "As you grow up, see if you can pick a person and borrow their shoes. Choose the person based on how different they are from you. Then borrow their shoes and see what they see, try to feel what they feel. I do this every day, and I have learned to understand how different, yet how similar we are. We might look or walk differently, but everybody needs to be seen and be loved."

Grandma does reversal games with me. Hypothetical situations that need a solution. Imagine the neighbor would cut all the trees that divides our garden from his without asking. The first reaction would then be, *stupid man, why did you do that, there is no fence anymore and your dogs run into our garden*. If you reverse it, you think, *great neighbor, now we can stroke your dogs and we have more sun.* In the first case, the neighbor would probably go into the defensive and it would start an argument. By reversing it the neighbor would probably apologize that he had not discussed it, and a possible solution would be discussed.

Totally frowned upon by the women of her age, but my grandma is a huge boxing fanatic. She has a tiny black and white TV that my dad had organized for her so she would not miss the boxing matches. She sets her alarm for the matches that take place in America (the middle of the night for her). She loves Cassius Clay, and when he converts to Islam, she explains to me that Malcolm X just has the brains, but Muhammad Ali has the brains and muscles. I respect Muhammad Ali for his path in life, as my grandma taught me.

While my grandma and I peel beans and dig the soil, she teaches me the essence of empathy, refraining from judging until you have seen the issue from more perspectives, and often, what looks like a problem is not the problem at all.

These practices form the basis of what I now call my *reverse design practices.* Probably not a correct term, but it is how I see the world. This world in which we are conditioned to identify problems and then fix them, without questioning the assumed problem. Every business plan starts with the question: what is the problem, and what is your unique solution? In this mentality, mobility devices are technical solutions for a body with a problem, completely disregarding the user experience.

Chapter 4

CHESS WITHOUT A BOARD...AND OTHER CURIOSITIES

As long as I can remember, people have commented on my tomboy behavior, the absence of dresses, the non-girly sports I play and the way I walk with my hands in my pockets. When I was very young my mum had to endure all those comments as if it was her fault that I behaved like I did. She also had to endure years of fighting with me as a little girl about my clothing, although she was the one who initiated these fights with me. Every morning my mum would try and dress me in a skirt or a dress, preferably the ones that she had made herself, but I fiercely refused to wear them. It was like I instinctively had an aversion to those clothes, the girly clothes. My memories are vivid.

I am five years old, and my mum tries to get me in a Scottish checkered skirt, to which I protest high and low, then my father comes between us and puts an end to these fights for good. "It is enough, the kid can wear what she wants. I will take the day off and go shopping with her. I am sick of having to listen to these silly fights over what to wear every single morning, today it will end," he says quite calmly but makes his point. He does not raise his voice or fight, but I beam inside that he's advocating for me. He is a very introverted man and keeps to himself, making our time together even more acute and special.

We go shopping and buy corduroy pants and a long-sleeved shirt with white and red mini checkers we both approve of.

My father is an extraordinary, smart man. His intelligence comes through his hands. Under my young watch, whatever he thinks, he makes, manifests. The hand-brain connected intelligence is a characteristic that my two brothers and I have all inherited. His mind works in a special way, guiding the unusual bedside stories and imagination games or rather, exercises he does with me. Only in retrospect I realize how unusual all that he taught me was—so unusual that I have come to discern that I have no boxes.

He asks me to imagine flipping the three-story building we live in on its side, then asks me what we need to change to make it livable again. So, the kitchen now hangs off the ceiling, the doors are 90 degrees rotated, and so on. We go in detail for many evenings following through all the changes—what we need to adjust, change, reconstruct to make it functional, and all that whilst identifying new opportunities, seeing the potential that presents itself. The living room window is now on the floor, over the grass. How about we take out the window and dig a pond? How cool to have a pond in the middle of the living room! We sift through every little detail and make the most amazing new home, all in our minds.

He takes me on his bike often, through the fields and forests, showing me the salt industry where he works. He was one of the first computer programmers, when a computer still filled a room, the spindles making that swooshing sound, and the programs being a stack of thick cards with punched rectangular holes in it. At home we cut the punched holes into slots and use the cards to build castles with.

The age of five is pivotal. He asks me a very unusual question. I feel the weight of his words and have always remembered them exactly, word by word. He looks at me as we are cutting the slots in the punch cards, and asks slowly with pauses after each part of the sentence: "What do you do...in order not to go crazy...when someone locks you up...for something that you think?" I am fascinated by the question, wondering how something that I think would be powerful enough for someone to want to lock me up for it. Can merely thoughts be that much of a threat?

In hindsight really, what he asked me is a mental preparation for being a political prisoner and not crumbling under the injustice of being locked up for something that I think. How do I keep my sanity in a situation that is highly unjust?

Following that question, my father teaches me how to play chess, all the pieces, special moves, openings, closings, special strategies, seeing multiple moves ahead, then asks me to scan the board and memorize it. Over time, he takes the board away. So, he teaches me to play chess...without a board! Soon, I could play chess, strategically as well as memorizing the whole game and the changing constellation after each move. I would say: "Horse B1 to C3." He looks at me, thinks, nods. Next day, next move. No board. Each time, we memorize the evolving game.

Chapter 5
FATEFUL PHOTOSHOOTS

I am five years old, and we are all sitting around our preschool teacher who addresses us for an upcoming event. There is excitement in all the wiggly bodies around me, as the teacher announces that there is a photo shoot tomorrow.

"Please make sure to wear neat and presentable clothing tomorrow, this picture is for the rest of your life."

I feel an upcoming anxiety, I feel separated from what they all feel, and I don't understand why I am not wiggly and excited. The teacher keeps talking as the thoughts in my head make her voice one in the background. "Girls, tell your parents to dress you in your prettiest dress, and boys, choose your nicest shirt and pants, you want to look good in the photo." Now, she pulls out a huge, ugly doll and a massive red plastic locomotive and proudly says, "The boys will take their photograph with this cool train, and the girls with this doll."

I panic, I do not want either. I want my bear, and my head starts frantically making pathways. I escape toward a photo I can already see in my head, me with the bear. I am not hearing anything the teacher says anymore, the kids are excited, and I get up and run to the toilet. I sit on the toilet, calm myself down and make a plan. A few minutes later, I feel confident that I can turn this nightmare around. I can breathe again. I walk home in my corduroy pants and long-sleeved, red-white checkered shirt my father helped me choose.

I walk around the back and enter our house through the old kitchen and see my mum. I barge in with my plan, and now excited about the photo shoot because I am confident that I can do this. I describe the photo I want. "Okay, well, if that is what you want to do, then we'll make that happen. Do you want me to come with you tomorrow?" my mum said. Step one of the plan in place; backup of my mum. *Check*. Next step, I storm upstairs, pick up Bear, the oldest animal in my collection. I make a hat for him from shiny green cardboard from my 'make-shit' corner. Finally, it is exactly how I want it, and I put it on his head. Step two complete. *Check*.

The next morning, I walk to school, I hold my bear close, I feel excited and a bit anxious. I actually do not remember how I told the teacher or how she accepted the fact that I would have the photo taken with me holding my bear, but somehow that was accepted. When the afternoon rolls around, the teacher announces that we must go up to the room where the photoshoot will take place. She tells us to line up and in the corner is where the photographer installed the lights and the settings with a little chair each of us must take place for the photo. I feel victorious and somehow that overrules the fact that I feel very exposed in front of all the other kids. I am aware, reflective, about how I transformed this experience to suit me, regardless of what others think or want me to do. It's an early victory.

Once, this teacher told me to stand in a trash bin, facing the corner, while the class had to chant, "Barbara is trash." I never understood why.

We moved from Hengelo to Borne. I am in the first two years of a Catholic preschool, and the teachers are mean. They separate me, ignore me, make fun of me for bringing my stuffed animals to school. They isolate me and punish me. I never knew what I did wrong, but on another day, I had to kneel on a sisal mat in the corner, while the class had to chant bad things about me. I am different and feel that is why I am being punished and ignored.

While the photo of me with my bear feels like my first gender victory, the first holy communion is definitely not. We are sort of raised as Catholics so when the event comes around, I have to attend and dress as a girl, no escape there. My mum must have seen her

40

chance to finally get me to wear one of her own creations. She had genuinely tried to make it as suitable for me as possible, made of light jeans fabric and I could throw it over my favourite shirt. I have butch shoes, big calves and my hands clumsily half hanging in the half-rounded pockets of the dress. The photo taken that day at age seven is probably of the unhappiest girl who has ever done her first holy communion. I resent that event and as soon as we arrive home where family is to visit,

I run upstairs and change back to my jeans.

At this age, I am not sure where such strong resistance comes from, but it is clear that it is particularly geared towards girly clothes and anything else expected of me just because I happen to be a girl. I know exactly what I want to wear and that I don't want to do anything just because that is what girls do. I am different. I feel strongly that I am different and express that with my resistance to dresses and skirts. Resistance sounds negative though. It is more that I just want to do what I feel. Generally, I am a very happy and positive child, sticking my nose in flowers to smell them, playing soccer with the boys, my knees always bruised, exploring my father's tools in the garage, fixing the bikes, welding stuff together and fantasizing how I will be a welder one day, making wood sculptures and playing with clay. I climb trees and hang out with the builders on the nearest building sites.

Only in reflection to the world around me, which is made very clear to me through continuous comments, the ways I am judged and regarded, I am different from others. Feeling different brings quite an ambiguous sensation; on one hand, it suits me because I AM different, and the acknowledgement is reassuring. It justifies my behavior; people think of me as different anyway so now, I can be free and behave differently. On the other hand, it makes me feel misunderstood and lonely.

The day of first communion also marks the last time I ever wear a dress or skirt in my life except two or three rare occasions, but these incidents are by sheer choice.

Chapter 6
MY FOREVER FATHER

When walking home I have my hands in my pockets, kick at rocks and spit on the ground. The neighbor, a retired school inspector, notices and shares with my parents. They transfer me to a public school, and I land in the class with Stan, my teacher, an artist (we remained friends over all these years).

I am seven years old, just in my new primary school and I am so happy, everything feels so much more spacious and freer. We do a game. Kids in a circle, one in the middle, eyes closed and spinning around while pointing one arm outward. *One, 2, 3, 4, 5, 6, 7,* who can I give a kiss (in Dutch this rhymes) … It's my turn to be in the center and I have a crush on a girl close by. I peak through my eyelashes to make sure I end up pointing at her, so I can kiss her.

I ride horses, carve wooden sticks, build stuff, ride my bike through forests and mud, wear pants and behave like what the world sees as boy stuff. Since Stan is my teacher, I can grow into being me. He lives on a little farm half an hour on my bike, and I go there nearly every day. He is a sculptor and ceramicist. He teaches me techniques and we do work around the farm.

We are on our way to the farm in Wijk en Aalburg again, a three-hour drive in our Renault 4 that doesn't go faster than 90K/hr unless the wind comes from behind. We are regular visitors at the farm from Auntie Trijn and Uncle Bas, two older farmers with five cows, and a veggie garden, land where they grow feeder beets for the cows and old-fashioned maize, the type with kernels in a variety of colours. I love them and love being there. Behind the farm, they had converted

43

some old stables to holiday rentals which gave them some income without the need for the hard physical labor.

My father is ill. We do not know what is wrong, but on a drive like this, he stops the car often, walks around to the grass roadside of the car to throw up. Over the past months, he did not tolerate unprocessed food anymore. It had to be milled, cooked long to make it soft and easy to digest. As time passes, he has to vomit more regularly.

My mum and dad behave as if it were normal, not saying a word to us, but every time he pukes, I feel nauseas and helpless. I took on the milling of his food, it made me feel better somehow, as I wanted to be part of the dire change and not just witness it happening and feeling excluded. So, I created a role for myself and started preparing his food.

He becomes thinner, which I notice because his big cable veins I always play with, pushing up the blood until I find a valve, are even more pronounced. By the time we go to the farm, he does not tolerate any food anymore. All he eats is porridge, and then only baby mix. He is so skinny, puking more life from him all the time.

This time, we stay in the front house, shared with Trijn and Bas. The house has more comfort than the refurbished stables, and my father is really sick. He always had a pocketknife in his pocket, a beautifully worn but well-maintained Herder-Solingen. We sit outside under the big oak tree, and he pulls out his knife. He looks at the knife on his hand palms, pauses, confirming that he has my attention. "This knife is from 1890," he says. "My grandfather got it from his parents for birthday or something, when he was still a kid. He used it his whole life, always had it in his pocket. Many years later, when my grandfather died, he gave it to my dad, who in turn, used it throughout his life." I am fascinated and in awe of the life span of this knife. He pauses for a moment, then says, "When my father died a few years ago, he gave it to me." He put his hands out to me, with the knife, holding it up for me to receive it. "And now I am giving it to you, my only daughter."

We lock eyes as I accept the knife. He looks so frail, his eyes fading to light blue. I know what this means. He is wearing his white pants and favourite dark red sweater. I get up and get on his lap, his arms around me, no words.

I sit on his bed; I don't want to sit on the chair next to the bed, which feels too much like a hospital. The texture of the blanket feels awkward, and I hate the fact that this too reminds me of being in a hospital. The blankets, the smell, the chair next to the bed, the tubes in his arm, visitors with very sad faces or fake smiles, the flowers, and the fruit on the cabinet on wheels. Everything makes it undoubtedly a hospital and that my father is there for a reason. Something is stronger than this terrible truth.

I hold the steering wheel of his bicycle, his arms around me holding the steering wheel by the handles. It's a bit windy, but a nice day at the beginning of spring. Some butterflies are out too early. On a Saturday, he often takes me by the hand, lifts me on his bicycle and we trek for a long tour, just the two of us. Days like nothing could go wrong, just me and him, capable of everything as long as we are together. Every second is precious. I am the happiest girl. We have an exclusive bond, just him and me; nobody else in the world.

I sniff every flower on the way through the fields of flowers we pick and put in a vase on the table at home. We witness how a cow gives birth to a calf, there in the field as we pass by. He explains everything to me, how things work in nature.

On a winter evening, he fills up a cup with water and puts it outside in the freezing night. The next morning, he explains that water expands when the temperature gets below 0 degrees Celsius and that is why that cup has cracks in it. Another time he retrieves a voltmeter and connects the wires with the "crocodile mouths" to a battery, explaining how electricity, plus and minus, volts, amperes work.

By the time I was five, I could fix a flat tire of a bicycle in the most efficient way, knew different tools and how to use them, how to paint a desk and a chair, how to stand on his feet while he walked around with me, my little hands in his beautiful hands with those fascinating veins. I always played with the veins on his hands. Found out that when you go in a certain direction, you discover a valve here and there, which prevents blood from streaming in the wrong direction.

In the process of going to bed he would count, from ten back to zero. At zero, I should be in my pajamas in bed, ready for a story. When I stretched the time, before hitting the bed, he started to use fractions, five, four and a half, four and a quarter, four, three and seven eighths, three and twelve sixteenths, and so on. This could take forever, and it was meant to take forever as the rules of our game. When I finally reached the horizontal position, he told me endless stories.

"Faraway from here in a land locked country, somewhere in the Middle East, lived people who were very different from us. They didn't have any clothes on, they built their huts a few meters above the ground between tree branches. They lived peacefully together there, prepared food from plants and fruit they grew on their land. They were an artistic group of people who made amazingly big sculptures from huge pieces of wood. The sculptures were all geometrical shapes, in fascinating compositions. Only timber from trees that had come down in a storm or so was used. This was a way to honour the trees after their lives. Trees were seen as the most important creatures in their environment.

"The tools they had were limited, all handmade and purely functional. They seemed to manage life with little possessions and live happily. Even an event like the death of a person was approached in a totally different way than what we are used to. Those people had no fear of death; they saw it as a part of the life cycle. The fact that life is ending, someday, was the reason to live life as fully and happily as possible.

"So, when someone died, they celebrated the fact that this person had lived such a wonderful life and had contributed so much to their community. The body was kept for three days under the favourite tree of that person, and then buried under the same tree. Trees were very important in their lives as they were seen as the womb of all the newborns. Babies were born out of a tree, and they saw that tree as their father. It was most likely that this tree became your favourite during your life and the tree you would return to after your death. They believed that the moment someone died, the spirit would transform into a butterfly and be around them. Loved ones would not disappear after death, you only had to re-recognize them."

After he finished the story, I always wanted to hear more, wanted to know more about those people, wanted to be with them. When he left the room, I kept staring in the dark, wondering about those people. The next morning, I always wondered why I could never remember the exact moment I fell asleep.

I resonated so well with the characters, time and space squeeze us together.

We move to another house in another town. I like it there; the house is light and airy, an open staircase in the middle of the house. My dad glues a beautiful dark wooden floor to the cement floor; no one had such a special floor! The first few months we sort of camp in the house, before all the furniture is in the right place. Quickly, I make friends with children living in the neighborhood, and often, I go outside to play. The school practically next to our house has a big football field. It's one of my favourite places to play. I ride on my bicycle, cycling around, looking for someone to play with. Suddenly a white butterfly lands on my hand. I have the feeling I know the butterfly. I am eight years old and not prepared to lose my father yet.

When my father died, 21st September 1972, it was without a doubt, the most determining event of my life. A death which has seen so many metamorphoses already and has had many faces and appearances. A death with many different characters. Every time this death pops up again, I have grown accustomed to it now and it has become a guide on my path through life. It supplies me with energy, and it has become my drive…no, I should say, I have turned it into the drive to live life to the fullest. I have come to appreciate death because with the certainty that our lives will end, one day, life becomes meaningful. Being born, dying, and in between trying to achieve happiness, knowing that we will die, that our existence here will end. The person dies, my father died, but his effect on my life continues. I have always had a father, physically not here anymore though after his death, but present, nevertheless.

At the funeral, people are very somber, and some are crying. They offer their condolences to my mother with sad faces and after that day, we are alone for a very long time. Life trudges on. People do not talk about it anymore. I feel as if we are being punished and I don't understand. If his death crops up in the conversation by accident, their uncomfortable feelings are clear, or they say what they think are comforting things to us or our mother.

"Be glad you still have your kids."

"Luckily, you are a Catholic and you go to church."

"Luckily, you still have the Lord!"

"You must look after your mother."

These comments are extremely irritating. I sort out how stupid and clumsy people are. Even our own family refrains for two years from regularly visiting us, too uncomfortable, not knowing what to talk about in the face of his death. As an eight-year-old, I understand that people choose their comfort over showing up for a young family with this majestic loss.

My father's death has severely confronted me as an eight-year-old child with the ignorance and clumsiness of the Dutch in dealing with sorrow. Precisely my father had told me about those people who do not mourn a deceased but celebrate his or her life and see everything in a lifecycle where people do not disappear but remain part of their community in another shape. Now, he is dead, and everything—from feelings and habits—I could relate to through his stories makes me yearn for those people and their customs. The longing to be in another country than the Netherlands is planted.

I learn about the storks and how they migrate to their other home country, I feel relieved! I am not stuck here, there is another home country.

Chapter 7

SEEKING REFUGE IN MOBY DICK

My mum feels like a failure raising us. She is judged by the people around us and has a really hard time. She is the first young widow in our community, and we are the first 'incomplete' family in our whole school. She gets judged instead of people showing up.

As our own family disappears, the parents of a boy in my brother's class engage with us, invite us over and we become part of their family. The Ettes have six kids and a blind horse that can't damage anything in their home. It is a safe haven for my mum and us. We spend every Christmas and holidays and Sundays with them. Being their friends makes my mum even more of outcast in that village of the judgy and mean. Such good Catholics!

The first few years after my father dies, my mum often disappears, goes on long trips to Russia and France, times when my grandma comes to stay with us. I love my grandma, and I often wish that my mum would stay away, and Grandma could live with us forever.

The farm of Stan and horseback riding at the stables next to the castle become my refuges.

A farmer who spoiled his horse after his wife died, gave his horse to us to train it and slim it down again. He had spoiled it to the point it did not fit between the booms of the plough anymore. Roodenburg, the cavalier lieutenant, who runs the stables, gives me the responsibility to train Moby Dick, as I called him. Every morning, I get up early and bike through the forest to the stables. Moby Dick is too fat for a saddle, so I put a single around him, a big leather strap with two handles on top. I learn that he loves jumping in the forest, and I train him. No one knows, but he loses weight. I love him and want him to be around as long as I am.

One day, there is the annual tournament, and the girl who normally commands the jumping competitions to represent the stable is ill. Roodenburg urges me to go. I agree only if I compete with Moby Dick. I am ten years old, and he has to surrender to the embarrassment of me going on a farmer's horse. But I win first prize!

I stand up against this military guy who also has loose hands. He grabs me in my crotch upstairs in the saddle room, and I instinctively swing a headset to his head; the metal mouthpiece smacks into his face. Another prize!

At a school outing, I am eleven, and Stan is still my teacher. I arrange for my whole class to do a day ride with the traditional horse carriages (the ones with the large wooden wheels and metal hoops around them) and the horses of my stable. I am managing Moby Dick as he fits back in the booms.

On another school outing, we gather in the forest and play games the whole day. The knife my father had given me in Wijk en Aalburg had since been in my jeans pocket. It felt as an important gift and with the story my father had told me, the knife felt like an ancestral responsibility. I cut apples, cakes, butter bread, cut wooden dolls, peel oranges. I use the knife for all possible things you can use a knife for. On one side the wood is lighter than on the other that is dark. My father had shown me how you can stick the knife in the ground and clean the blade on the soil. I kept the blade clean like this, I sharpened it carefully on an old whetstone and I lubricated the wood with natural linseed oil—it was always with me.

During the school outing, there is a great deal of activity in the woods with the other children. I cut off branches with the knife and carve out dolls and little animals. The next day, I don't feel the knife in my pocket. It's gone! I panic. My father's knife...gone. I cannot imagine I had been so stupid as to leave it in the woods. Cycling back through the woods, heart thumping in my chest, I dig under all the leaves, survey the perimeter like a detailed geologist, but there is no trace of the knife. I ask everyone if they had seen it. Nothing. I can't let go, the thoughts continue to torture me that I had forgotten something, a movement, a spot. It lasts a year or so, thinking how careless I had been. The thoughts do not stop; they become less prevalent but never exit my mind.

I decide to look for another knife Herder-Solingen shape and the different colours of the wood, making my rounds at all the hardware shops. Those knifes do not come cheap, so I save pocket money. This hunt is symbolic. It won't be the same knife, but my father will know of my great chase. At last, I find the knife in a hardware shop in Hengelo, exactly what I want, the same shape, the exact colours of the wood. It cost 48 guilders, and I will have to save for a bit, but I am pleased to have found that knife because it looks exactly the same. I ask the shop attendants if they can keep the knife for me, explaining the significance, vowing to save enough to buy it. How can they turn me down with the desperation in my little face?

After another few months, I have the money. I race my bike to Hengelo ready to pay up for my treasure. The man smiles warmly again and retrieves the knife from under the counter. I touch it. I am so pleased, as if a debt had been settled. This knife, with the same features as my father's, holds the weight of ten knives, it feels more valuable than gold.

I needed a wee when I got home and sat on the loo relaxed and took the knife out of my pocket to look at it. I conjure up an image in my head of the space above the wardrobes in the bedroom, with a yellow rucksack behind it and my father's knife in the left side pocket. I am a bit confused, as if I had been daydreaming. I get off the loo, wipe off...I think...and climb on a chair to inspect the space. There is a yellow rucksack. I look in the left side pocket. My hand grasps my father's knife. I have it back. It is there where I had seen it in my mind's eye! The funny thing is I never see the new knife again, never find it, but my own knife is back in my pocket.

Chapter 8

YOUNGEST MEMBER OF THE ORCHESTRA

I am eleven years old, and my mum takes us on a holiday to Denmark. We drive in the Renault 4, and she arranges for us to stay in a pension where other families stay as well. A girl my age and I go out to the forest, out on the water, and are in our own world. We stay friends, she is like me, a boy-girl. We live far apart, but are pen pals, and visit sometimes. In early high school, we lose contact.

Laurence is my school friend, and we take bikes apart and build boats from wood, with sails. One day, we play with the three-masted ship we built, and a whole bunch of older kids throw rocks at it till it sinks, then they beat us up, badly. We are black and blue, our clothes shredded in sync with our bleeding cuts and noses.

I want to play the bassoon. In primary school, the teacher had played us a record of "Peter and the Wolf" by Prokofiev. The fairy tale where every instrument represents a person or an animal, so-called *programmatic music*. I can hear the happy melody of Peter played by the violins just by thinking about it. Grandfather was a bassoon, and I was enthralled by the deep, almost hoarse sound that cannot be compared to anything else. *Po dom po dom.* I immediately knew I wanted to play it.

Two houses down lives Gerard, the conductor of the Twents Youth Harmony Orchestra, and my mother says I should ask him, maybe with the idea that my continuous talking about bassoons will stop then. I eagerly walk to Gerard's house. *I am going to arrange it. I will play the bassoon.* I can picture it.

I know Gerard and his family well because I often take their dog for a walk, so I ring the doorbell and Gerard opens it. He automatically picks up the leash because he thinks I am going to walk Anoesha, but I tell him I want to play the bassoon and ask him if he can help me. Quite surprised, but with a grin on his always friendly face, he instructs, "Show me your hands because a bassoon is quite big, and you probably are still a bit young." I hold up my hands to him. I have big fists, "fumbling hands", as my mother calls them. Gerard notices with a grin that they are big enough to reach the holes and valves of the bassoon. I am so pleased!

He promises me that he will find out if there is a bassoon available at the music school and let me know. I run home and I shout to my mother that it is possible, I will play the bassoon. It already feels like a victory.

The next day, I go to Gerard's house to walk the dog, hoping that I will see Gerard armed with the magnificent news. He is in and tells me what I hoped for. He's reserved an old bassoon that will be available in a few weeks. Gerard clearly is pleased I was so determined about what I wanted and came to him to arrange it.

Ottomar Schulze, how could you forget a name like that, is my lucky teacher. A short, fat man with a shiny bald head and very strict. I am always a bit scared of him and a lot if I had not practiced, but he is passionate about the bassoon and making his pupils into virtuosos and he sees it as a personal insult when I have not practiced. Actually, he is a bit like a bassoon himself.

The first weeks, he only teaches me to breathe from my abdomen; I have to learn to give support from my midriff because you become light-headed if your breathing is too high. I am so nervous, the memory of Roodenburg groping me; he puts his hand on my belly and one on my back. I then breathe in his hands, and he "empties" me when I exhale. He calls that "support from the belly, use your midriff".

My patience is tested because I immediately want to blow into that thing, but the master decides that I must wait. Breathing first and then further. I am so proud that I am going to play that hoarse pipe; I cannot wait to blow it. I put the case with the old Adler bassoon next to my bed and continuously put it together and dismantle it, like Ottomar taught me. This is quite a task because there are four wooden parts with valves and things that need to be joined if you place one pipe in the other and then the silver bocal, the S-bend and all parts can only be assembled in a certain order. When the pipes are assembled, the handle for the right hand you have to assemble, the silver L-pin to keep the two long pipes together and finally, the reed. The old case smells like camphor and every time I smell that somewhere, I return to that case in my room.

One year later, I play in the orchestra as one of its youngest members, just eleven—with an instrument almost as tall as me. Usually, the bassoons are at the back of the orchestra, but because I am so new to the instrument, Gerard places me next to the conductor's pedestal to indicate the measures when I lose track.

The first concert I experience is in Zwijndrecht in a big sports hall. My God, I'm part of an orchestra playing concerts! We travel with seventy people in two busses, and I study the sheet music to follow it better. I have no idea how to study music without playing the notes, but I try to hear the notes in my head and count the measures. We have a very special repertoire for a harmony orchestra and Gerard motivates the whole lot. The orchestra has a reputation (in Twente, at least) because Gerard did everything not to exclude anybody and always chose special music, we often swinged, but also had classical pieces, pop, jazz and blues. A bit of everything. The concert goes well. I had been quite nervous, but it was over now, and we could relax.

There is a long applause. I am very impressed by the whole event. Imagine all those people clapping for us. Gerard gestured to us to stand, and the whole orchestra follows in one wave. With our instruments in our hands, we bow and listen to the applause. It goes on and on. I stand there dead proud with my bassoon around my neck in the front row of the orchestra, next to Gerard. People do not stop clapping. The clapping intensifies until I suddenly notice they are clapping for me alone. I had not noticed that Gerard had already given the sign to sit down again.

Chapter 9

SOMETHING IN THE WATER

I am twelve years old and off to the high school, the coolest (left progressive) of the three in Hengelo, the city I was born in, and half an hour on our bikes from Borne where we moved to a couple of years before my father died.

Three years later, I am with the rest of my water polo team in the pool. We train, swim laps, do exercises to push ourselves up to rise above the water. I am the goalkeeper and am training to kick my complete upper body above the water, so I can catch the flying balls coming at me. I love being in the water, I am in flow with my body, I feel strong and good.

Our trainer is a woman with red hair, she is cool, I really like her. I might have a 'baby dyke' crush on her, like the young, awakening lesbian girl and the famous gym teacher. The training is over, and everyone leaves the water to get dressed. She waves to come over to her. I swim a few strong breast strokes and hang in the water, my arms on the edge, looking up at her curious why she called me over. "You might want to start wearing a top," she says. "They start showing." I want to sink to the bottom to never come up. I have no air in my lungs, I feel so humiliated!

I am fifteen and yes, my breasts are late to develop. I wished God had skipped me and would never grow them. Crushed and in a slight panic, I am thinking, *if she can see that they are there, then everybody can see that. So, how am I expected to get out of the pool and walk around half naked with a body that clearly needs to be covered?* I have a very cool bathing suit that I carefully selected of which I only wear the bottom. It is yellow and white and different, with longer pipes. As all female swimsuits did, it contained a top part, but I threw it out because that part was not for me. I am exposed, called out, humiliated, and embarrassed of trying to ignore that this is happening to me. With the external identifiers growing more visible, the freedom of being a kid in flow with my own body was stripped away. I feel so ripped off!

In my high school, we have some classes where we get introduced to or made aware of issues relating to our society, social classes. During those classes, issues like drugs, sexuality, religions, cults and sects, career paths to choose from, police and justice are addressed to prepare us to be conscious human beings in a world where we will have to make a lot of choices. Twickel College is quite an extraordinary high school, with a widespread reputation of being politically left wing-minded, actively anti-war and nukes, with anarchistic and experimental education approaches. Parents would either specifically choose to send their children there or absolutely not.

One of the subjects in these social awareness classes is homosexuality, which means that they actually invite homosexuals to come and explain how they discovered that they were gay. These classes are meant to reduce the prejudices and to ease the way for the ones amongst us who are possibly dealing with these issues in their own lives. At fifteen, I don't identify as gay; it is more like I slowly start to see, in reflection to the world around me, that all the others are not as normal as me!

This awareness process took place in me years before we have these classes and to me, being ahead of what these classes are supposed to bring, it seems like a bizarre spectacle to invite gays from outside the school while we have gays inside our school community as well. When you invite people from outside, in an attempt to normalize the phenomena, it simultaneously gives the message of being something alien, as if it doesn't exist within our own school community with its 1,200 students and ninety teachers.

Contemplating about how this situation could be improved, the idea roots in my head that I could be one of the gays doing these classes myself, facilitating them with Nicole, who had just moved from Groningen to Hengelo and landed in my class. The moment she was introduced in our class as the new student, we had recognized each other as 'family' and connected straight away—both having been confronted with being gay and how that impacted our relation to the world, emotionally far ahead and more mature than most of our fellow students.

Nicole is all in favor of doing the classes and together, we propose the idea to Ineke, the teacher.

We inform her how we can substitute the homosexuals from outside and do the classes ourselves, explaining all the benefits, not leaving her much space to object to it. We are quite the rebels. We have the heroic idea that we can be an example for our fellow students who are only just discovering their own homosexual feelings. We feel the adrenaline pumping by just the thought of climbing on the barricades to change the world and be at the forefront, not afraid of anything. Mind you, these are times that homosexuality is not really accepted as a normal thing. The word, *homosexual*, is still regarded as a disease by many people, something dirty, disgusting and punishable. Even curable.

At this age, emotions are very complicated and challenging, and we think it can help other young people who are struggling with their emotions in fear of being rejected, if they can identify with people their own age who have come out. As a teenager, I am unpolished, reckless and provocative. The crudeness of this age makes the process all the more interesting, mainly in the interactions with people who are beyond their teenage years.

61

The older people who are open to recognize and remember their own youth are okay, but the older people who now merely judge everything relating to teenager behavior are a potential source of frustration.

Ineke belongs to the first category and is quite amused and inspired, eliciting our input in her classes. She will need to run our big idea past the headmaster and the head of the section. It turns out they are scared for our safety, suggesting we could be yelled at, or even that our bike tires could be punctured.

Wouldn't it be wiser, after all, to invite the homosexuals from outside? The headmaster did not want to feel responsible for possible negative reactions. Nicole and I are determined though, arguing that if the reactions are so negative, it will support our initiative even more. Wasn't the purpose of the classes to advocate acceptance and normalcy for homosexuality?

We argue our case well and finally, they all support our appearance in the role of 'educators' during these classes. I tell my mum what we are going to do, and she thinks it is ridiculous that we need to be put on the spot. "Why do homosexuals have to explain themselves? Why don't they ask me how I discovered that I was a heterosexual?"

The following weeks, we are excused from the regular classes while we make our appearance as the gay educators. Word spreads around the school what we are doing, and it actually earns us a good reputation, we are regarded as brave and cool. None of the fears the headmaster had previously expressed materialize.

In that period, we are also engaged in career path classes to get professional advice to prepare for the course packages we have to choose in the third year. The aim of the professional advice is, of course, to give us a comprehensive view of the job opportunities for a well-grounded choice of studies, which would allow us to make an informed choice about the courses.

In the first hour of the professional advice, the teacher fires a round of questions about the professions of our parents. After my classmate, Jeanette says, "My dad is a policeman, and my mum is a housewife," it is my turn. I say, "My dad is dead, but he was—" She cuts me off. She looks at the next person and says, "Your dad…?" I want to get up and leave. I feel ignored, insulted, dismissed, and ridiculed. I am angry at her, her ignorance; and I have nowhere to go with it.

I learn to avoid talking about death, as people are clumsy and not willing to be in conversations about death. I feel misunderstood and like an outcast, isolated. It feels like I am being punished for having a dead father. It's endlessly lonely. My first thoughts of leaving develop. Leaving life, leaving to another country, anything but being here.

Jeroen and Hans are classmates who recently join from another school. We form a circle of friends around them. They are a bit older, and Hans has already served in the army. I am introduced to hashish and start smoking joints. I found an escape from being here.

Chapter 10

LOVE AND LOSS ARE FOUR-LETTER WORDS, TOO

During the summer holidays, my mum sends me to music camps, with one-third of kids with disabilities playing adapted instruments. We dance and sing and play in orchestra. Karsten and Dan, the two brothers, both with quite advanced muscular dystrophy, have wheelchair races in the hallway. Marcel accidentally drops one of his glass eyes and the slightly smaller spare rolls in his head; he tunes the milk bottles during lunch. Hanneke, who has no knee and elbow joints, beats me and all others with table tennis. Dommeltje is the daughter of a famous Dutch author and is brighter than pure light. In these camps, I don't feel like the only weirdo—I have a strange familiarity with the disabled kids, as they understand my experience of being different. But they are also kids from affluent families, and I am not, being from the east and the only kid from farmland. Many of their references sound like from a movie, and as a kid from the poor class, I am still an outsider, learning about other levels of being an outsider.

During the first camp, I meet Pat, who's also from the east and lives near me. We start seeing each other. She refers to her parents as *X* and *Y*. Something is wrong. I don't have the words for it, but abuse is an issue in her family. Shiny from the outside, playing violins and all, Pat is emotionally compromised, and she starts leaning on me. She often threatens to kill herself, and I do not know what to do other than to be there as much as I can, and distract the family dynamics by just being there, which is 40km on my bike.

When the favorite girls are invited by one of the music camp leaders to Paul's house, I feel rejected, not girl enough to be invited. Only years later, I learn that he was a sexual predator, inviting the girls into his home to abuse them. Not being girl enough had advantages.

I am in a European music competition in Neerpelt and win the first prize with the bassoon duo. I play in the orchestra, and we do an international tour, where one of the musicians becomes more than a friend. I want to fit in.

He is a tall, blond guy, sits next to me in the youth orchestra I play second bassoon in. I am over the moon to have a boyfriend, though we have not even exchanged as much as a kiss. Everybody else in the orchestra is trying to date since with a boyfriend, you are part of the cool group. I don't belong and trying to have a boyfriend is an attempt to fit it, while always feeling like a fraud inside. Having only played the bassoon for two years now, I am too young for this seat, but I am working hard. He is a good number of years older than me, tells me when to turn the page, points at the bar when I lose count so I can catch up. I notice how the girls get envious that he pays attention to me.

I wake up and get up to go to the bathroom. I open my bedroom door, and he comes out of my mum's bedroom. I stumble and try to pretend this did not just happen. "Uh, we need to talk," he utters, nearly naked, and I say, "No, if anybody, my mum needs to talk to me." For the record, she never does!

New neighbors move in a couple of houses up, a young couple. I like her, Lidy. She is the first woman I fall in love with. Through her, I realize I love women. She is twenty-six and pregnant, I am fourteen. Her husband is a bit of a loser, a weak guy. When Lianne is born, I spend a lot of time with Lidy and the baby. Lidy has a postnatal depression and does not get the help she needs. I am close with Lidy, and she tells me that it feels like she is in a glass bell jar and all she says bounces back to her, and everything people outside the bell jar say, bounces back to them, but I am in the bell jar with her, the only one who understands her. She shares her feelings with me, explaining what a postnatal depression is. "When a mother has not landed properly when she was born, making a transition from other realms to earth, she experiences that again when she must land again as she is there to birth the baby."

I am every day after school with Lidy and she gets more and more depressed. She feels more and more isolated and "crazy", as the people around her start calling her. First, she is admitted in psychiatric daycare where the psychiatrist abuses his patients, as it turns out later. The situation spins out of control and Lidy is admitted in a psychiatric clinic, and I am not allowed to visit her.

I've turned sixteen, and the adults 'dealing with' Lidy do not acknowledge my closeness with Lidy; I have no access. Finally, I negotiate with my mum that I can go and visit her for her birthday, and Lidy knows I am coming. I am ecstatic that I will finally see her again. Two days before her birthday, Jan enters our house. I am upstairs and I hear him tell my mum that Lidy has committed suicide. She walked in the water and left this life. I close my bedroom door and withdraw from all life.

I stop eating, lose weight, energy, to the point of fainting on the floor of the canteen. Vilja, my Dutch teacher, is called to find me. She takes me to her flat and serves me a large plate of mashed potatoes and cabbage. She helps me dress in her clothes, and I sleep there. I feel so safe with Vilja, who calls my mum to explain that I will stay with her for a few weeks. Over the years, our teacher-pupil relationship changes into a deep friendship and I will forever cherish my love for who she is to me.

I smoke, skip school, play billiards, smoke pot, am an activist on pink Saturdays, supporting Greenpeace and anti-nuclear missile installations, drink and have a few lesbian friends.

As a youngster in secondary school, I participate in the Pax Christi pilgrimage and meet Judith. I get into my first relationship and am so innocent. For the first four years, there is no sex, just intimacy. (Loved that pace!)

I stand there, not sure if I really want to be there, filled with nervousness. But at the same time, I am glad, as it's exciting. My older niece and nephew have come here a few years and always returned wildly enthusiastic, and now, I'm here too, at last. The Pax Christi hikes are a must if you call yourself slightly alternative, and politically aware, against nuclear power, against racism and sexism, for peace and believe in equal human rights.

"Alternative" signifies a whole outfit of ripped jeans, T-shirts with political slogans, Indian scarves, patchouli, Jesus sandals, earrings, long unwashed and uncombed hair, hip hats and tobacco bags, SAMSON with red RIZLA in the back pocket of the worn jeans with the king-size filters to roll a joint from time to time. The additional equipment for a hike like this is old army chests and a secondhand rucksack.

It's October and rainy. I arrive early at the meeting point near the 'Brabant halls' in Den Bosch. I know my group is No. 84 so I scan the crowd for a sign with the number. I soon spot it, and I'm the first of the group to be formed in the next half hour. The woman holding the sign is older and seems to be one of the group leaders. She is pleased I am there because she has to pick something up, so she hands me the sign and disappears.

I stand there alone and quietly waiting for what's coming, moving people all around me, screams of people seeing each other again after a year, excited and shy new people. Everybody caters to the happy atmosphere, as the big square is filled with at least 2,000 young people from the whole country trying to find their groups of old acquaintances from past hikes.

At go time, the groups of fifteen, with two leaders each, walk in different directions. We sleep in farms, schools, barns or factory spaces organized along the various routes. A number of groups share the same accommodation each night, easier for the organization of meals. The whole idea is to bring young people together to talk and exchange about big topics like world peace, personal development and hashish.

In the crowd, a woman walks towards me, towards the sign, of course, to join our group. She has curly, chestnut, shoulder-length hair, and she's wearing a bright yellow raincoat, round glasses, lilac shirt, torn jeans, and old, worn suede shoes. She has an air of nonchalance, almost indifference.

She finds a spot. Looking shy, it is clear she tries to puff up an attitude because she feels uncomfortable in the situation. She takes her tobacco and starts to roll a cigarette nice and tight with a belly in the middle. I know she is for life—I completely fall in love in a few seconds. I start walking near her in the first kilometers. I so want to talk with her but am so nervous, words are not coming easy. I take an apple from the pocket of my raincoat, asking if she wants a bite. She seems pleased I spoke to her! She does want a bite of my apple, but she's sensing double meaning in my question. I'm Innocent and had not grown up with the *Bible*, so I had no idea. Judith, who grew up in the far south of Limburg, knew more about those things. Later, we laugh about the ultimate chat-up line our relationship started with.

Four months later, we are in Boxtel for the reunion of the Pax hike on January 10. Four months of not concentrating at school, I am so in love. Four months that trebled my mother's phone bill. Four months in which I have become a permanent member of her family. Four months of travelling by train three hours each way between St-Joost and Borne to see each other every weekend. Four months of still not being able to suss her out, to evaluate her feelings.

Marian, who had organized the reunion, is a daughter of affluent and educated people, living in the best neighborhood of Boxtel in an elegant, old city house. Everyone can sleep in the enormous attic under the beautiful roof of the old house. The whole attic is full of camping mats and sleeping bags. It's freezing with lots of snow outside and we also use the sleeping bags to sit in. Near the stairwell is a record player that can't be nearer because the extension cord is too short. The music of Janis Joplin, Patty Smith, Pink Floyd, the Doors and more timeless sounds play on. There is plenty to eat and to drink, everybody talking about the months after the hike, with a joint here and there.

By midnight, I want to go out in the snow. Judith and I walk down the stairs and out the door, slightly drunk and a bit stoned. We walk and walk, giggling but not saying a lot. Buildings are getting sparse and slowly, the village is behind us. It starts snowing again under a full moon and frigid mist.

The sound of the fresh, crispy snow is all we can hear. We walk over a round bridge looking like the entrance of a park or something. We stop in the middle of the high bridge, lean over the railing and peer down at the cracks in the ice. The fresh snow covered the ice, the water rose through the cracks and the cracks looked like big, deep black arteries in the fresh snow lit by the full moon. We walk further, our steps in the snow the only proof of life on earth.

We suddenly see a castle through the trees. How can that be? Eerily lit in the moonlight in the grey shades of the night, we ask ourselves if we are imagining it because we are stoned or if it's real, but we immediately abandon the reality check and decide to approach it. We decide we would walk into a fairy tale. We get near the castle, with a wide moat and a draw bridge. The bridge is down. It is all so unreal, dragons flying out of the towers with flames in their big nostrils. Little creatures could lift their heads through the cracks in the ice of the moat anytime now. The holes and cracks in the ice are so jet black that we cannot help but imagine a whole world underneath. The walls of the castle seem alive. Ivy turns its leaves and looks at us, the windows are liquid and reflecting the moon. The full moon is blindingly white. We imagine that the cosmos is a huge balloon, a type of membrane with the moon and stars as holes to see the light outside the balloon.

Inspired, I say, "A cell of the human body has a core with rings around it, on which all sorts of atoms and plutons jump, dance to the impulses it gets. Imagine that our whole solar system, with a core and all the planets around it, is just one cell of a much bigger gigantic body. Imagine how small we are then. Who knows, there are so many things we do not know yet. We think that we humans are so important, more intelligent and better than the rest, but think how stupid we would be to think we matter."

Judith looks at the moon, blowing the smoke of her roll-up, but the smoke continues to come. You cannot see the difference between the cigarette smoke and the breath in the cold night. Judith empties her lungs more than usual, because she wants to breathe out the smoke.

Suddenly it becomes darker, the grey shades deepen, and the lighter greys disappear. The moon disappears slowly by a black disc that slides in front of the moon, until the moon is no more than a light hue behind a perfect black ball. It makes us giggle again because the park becomes even more enchanted in the dark grey shades at the times the moon is fully eclipsed. So surreal.

I am seventeen years old, completely in love and that is when I tell her I love her for the first time. I have rehearsed it countless times in my head, but never expected it would come out just like that. She looks at me, gives me my first kiss and starts giggling again. The giggling turns into laughter and is so contagious that I start too, giggling, laughing, louder and louder, I am so unbelievably happy. Her whole face is a laugh, and our jaws start aching from laughing. She holds her belly and has to sit down. In the snow, we have lost control.

We lie down in the fresh snow and move our arms and legs to create angels, the arms, wings, the legs, the dresses.

When we finally leave the park, the snow between all the trees in the castle gardens is covered in angels. We giggle, imagining what the castle residents will think the next day when they look out of the window and are surrounded by angels. When we return to the attic, we have to be really quiet because everybody is sleeping. We zip our sleeping bags together and crawl in them. We warm each other up and fall into a deep sleep very close to each other.

Chapter 11
THE BALD ARTIST

1981

It's the summer holidays after HAVO (higher general continued education, ages twelve to seventeen, in the Dutch system), and I work a few weeks in Amersfoort in the live-in working commune, de Kromme Spaak ("The Bent Spoke") in the Kromme straat, where we specialize in old delivery tricycles and transport bicycles. It's a beautiful, old house filled with parts of old and often antique bicycles. Janos and Barend work in the cycle workshop and there are two other residents whose names escape me. Everything is handmade in the house, recycled wood, salvaged parts used for furniture, and we bake our own bread. Everything we eat is organic and of course, we do not eat meat. We take turns cooking, and I'm very happy here.

Janos is a very quiet man, I think in his late twenties, who stutters a bit but more out of shyness than through a speech deficiency. Janos and I work well together, and he likes me, too much, which is also the reason I can't become one of the permanent residents after my trial period of a month is up. It's terrible to think of leaving, as the remaining time to search for a course is very short, indeed, and finding an arts academy that still has selection days only leaves the one in Kampen. We have to draw still lives the whole day, make a portrait in wax, show samples of our own work and go through an interview about our motivation to attend.

The arts academy is located in the former van Heutz barracks on the IJssel, a heritage building with two wings square onto the central building. As a joke, I say to one of the other applicants that if they would not accept me, I set fire to the school.

Back at my mum's in Borne that evening, I see on the NOS news that the right wing of the van Heutz barracks burnt down. It's hard to believe what I'm seeing on the television. I feel horrible for joking about such a thing. I resolve never to say such things again, and I get accepted into the academy.

Janos gives me a very old frame of a motor tricycle, cargo bike as a goodbye present, a very unusual frame. A three-sided steel beam connects the saddle part with the wheel axis. Everything is rusty through and through, but still good enough to restore.

Janos must have understood me really well to give me that old frame as a gift, he delivered it with his old HIJ bus in Borne to my mother's home, triggering me to create in the garage day and night. I clean off the rust of every separate part, rig replacements for all wires, pedals, ball bearings, brakes in the drums, tires and lights. I have to completely dismantle the leaf springs and remove the heavy rust from them one by one. I manage to restore the heavy rounded metal mudguards and adapt the brake system and because there's no longer an engine, it becomes a push bike. A heavy chain, cranks, hubs, gear wheels and the old leather saddle are restored, and the chassis is ready. Of course, I visit the Kromme Spaak for the parts and to spoke the wheels with their special tools.

The frame has a strange proportion because the engine block was placed in front of the saddle pin, which makes the frame lower than usual. I fit the beams on the repaired and renovated springs with screwed steel strips I bent in such a way that I can fit a piece of round wood through them to be used as handlebars. Everything has to fit perfectly in order for the bike to be comfortable. I build the cart on wooden beams, narrower than for a normal cargo bike, to be fitted between the heavy mudguards and much longer. The metal and wood are black. I spray the metal parts or have them baked, depending on their size. The frame is too large to powder coat, so I have it sprayed, but the rest is better protected by the harder powder coat layer as it is actually burnt in with heat. Finally, a big ding-dong bell. My cargo bike is ready!

With no time to choose another academy, I start at the Christian Academy for the Arts, sculpting. However, when the anti-discrimination law is voted on, and my show of a pink triangle is not appreciated, they degrade me, making sure I will not get to the second year.

I am bald, finally daring to shave everything off, after contemplating it for years. Albert, the friend from the art academy, had enthusiastically started cutting with scissors and then Anneke, also a classmate, had fun shaving the stubble off. It was unreal and exciting. Bald. Completely bald. It feels great, and I can't stop touching it. If it would not have such a huge social impact, I would always be bald.

My father studied in Delft in the past and my mother told the story of the hazing he endured. He had been shaved bald after which he got curly hair. In the search for my identity, I wanted to explore if I was like my father in that respect. I needed to know, so I had to try.

It's my mother's birthday, though, and she's not impressed to see her daughter with a bald head. When Willem, my oldest brother, arrives bald as well, for the same reason apparently, it appears that we've ruined my mum's birthday.

Aunt Rie, my father's only sister, comes for coffee and asks, quite surprised, why we are both bald. Timidly, we tell her we will get curls just like dad after that initiation. Aunt Rie starts laughing with her trademark covering of her mouth to hide her slightly wonky teeth. The corners of her eyes are droopy, and she doesn't laugh much so it's even more pronounced when she does. "He always had curly hair!" she howls.

Chapter 12
SAY YES TO THE DRESS!

Working in the Moriaan, a cultural grand café and restaurant in Kampen, I've been able to be me—or at least, the parts I've pieced together as a teen. I want to venture out. I'm preparing my intended journey by bicycle to France, so I announce my last 'on duty' evening to Martin, who has been my wonderful colleague. He's a forty-five-year-old, flamboyant, gay man who has called me "his sister in the struggle". I don't know which struggle he means, but it's one of those phrases that has wings. It flies around once in a while, and it gives me the feeling that I am special to him.

The Moriaan is a strange place in a strange town. Kampen is an ultra-conservative Protestant stronghold that has recently opened up to the world by the sudden establishment of the Art, Journalism, Social and Expression-Drama-Theatre and Theology academies, all academies that tend to attract the more alternative and left wing—certainly not religious—students. In the first years, much tension and street fights between students and Kampen youth occurred frequently. Even after five or six years, the original population is still defensive and regards the students as unwelcome intruders, bringing evil to town with their anti-religious and pagan behavior. The students changed everything and the Kampen population did not want change; they still live in the Dark Ages and like it that way. "Black-stockings-people" we call them and in fact, it's their official nickname, which refers to the black clothing they wear to church while their women must cover their heads and faces with black lace veils. Also, the doom-and-gloom atmosphere is pervasive around them, as openly enjoying or having fun is obviously out of the question. They were born sinners and guilty by existence, so they sulk through life with this massive weight on their shoulders, the weight of guilt and payback time.

The city has separate student areas, and even cafés and other establishments are clearly earmarked for either students or natives, and if you dare to mix or challenge the unmentioned but recognized boundaries, then trouble abounds. There is an exception though. I made it a habit to play billiards in 'the Centre', a clearly Kampen café, just because I like to play billiards and these locals know how to play, have a beer and concentrate on a game instead of getting side-tracked by local issues. They condone me, but this is highly exceptional. I don't like scenes or division based on race or other differences and in a natural way, I always seem to maneuver between different groups without offending people.

The Moriaan is clearly a student café, one of the few but the largest. It is a substitute for the lack of living rooms in the student housing, a cozy atmosphere with a huge table with candles, newspapers and magazines framed by dramatic, large windows. Right after opening time, the table is surrounded by the regular customers having their coffee or other habitual drinks. The bartenders fold napkins or roll the cutlery in napkins in preparation of the evening. Coffee bubbles away continuously in the percolator and its aroma draws in more customers. While Herman does all the preparatory work for dinner in the kitchen, me and Martin prepare the beer barrels, check the bottles and fill the shelves, clean the glasses and refill the cellar. The bar dominates the front space, tables at the center and in the far back, a stage calls to performers and wanna-be stars. We organize regular cultural evenings, live music gigs, political talks and special film screenings. The wooden floors and the gentle green wainscoting give the place a pleasant atmosphere; it is a second home for many students.

The Moriaan is adjacent to the local cinema and next door to the illegal brothels, embedded in the native zones in the back alleys of Kampen, a block behind the local theatre and the central church. Walk from the church, with the café behind you, parallel to the one shopping main street, take a left, then you immediately see the beautiful, old façade of the Moriaan, which had been an upper-class hotel in earlier years. Kampen used to be a great trading place and when businesspeople came to visit. They stayed in the Moriaan.

Kampen is one of the 'Hanze' cities, cities along the rivers that were once actively involved in trading goods over the river and flourished. Kampen is situated on the IJssel, one of those rivers flowing through the Netherlands. In memory of its heritage and trading past, Kampen still had a large fleet of the so-called "flat bottoms", the old wooden and steel boats used to transport goods from one end of the country to the other and between Rotterdam harbor and German cities. The flat bottoms allowed for sailing quite shallow waters and in recent times, these old boats were converted to leisure sailing boats. Groups of up to twenty people could hire them for a weekend or a week to go sailing on the IJsselmeer. Some even sail the North Sea to reach the islands on the north coast of the Netherlands.

On Fridays and Sundays, when the boats return to Kampen, the sailors bring their groups to the Moriaan to have dinner at the end of their journeys. The Moriaan has space for around eighty people dining at one time and on these evenings, the place is jam-packed, with people waiting to get the tables for the next service. While Herman and his assistant are cooking at top speed in the kitchen preparing the orders, me and Martin, assisted by Johan and Jet, work our asses off to get all the plates from the kitchen to each group at the same time. We fly through the heavy double swinging doors with our arms fully loaded with plates of steaming food. We never run into each other, we are a well-oiled engine, working better the busier it gets.

With movie night next door, Tuesday evenings are full speed ahead. As the doors open, 200 people crowd in for a drink at the same time. Martin and I juggle bottles to each other, shove the right glasses over the bar, and exchange half a word, enough to see what the other needs. I love the high-speed work behind the bar with Martin, eyes and ears wide open and reacting to the people on the other side of the bar. When, for example, Maarten appears through the door, I pour his red and hand it to him as friendly acknowledgment while taking peoples' orders. He knows he is felt and seen before we lube up the crowd. The Moriaan, a home-away-from-home for students and other artists in quite a hostile town.

Nearing graduation at my carpentry school, the idea of going by bike to France starts taking shape. I pick a date to leave, the night of the 28th of September, a full moon night, for me to start biking away from Kampen. I've been working in the Moriaan for the past one-and-a-half years and now, it's time to say goodbye. In a crazy mood, I had promised Martin that I would work all dressed up as a woman on my last evening but with his brain perhaps drowning in excessive alcohol intake, he forgot my promise.

Loes is a student at the academy for Expression and Drama and certainly a regular in the Moriaan, a friend and all-out doll with her heavy Limburg accent (southern with a soft G, like "Judith"), blond, wild, curly hair and always excited, happy and light-hearted demeanor, a joy to be around. I fill her in on the promise I made to Martin, and she gets psyched that she can dress me up as a woman. Nobody is to find out before the break of the evening, the moment I am entering the Moriaan as I have never done before. Loes has all the gear for the dressing event.

Loes goes through her wardrobe of possibilities, mumbling something about my short hair, then grabs a garment and holds it in front of me. She shakes her head and shuffles to the next piece. I trust Loes, the expert, since I have nothing useful to bring to the table in the way of women's outfits. She concludes that a professional-type outfit will best suit me: a pencil skirt with a subtle slit on each side, a billowing, dark grey silk blouse with a gentle pink-reddish flower print, tights with a seam on the back, pumps and big, round ear clips. I only have a hole in my left ear from piercing it, then filling it with half a paperclip when I was fourteen years old.

Loes dresses me, schools me on what to do, how to walk, gels and sprays my hair, hands me accessories like thin gloves to hide my working hands and a small handbag that makes it all look chic. She sits me down to apply minimal makeup not to overdo it. She steps back to examine her masterpiece, a little adjustment here and there, and here I am, a living doll.

Finally, I look in the mirror, which she had prevented me from doing before because she knows damn well that when she lets me have any say, it will ultimately not happen at all. Now I can only gaze at the mirror, see the end result and accept what I see, no time left to object. Loes takes my hand and walks me over to the Moriaan. As I stroll through the streets of Kampen, weirdly comfortable in the high heels, which surprises me, I notice reactions from people being different than I'm used to. By the time we arrive in the Moriaan, I have completely taken on the role of this new person. I enjoy it. I feel confident.

Loes enters a few minutes ahead of me. As I make my entrance, I notice that none of my friends or colleagues recognize me. Martin approaches me and asks what I would like to drink. I twist my voice a little, tweak higher than my own voice and respond, "A red wine please." When he returns, he stops in his tracks, taking me in to full recognition but immediately swallows his reaction to let others find out for themselves. He grabs a chair and sits next to me. "Darling, what a difference, I can't believe it is you." He can't get over the transformation. It becomes a celebration, as he starts playing dance music, turns it up loud and invites me to ballroom dance with him, something I had no experience with, but Martin is an excellent dancer who leads me on the floor like it's only natural. Similar to the responses of regulars and friends who slowly start realizing that it is their bartender who they only know in jeans and butch shirts, they comment I'm a "good transvestite" or I "look like a cross-dresser" and so on. I don't feel like a woman. I feel like a man dressed as a woman! I internalize these comments with confused feelings, but the comments are congruent with what I feel.

It turns out to be a great night with lots of dancing till the night sisters on horseback ride in (how Martin refers to the police officers who always come to check if we close on time). Rules are rules, and in Kampen, this is something to be taken seriously. We close the curtains, turn the music down and have a crowd of people helping us to clean up, count the cash, and drink more. We're not finished with the evening. We have plans to continue on to the next café, not a typical students' pub, but more a place for everybody out and about past 2:00 a.m.

Martin calls Rinus, the owner of Boogschutter, which is located on the river quay, announcing our arrival. "Hey, guess what, Rinus, Babs looks a bit different tonight. Just play along, okay?" Playing dress-up or not, I have an outstanding issue with Rinus about a large dormer to be constructed on his house and this is the perfect opportunity to discuss it with him at the bar.

I don't waste any time once we arrive. I stand tall in my pumps. "Hey Rinus, about that roof light and the rest of the refurbishment of the attic you asked me to do? When do you want to get that done? And we need to talk about my pay, winter is coming closer you know, we need to get moving on this; otherwise, it is too late to open the roof up." The regulars who, hours ago, left their state of soberness, nearly fall off their stools when they hear Rinus discussing technical stuff with this finely dressed lady. Martin and the rest of the crowd watch from just behind the regulars and piss themselves laughing. I have problems keeping a straight face.

Martin had mentioned her in numerous conversations, so I felt I knew her before I ever met her. My back is to the door, but I feel a presence entering. I watch over my shoulder. This must be Colet. A deep, long breath, as a sigh, numbs all the babbling for a moment. A breathtaking woman, tall, who from under her heavily but exquisitely colored eyelids, scans the room. From top to bottom, she's tastefully dressed, not missing one detail. Her clothing is rather chic, her hair neatly tied up whereby every hair seems to be meticulously placed. She wears a light blue dress with an endless number of tiny folds, the finest fabric, a white thinly woven, tight vest and gorgeous high heels at the end of her strong, long legs draped in perfect tights. Matching earrings and a collar with a white oval medallion with a carved little silhouette, like the face of the queen on a coin. Her perfume barely noticeable but just enough to attract you and give you the notion of being around someone very special.

Martin introduces her for formality's sake only, as her presence needs no prelude. Her voice is like a soft spring rain against a shy sun shining from under the evening clouds, dark but endlessly attractive. Turns out she has an impertinent sense of humor, often harboring cynicism, hilariously funny. Her nimble way of telling stories makes everybody hang on to her lips, hungry for more stories. She tells amazing vignettes about her past when she still had the body of a man, her well-manicured hands moving with incredible elegance. In her late forties, born with a male body, Colet is the first woman in the Netherlands to have gone through the complete transition from male to female, matching with who she felt she was. I feel strangely connected to her.

Chapter 13

CAVE DWELLING

On New Year's Eve, I often make deals with those I share the
most important day of the year with. It's the first year after leaving
home. I live in Kampen and celebrate with Willem, my brother, and
we create a plan for what we will do in the New Year. It has to be
related to a house, something with natural materials, and it can't cost
anything. After some talking, we decide that we have to build a house
somewhere. It can be a model, built in natural materials, present on
the building spot, and the big challenge is that it must be a house
suited and hard-wearing for the climate where it is built. And again, it
can't cost anything.

I am crazy about Hungarian oven systems and in Den Andel, a
hippy village in the north of the Netherlands where I often spend
holidays with Joke, the oldest daughter of the Ettes family, who lives
there with her boyfriend, we build tiled stoves. We build them through
the walls, so they heat several rooms at the same time. Historically,
they were built in castles. I want to combine Hungarian oven systems
with tiled stoves but do not exactly know how. I develop a system,
with baking as a starting point, but I reverse the oven. That reversal is
the solution. Instead of baking things in the oven, I will bake the oven
itself. The oven is then the home I want to build. If I build the house
in clay, fill it with dry flammable material, cover it with another layer
of dry material of approximately one meter, and then cover it with
another layer of clay, I can actually bake the whole house. I want to
build the house with a stove inside, also in clay, which will form smoke
ducts and the chimney through the benches, like in tiled stoves where
the hot air is led down with the smoke through a system of smoke

ducts to obtain as much heat as possible, which would otherwise escape via the chimney.

I will build the smoke ducts along the walls. All in wet clay, leave to dry, and then fill with the dry flammable material, seal and cover with the outer layer, leave to dry and light. When I light the unit from above and provide enough air supply from below, it should be possible to bake the whole house in a day or two, like a raku oven system, which does not reach very high temperatures, but can heat flimsy material sufficiently to turn clay into stone. After baking, I can then break off the outer shell and the baked house will appear. A reverse oven, in fact.

I'm determined to test-build the house in France and convince my friend, Albert, to come along. We hitchhike our way south on the Easter holiday, no idea where we are going, only that we have to find a river where we can build the house.

We find a spot on the river near Vallon-Pont-d'Arc where the Ardêche river flows under a huge bend; the river is sinuous there and deposits lots of clay in the bends. We buy a cheap 10-liter pack of red wine and twenty coconuts, some aluminum foil, lemons and salt, fishing hooks and line. Otherwise, we only have tobacco and lighters on us. We sleep in a hole in the rock wall in a wide bend of the river. We call ourselves cave dwellers, make fires and fish with flimsy lines. We even succeed in catching a rainbow trout! We bake the fish in aluminum foil filled with lemon and salt and drink the cheap wine that tastes like the best we ever had. We invent our own language, *Khaskum Khaum*, meaning "I want to go home", and *Khabung*, "I'm hungry."

Albert and I camp there for two weeks in the cave and build the house. I honor the deal with my brother. It's only a model and not as big as we aspired, but it worked.

You can bake a whole house, and within days, you can, in fact, have a stone house.

Chapter 14

FIGHTING FOR A CAUSE WHILE FIGHTING OFF RAPE

1983

I am nineteen, and hitchhike with others to Sicily for a court case against twelve women who demonstrated in Comiso, one of Europe's women's peace camps in the time in which the nuclear cruise missiles on the American bases are made operational.

Late in the afternoon, we catch a lift in the Po Valley by a man in a red Ferrari on his way to Rome. We're so relieved since hitchhiking has not been good. He drives very fast, around 200k/hr, it doesn't feel that he is in control, but getting out is crazy. He'll get us to Rome in no time. Even so, I still decide to ask him to stop, and he drops us at a gas station. Heleen is livid I made this executive decision for both of us, but I don't care. Almost immediately another car going to Rome stops. Not even ten minutes later, we get stuck in traffic. There's been an accident. When we drive past, I see a completely wrecked red Ferrari against the safety rails. The driver is dead.

I'm rattled. The court case we're attending is against twelve women from seven different countries. Women who had, two years prior, chained themselves to the railings of the American military base in Comiso to protest the stationed cruise missiles there. The demonstrations had not ended peacefully, and the women were arrested, jailed and extradited. Because they were punished twice, in effect, they started proceedings against the Italian state; the extradition should not have happened because they had already

87

served time in prison. I hear about this court case around the campfire in Volkel, the women's peace camp, just opposite the entrance of the American base on a plot of wasteland that I helped install. We made tents based on the example of the "benders" that the women of Greenham Common made, Greenham Common, the big women's peace camp in England, the mother of all camps near military bases where nuclear cruise missiles were made operational. We stuck bent branches into the ground, tied them together and covered them with blankets, layer upon layer, insulated well under the agricultural plastic. A thick layer of straw and hay on the floor covered in plastic with a pile of blankets instead of mattresses. The huts were cozy and very comfortable. It was winter and freezing. We sat around the fire with a group of women, warm at the front, our backs ice cold.

We often had visitors, fun sometimes, but sometimes also aggressive visitors who felt threatened by some women in a women's camp. One night during carnival, we were sitting around the fire and a car stopped next to the piles of wood that sheltered us from the road. It was late and most women were already asleep in the benders. From the car, four visibly drunk men threw something in the wood. We peered through the dark to see what was happening. Only three of the women still sat around the fire. An arm threw a lit match from the back window and *woosh*, the wood started burning immediately, the car raced away, the men shouting obscenities. I ran to the fire and saw what they had done. It seemed they had filled a milk carton with petrol and thrown it into the wood. I quickly assessed the situation; the carton had landed upright in the brush and most of the petrol was still in the carton. The fire around the carton ebbed away because it was only some spilled petrol that had caught fire. I took the carton carefully from the flames, fire on petrol, aware it could explode if it moved more and too much evaporated. I carefully walked to the road with the carton, and at a safe distance from the camp, I threw the flaming carton away...*woosh*, and the danger was gone.

While I fully focused on removing the danger, because women were asleep just behind the wood, I heard two other women scream in panic and wake others. Now that it was over, everyone was cozily talking about the incident while I shook with fear, processing what just happened. Women from other camps visited, often from other countries, who then stayed a few days, helped us to prepare actions or brought news about activities in the other women's camps.

When women from Greenham on their journey to Sicily to attend and publicize the court case informed us what was happening, Heleen, one of the "permanent" camp residents, and I agreed quickly that we wanted to go too. Heleen with her accordion and me with my guitar. We earned money by busking. We traveled through South Germany where I had friends, who I knew from the international music weeks that I participated in during high school. I cashed a cheque of 500 guilders—without credit at the time, but I vowed to pay it back later and I did. We hitchhiked to Baden Baden, Laufenburg, Zurich, Torino, Syracuse.

And here we are in the last leg of this important journey.

After the shock of seeing the red Ferrari crash into the safety rails, we arrive in Rome to stay a few days. We play on squares and earn our daily bread, or rather, pizza. We sleep in a women's house, a beautiful, old building with an inner courtyard. The street entrance is a big portal followed by a tunnel. A fabulous barrel arch with handmade bricks that are seamlessly joint. A courtyard with galleries on the floors that you can walk around in, arches and crossed arches, entrances and stairs to the next floor, peeling paint and rough, sober mosaic tiles on the floors. A courtyard where Italian women yell at each other while hanging up the washing on lines you can move on rolls. The rooms on the ground floor belong to the women's house.

There are more women staying in the women's house on their way to Comiso, Sicily and we get to know many, singing songs together while the courtyard resounds with the sound of Heleen's accordion.

The old bricks are covered in moss. There are women everywhere, wild women. Those on the balconies are silent when we're singing until they are inspired to hum along.

Hitchhiking is not without risk in Italy, as we discover. I quickly surmise that all men here ask you to have sex sooner or later. A simple "no thank you, not today" has done the trick a few times, but when we hitch a lift with two trucks, things are different. We are nineteen years old, naive and inexperienced. Heleen and I hop into separate trucks, which we never should have done. It does not feel right, but they convince us.

Early in the evening, the driver starts to make comments that crawl under my skin, talking to me in Italian. I try to find English words I can say with an Italian accent to explain I'm not interested. He becomes more and more insistent, and I want out. I demand for him to stop the truck for me to get out. I almost panic. He grins and tries to touch me.

I start raising my voice to which he only replies with more insinuations and comments about sex (that much I can understand in a foreign language!). He's not listening, not stopping. He points to his crotch and my breasts. I can just avoid him physically—the steering wheel is too far away to touch me. Trapped against the door, I desperately contemplate how I can make him stop and then flee. Suddenly, he opens his fly and an enormous cock appears, which he starts to pull on wildly. My panic disappears. A huge disgust comes over me. Now, I change my tune to loud swearing in Dutch, seething. How dare he, the dirty bastard. I despise him. I'm truly scared, angrier because my body reacts as a defense to the threat of rape, I am aroused and feel betrayed by my own body, but I don't know that yet. I scream over it. I feel fucked by him and myself. My anger jolts him into getting confused and asking for explanations. I continue to swear and speak Dutch nonstop. "Today, we have carrots and a soy schnitzel, and we buy it in the health food shop every Friday after the market where we buy fresh vegetables at the end of the market..."

I talk gibberish, anything that comes to mind, to not hear a second of silence, not a second. I'm ice cold, my voice loud but no longer screaming, every word a bullet I fire at him. I go on and on, word after word, no second of rest, until he has no chance. The more confused he is, the calmer I become. My voice cools down as I regain control and feel less threatened. He buttons up his fly sheepishly. He appears helpless. I talk like a waterfall until he stops the truck at the next gas station. I feel a massive relief.

I jump out, grab my rucksack and run to the second truck that had been following close behind during this whole ordeal. Heleen jumps out. She tries to argue that they will drive further, and we'll miss a good ride, but I do not let her finish. My anger is now focused on her because she starts arguing with me in front of the truck drivers, the idiot. I hardly know Heleen, only from a few weeks in Volkel, from the women's camp, but this hitchhiking experience immediately slices a big rift in the trust to travel together. I don't see an option to travel alone though. I feel trapped but think of Comiso, where there will be other women to connect with.

This is a lesson. When we boarded the truck, it didn't feel right, like with the Ferrari, but this time, Heleen convinced me we take the ride as it would get us 800km further. I ignored my gut feeling and paid the price. I learned that I do not need a solid argument, I need to trust my gut.

The court case lasts three days, along with our hunger strike with a Buddhist monk who meditates outside the courtroom. We join out of solidarity. At the same time, women from all over the world attract attention to the court case. The women's camp, La Ragnatela, overflows in those days.

One evening, we sit around the fire, sharing bread and wine. Someone plays guitar beautifully and not just a few chords thrown together. She sings and it is quiet, as everyone is breathless around her, staring at her or the fire. A shy but very powerful woman makes

91

a strong impression on me with her voice. A passionate, raw, husky, beautifully dramatic voice. Catching and emotionally unpolished.

A few months later, I am watching the German music show, "Rockpalast", at my mother's house when suddenly Gianna Nannini takes the stage, the woman with that magnificent voice! How beautiful and brilliant that the Italian women who surely must have known who she is did not make a song and dance of it. We just enjoyed her songs around the fire. She could just be herself there, all present for the same cause.

Chapter 15

I, WOMAN
WOODWORKER

After getting media attention and fighting through a male-dominated system, as the first woman ever, I start my carpentry training, becoming an all-round woodworker, summoning my dad.

In Kampen, I had kicked up a stink at the employment agency because they said I could not do the carpentry training as a woman. The agent called it an "unreasonable offer" if a woman wanted to work as a carpenter. The anti-discrimination legislation was on the agenda in The Hague at the time, the law designed to protect homosexual teachers from dismissal on the basis of their sexual preference, for example. That law was also the reason I had to leave the arts academy after the first year. I thought it was necessary to walk around with a pink triangle in the time of those debates and that was not appreciated at this Christian Arts Academy, where I only enrolled because of the late selection days. The Christian character of this academy that I had had to accept, had prevailed.

I start the carpentry training as the first woman at the Centre for Adult Vocational Training in Zwolle. My outburst sparks the employment agency to give me a chance. Not with much conviction, mind you, but they do not want more articles in the papers. I had already started to criticize their practices of unequal treatment.

It is a retraining for adults although I am only nineteen. I meet Appie there, a magical gay human being, who had lived in India and built his houseboat from scratch, and we become dear friends. One morning, Ap and I have to do a roofing task, rules on a roof siding,

60cm apart, calculate the distance between the laths, by placing 10 pan tiles on each other, dividing the total dimension by eleven. Then we run out of nails. It is still very early; we always start at 7:00 a.m. It's a beautiful, sunny day in late spring. As is customary, Ap and I smoke a joint before starting work. Ap goes to fetch nails and I wait, lying between the rules, my heels resting on the lowest lath, until he comes back. I wake up mid-afternoon with my head slightly burnt. Ap had let me sleep. He calls out the other students and instructors to "exhibit me" and can't stop laughing.

I thrive in the course, love learning to master the tools and machines, learn about various timbers and joints. Towards the end of the course, I arrange with the metal department to weld the frame for a cycle cart. I buy strips of steel and make a design of what I want: Weld a horizontal strip vertically with two clamps. Drill holes for the axis of the cycle wheels I fit in between. Another strip leads to the cycle cart hook I fit under the saddle of my second-hand Raleigh racing bike. A plywood basket with a lid, piano hinges and a chain to stop it from flapping when the lid opens, Ghandi painted on the back, and I am ready to cycle in the damned Alps.

Chapter 16

BONJOUR, FATHER

In the small Renault 4, "Tonneke" (I have never called her "Mother") and I drive to the South of France to take part in a walking trip of the "pilgrims". The pilgrims are a group of people who get together every year in the spirit of St. Francis of Assisi and then go walking for ten days with a rucksack on their backs. Simple living and exchanges between known and unknown people are the aim of the walk. My group consists of fifteen people, Dutch, Belgian, Swiss and French, young and old. It's like the Pax Christi for grown-ups. My school French is very limited, just enough to buy lait, fromage and pain ("milk, cheese and bread"), and that is the end of it.

Bernard is quiet, often walking alone. In his early fifties, tanned and etched face, jeans and an old shirt. Old-fashioned specs with dark glasses and dark, bushy eyebrows. I never stop looking at his hands, beautiful, working hands that touch me by the way he moves them. Anything he touches he truly touches. Always an Opinel knife in his pocket that he uses to make a cross on the bread before cutting it— this is the only thing to indicate he is the priest in the group.

When we cook in the evenings, Bernard helps with slicing vegetables, fetching water, making a fire, everything without many words. We often walk together in a silence that is not necessarily a choice but simply by the lack of a mutual language. He makes a lot of effort to make me understand what he wants to say and with many gestures, drawings in the sand and facial expressions we manage to understand.

I learn that Bernard grew up in the mountains, a farmer's son, became a carpenter, fought in the Independence War with Algeria as a young man. The horrors of that war made him realize that he wanted to do something about bad things. He became a priest, but one who never preached on the elevated altar area, always in the alleys amongst the people.

He spent his Christmases with the homeless people, had his friends amongst the shepherds of the Plateau du Larzac, an elevated plateau with an ecosystem like the high Alps that generated the most delicious honey I have ever tasted! Back in the seventies, the army wanted to take over for strategic exercises. Bernard and the shepherds did numerous non-violence actions to keep the army away from this plateau in the deep South of France. The action he told me about that really stirred my imagination is the one where they, as a last desperate attempt to get attention, decided to load all their sheep in trucks, drive to Paris in the night, release them under the Eiffel Tower, with signs around their necks that said: "We come to eat the last green of Paris, cause we are being chased away from our plateau." When Paris woke up it became world news.

This action turned out to be the final stroke against the army. All the international attention made it impossible for the army to just take over their plateau, their home ground. Bernard was the brain behind these powerful actions. Whatever he did, he always stayed humble, a simple man who just did his own thing.

I think I have always had a special nostalgia for a bond with older men, who could be my father. I decide to visit Bernard in France.

My carpentry course is nearing the end, but in the current environment of a construction world in desperate need for form workers, the carpenters who make the concrete casing for concrete pours, I have no intention of getting my certificate and being forced into a job. This is a course paid for by the labor department, so the idea is to train people to fill the job requirements. The whistling at passing girls itself is not the big deterrent; the mentality of the construction workers who whistled is.

It is 1984 and I make plans to leave the Netherlands. I want to be with Bernard. A deep longing to be with a man my father's age and explore who I am in relation to a father-like person, feel what it feels like to be in the role of a youngster who needs to learn life, yearn for a teacher, with the guidance and love of an older man. I miss my father; I miss having a father. I am a bit lost understanding who I am in his absence, so I decide to leave. I mail a letter to Bernard announcing my plans. He writes back with a simple note of "welcome" and his address. My French is still virtually non-existent, so a phone call is not really an option. Letters take around a week to get from the Netherlands to France, so I take his welcome letter as good enough to go on.

I have his address. I buy maps that will help me navigate to his house address in Roanne, France.

The last weeks of the carpentry course, I spend most of my time in the welding department of the adult education vocational training center, cutting, bending, and welding a carry-on frame for behind my bike. Just before the final exam, I announce to my supervisor that I am leaving. He simply smiles.

I have to find myself, have no idea of what I want, and am still mourning my father's death, which is only amplified by Lidy's suicide, the neighbor I was so crazy about. I feel as though I am living to be liked by others, and I need find out who I am, to give missing my father and Lidy a place and start living for myself, not for the opinion of others.

I organize a last supper, make corn soup and sell all my things: furniture, records, sound system and mattress, kitchen and drawing tools. It all has to be drastic and dramatic; otherwise, I will not do it. I must force myself to face an extreme challenge in order for this time of my life to become some sort of turning point.

I put personal things in the Renault 4 with Tonneke to take to Borne. The bassoon, my carpentry tools and diaries, all of Judith's letters and photographs.

The last supper ends around midnight, on 28 September, with a full moon and farewell to friends. I start the nightly trip on a cold autumn night to Borne. Moonlight changes all colours in the night into endless shades of grey, very dark, almost black to all the shades that are almost as white as the light of the moon itself.

Jenny cycles a bit further with me. She's the owner of the pub a few blocks up from the Moriaan, a friend I share books, Valerie Lagrange's music and poetry with. We smoke a last roll-up in the vegetable gardens just outside Kampen and then I am alone on this night that feels like a new beginning.

I cycle many miles per day, and I quickly become exhausted, being untrained. Judith lives in Paris, my first glorious destination, my first rest.

Via Eindhoven, Sint-Truiden, Namen, Dinant and Charleville-Mézières, knocking on strangers' doors to find a place for the night, I am on my way to Paris, with Reims, the cathedral with the large round window between the towers like the Notre Dame, on the route. I may not make it, however. I'm suffering through exhaustion and pain. Everything hurts. It's hot to cycle, I sweat like mad, but as soon as I stop to eat or drink, it is clear that October has arrived and brings early winter notes with it and I catch a cold. I cough and have a slight fever.

I cross a hill and at last, see Reims in the valley below. As a kid, I made full-scale models of the cathedral and studied the books of Macaulay. Instead of the ecstatic feeling I expected to feel as soon as I would see Reims at the horizon, I'm overwhelmed by a suffocating feeling. I have no control over it. I'm scared. I can't breathe and panic, thinking I have to ride on to that city. I sweat, now without cycling, I have fearful images in my head and a physical resistance against the city I see in the distance that takes me by surprise. I sense something very dark; it stops me. I can't continue. I'm crying next to my cycle and cart on the side of the road.

It seems like hours later, I am still sitting next to my bike, looking at Reims, which stares at me from the darkness. I can't stay here. I have to do something. I decide to hitchhike and a few seconds later, a small bus stops. A friendly man gets out and without words, places my bike and cart at the back of the empty bus and drives me to Paris. He drops me and my load near Père Lachaise, the cemetery that's a five-minute walk from Judith's house.

Half a year later, I would find myself at the table of a clairvoyant in the Netherlands who tells me that in a previous life during the Middle Ages, I was a knight and was beheaded in front of a large cathedral.

In Paris with Judith, I'm itching to cycle again after just five days. Not that I want to leave Judith, but I had to force myself so much to leave Kampen, I don't want to risk feeling too comfortable together. I still have a lot of travelling to do.

It takes almost a whole day to get through all the outskirts of Paris and finally see some greenery around me. The outskirts of such a big city with its industrial zones are often so soulless, only concrete, glass and ugly buildings. I reach Fontainebleau that day via Evry and Melun, only 40km south of Paris.

I cycle with the cart, which now seems too immense to carry into Fontainebleau. I spot a young woman with a pram on the sidewalk. I accost her and ask her if she knows a place to stay overnight. She informs me she is an au-pair with a family a few streets further, gives me directions and a few minutes later, I ring the doorbell at a porch overgrown with ivy.

A window opens upstairs and a woman peers out. I declare who I am, that I'm looking for a place for the night. "Come in," she says, "start shelling the beans in the kitchen. I'll be there soon."

I open the porch, ride in the cycle with the cart and walk into the house. A huge female bronze breast stands in the center of the living room. Silvie is married to Charles, a sculptor. The walls are covered with pictures of Grace Jones and other familiar faces. I go to the kitchen and start to shell the beans. Not long afterwards, Charles comes home, the au-pair girl returns from a walk and Silvie arrives downstairs to hug me. The house is narrow and long with a hearth at the end where Charles is starting a fire.

He leads me to the garden where he has built his workshop. As I walk into the garden and see the building, I become light-headed. During my time in Paris with Judith, I had been fantasizing about the house I would build one day and how it would look. I am now looking at a literal manifestation of it! The whole building is shaped like a rhinoceros whose legs are below ground, its whole body and head covered in black bitumen as if it were the skin of the huge animal. When you walk in through the round doors you reach a solid white space, covered with hand-smeared plaster. The bookshelves on the curving walls are shaped like tree branches, all in plaster. The whole inside of the beast is a web of tree branches in plaster. Books everywhere. A chair made of textile appears as if an enormous voluptuous woman is sitting there, a sort of beanbag shaped like a fat woman you can sink into. Everything, every detail is as I described to Judith the week before.

After dinner, Charles invites me to take a bath with him, and as if it's the most normal thing in the world, we hop into the tub moments later, in our underpants. Around the bath there are big glass bell jars with collections of weird objects, ivy lusciously grown throughout the bathroom, walls of glass shards and mirrors, but nothing kitsch. Charles takes his three-toothed stave in his right hand and places his Zeus wings in a band around his head behind his ears. I am sitting in a bathtub with a man who thinks he is Zeus!

I'm coughing up blood. My stools contain blood, too.

Charles and Silvie show me the way to a friend who lives 50km south, a safe place to stay the next night. They phone Roger, and he expects me. The next day, I cycle away and have a very special feeling about these people. It's so difficult to leave.

It takes an incredible amount of effort to reach Roger Bus's house. I cross a little bridge that leads through a porch as if you are entering a small castle. The tiny courtyard is filled with roses. A mini heaven. Roger guides me inside.

He has a furniture upholstering workshop, every corner exuding the old craft. It's like going hundreds of years back in time. I watch him for two days, every movement, every nail he fishes out of his mouth with the magnetic hammer, his mouth full of those vicious, little nails he then hammers in the bottom of the chair's frame. Everything with incredible dedication, looking out over his half spectacles, love for every movement he makes. He picks from a bunch of horsehair and fumbles with it until the mat has the right thickness and strength to be placed between the one and the next burlap layer. There is a strict sequence of layers and materials, which ultimately provide perfect seating.

Roger lets me watch him work. Sometimes he makes coffee, sometimes his wife comes in to eat something, and regularly he walks to the pot-bellied stove to put more wood in, always modest and without many words, but like a bed of warmth and tranquility. I stay with Roger for three days in a little room above the workshop, in a bed with an old, thick mattress in kapok where I can roll myself in completely. Thick cotton sheets, starched, every piece of material in the house is precious. As I intensely watch Roger's actions, I think how great it must be to be so good at something in your life and to be perfectly happy with it, be such a master, like some sort of calling. I wonder if I will ever find that.

Too ill to continue cycling, I call Tonneke, who asks me if she should pick me up, but then she will take me home, not to Bernard's. I've gone too far already to give up here. I tell her that I will go by train to Bernard and then continue the journey. She knows I have to continue, leaving the choice up to me. Roger arranges a train ticket and puts me with my bike and all on the train to Roanne.

I wake up from a night full of dreams, as usual. The dogs are scratching at the door; *they must be hungry*, I muse. It's after 9:00 already. The dreams have kept me busy, preventing me from waking up at 7:00 a.m., my usual time. I slip on my trousers, pull a warm shirt over my head and grab some thick socks. There is ice on the inside of my windows with beautiful patterns. "Ice flowers", my dad used to call them.

I head downstairs to start the fire in the fireplace. It's dark inside because at night I close the shutters to keep in the warmth. I put the kettle on to make coffee, quickly open the door to let the dogs in. They snuggle against my legs, and I scratch them behind the ears. Diogenes, the smartest, sits by the fire; he knows that I don't like begging. Neligane, the big and rather dumb rottweiler, tries to step on Pipo to prevent him from getting my attention. Pipo is an elderly cocker spaniel showing strong signs of dementia. Often, Pipo runs in little circles and makes all sorts of noises, sometimes sad, sometimes happy, or angry. It looks like he is playing films in his little head of days that have long gone. He projects his own little show there, all by himself; the rest of the world around him seems to disappear. Sometimes when the film doesn't seem too pleasant, I stop him from running in circles and then he sits down on my feet and wants to be as close to me as possible. After a few minutes, he starts his rounds again and when the film seems to be a better one, I let him do his thing. Neligane is jealous and bigger than he can handle, which makes him quite clumsy. With a loud sigh, he finally settles down next to Diogenes by the fire, while I have my coffee and try to catch the images of the dreams that have made my night so long. Perhaps opening the shutters will help me to wake up. So, I slip on my boots, throw a scarf around my neck and go outside, the dogs literally on my heels.

The sun is hot and so bright that it blinds me. My little house stands on a mountain; on the very top of the mountain and at this moment, it is completely surrounded by clouds. The blinding reflection of the sun on the white clouds gives the whole scene a surrealistic atmosphere. I'm almost thrown back in a dream state. Diogenes runs through the garden and disappears in the clouds. As far as I can see, there are only white clouds and the bright sun. It is winter, with half a meter of fresh snow on the ground. I'm alone in this world. I stand there thinking that I should drink in every pixel of this image, the full sensation of this moment, every distinct smell, to memorize it. I am aware that this is one of the most wonderful experiences I have ever had.

I hear a distant sound of a car, far away on the other side of the valley, far below the clouds. The sound comes closer, and I hope that it is Bernard. I have been hoping for him to show up for the last two weeks, but the winter circumstances make it hard to come up the mountain. Even the mailman has not managed to get to my house. I've not seen a human being for over two weeks now, no human contact at all. Suddenly I realize why Diogenes has run through the garden to the road. Diogenes knows who it is. From under the clouds, I hear Diogenes making his happy, welcoming sounds to Bernard.

A minute before, it seemed that I was alone in this world and that even if there was a world beneath the clouds, mine was nicer, warmer and more beautiful. Now that Bernard and Diogenes are in the world under the clouds, it loses its appeal. I don't want to be above the clouds anymore. It takes another twenty minutes before Bernard drives up to the gate of my house. The clouds have risen, I haven't moved, but I'm now in the world under the clouds with Bernard and

103

Diogenes. I walk to the gate and open it so Bernard can drive his ancient Citroën 2CV in the yard. Diogenes, who sits on Bernard's lap, jumps out of the car. Neligane bangs his head against the opening door and Pipo starts running his rounds around Bernard's legs, making his cute, little howling sounds.

Before I can even greet Bernard, he rambles in French way too fast for my comprehension. I love his stories; I love listening to his voice even though I only get maybe half of it. The sound of his voice is very soothing to listen to. I love watching him and the way he uses his hands to make his stories better understood. Once we sit down at the table to have coffee together, he makes a big effort to be understood. I am so excited to hear a human talk again!

It has been over two weeks in which, if I think of myself as a house, with many rooms, storages, attics, basements, that as a matter of speech, it guided me through each and every one of the rooms. Every night I dreamed non-stop. The following day had the complete same atmosphere as the dreams had; if it was a bad dream, my day would be a hard one, if it was a very sweet dream, my day would be very gentle. The atmospheres of the dreams had become so strong in those weeks that I didn't seem to be in control of my moods anymore. The dreams took control of my life, and I surrendered to them. The difference between the days and the nights became virtually nonexistent, a kind of altered state.

I had to think hard if this was real or that it was a dream, whether I was awake or asleep. The animals kept me grounded a little bit. I had to make rice soup for the dogs and let Canelle in and out of her stable and feed her. Canelle was a cow, only one year old and mad. She was behaving more like the dogs, chasing the cats in the yard and standing up to the gate with her front legs when Bernard arrived. She came for walks when I went with the dogs. The three cats appeared as much in my dreams as they did during the days, besides, I didn't have to feed them, so they were not much help in that matter. The lack of distinction between days and nights didn't matter anymore; all was just one flow of images and emotions. Emotions in their most extreme appearance.

I walk up those massive stairs, black shiny granite, worn out steps from the millions of feet that had passed there, over the centuries this church had been there. Now, no one else, I am the only person going up there. At the top of the stairs, I make a 90-degree turn to the right and enter the porch of the church. Through the open double wooden doors, I see Bernard preaching, all dressed in white, the church is filled with radiant white light. I turn back and look outside and down the stairs. Two long staircases down, one to the left, a small landing and then one to the right, there is a big square landing with a sober bank on it. There, my father is sitting! He is looking up to me.

Now, I see that behind him a staircase descends. It goes on and on and I cannot see the end of it. My father stands up and starts walking towards the stairs leading to the church. He is wearing his favorite sweater, the dark red one, his creamy-white trousers and he is barefoot. The moment he approaches me I start crying. I am so deeply happy to see him again, but at the same time, I know that being with him will mean saying goodbye to everything I have. I stumble down the stairs, crying out loud, leaning my head against the walls of the building, desperate, not knowing what to do. My father doesn't take his eyes off me, he has this intensely satisfied expression on his face, an expression you don't see with living people. He comes closer, now on the same stairs as me. The closer he comes, the more I am torn apart, desperately crying.

In these moments, I feel all the pain of missing him, all the pain of learning to live without him. He comes up to me and puts my head against his chest, I wrap my arms around his waist and squeeze him; his hands on my back and head. We stand there, it feels so good, but I must make a Goddamn decision! After a while, my father lets go of me, looks once again at me with his light-blue eyes and satisfied face, turns around and slowly walks down the same stairs. Do I follow him? Do I go back up? What the hell should I do? My eyes follow my father going further and further down, across the big landing, turning to the left and starting the endless staircase, not once looking back at me. I stumble a few steps up, just to make a step, knowing that I will not follow him. I have not stopped crying, nor has the feeling of being ripped in two left my body.

I wake up because Moumous, who has apparently slept on my bed, licks the salty tears of my cheeks. I stroke her on the head, and she nests herself under my chin and along the left side of my face. She puts one paw on my cheek, now licking my eyes. She calms me down a bit; she is such a special cat. I stay there with Moumous for I don't know how long, thinking about the dream. My hands remember the feel of my father's sweater. This feels so much stronger than a dream. I have the feeling that he visited me, he was here, or I was there.

When Bernard is with me in this house he does his own things. When we eat together, he talks and explains things, or I will tell him stories or ask him things, but he completely leaves me to do whatever I do. He's never judgmental. He never asks what I am going to do, or why I did or didn't do something. I have the freedom to do whatever I want to do. It makes me feel hopeless sometimes, as I want him to tell me what to do, or what to cook, or what time to get out of bed. Some days when I feel sad after a dream, I want him to put an arm around my shoulder, but that never happens.

Today, startled by the intensity of the dream, I wait the whole day for him to say something and comfort me. At supper, he finally says, "Tu n'a pas ton jour aujourd'hui, n'est-ce-pas?" (You don't have your day today, hey?) That is all, but it makes me realize how he has seen me the whole day. An arm around my shoulder would not have solved my sadness. I need to go through these things all by myself, and he knows it. At times, he stays overnight in my little house and sleeps in the bedroom next to mine.

Sometimes he wakes me up with his screaming. I have come to understand that these nightmares are about his time as a French soldier during the independence war in Algeria. When I ask him about the dreams, he gets very emotional, telling me that if he could turn anything back in his life that he would have rather gone to jail than be part of that war. That war quiets him in the daytime and haunts him at night. When he has another nightmare, I quietly enter his bedroom and silently lay behind him, hold him without waking him up. I wait till his breathing becomes calm again and return to my own bed.

Living in Le Saule, in the little house on the mountain next to the willow, I do not listen to or play music. It's a rare period in my life without music. I only hear the silence and smell the land and the hearth fire in the house. I still taste the Larzac honey and the morning coffee, but there is no music.

Chapter 17

LIVING IN EARTHLING

Judith moves to Amsterdam after living in Paris for a year. I arrive from Sydney at Schiphol in December 1985. I nearly freeze to death in my much too thin clothes. I departed from the summer in Australia and while here in the Netherlands, it is an unusually cold winter, with strong winds and minus-twenty degrees temperatures. The canals look magnificent though, so Judith and I skate away many evening hours on the illuminated canals. The rickety Aladdin oil stove only makes the little room in the Albert Cuyp neighborhood clammy and never really warm enough. We usually spend all day under mountains of damp blankets to keep warm. Judith is sharing a floor with an older single, rather troubled woman. I cannot stay here. I must sort out my own life…fast.

I meet someone at a cultural evening who has a bus on the land behind Artis. Pip wants to sell the 1964 DAF touring bus, the same year of manufacturing as me, and I'm interested. On the previous New Year's Eve that I spent with Judith in my house in France, we made my annual deal: we would live in busses this new year.

The next day, I immediately venture to Artis and walk on the land there. It is a meeting point for drifters, lefties, freaks and other hippies, I fall for the place. There is a path with grass overgrown paving stones from the moment you turn the corner and walk into the plot behind Artis. The rails tracks are here as silent witnesses, holding a heaviness that I feel when I walk on the land.

The plot of land behind the Artis Zoo is a barren strip of land between the back walls of the zoo and the pack-houses of the Êntrepotdock. Houseboats tied along the rampart, pack-houses awaiting their future destination. Here ended the first harbor-railway track, the so-called Old Dock-line, starting at the Weesperpoort Station and going all the way to the Êntrepotdock behind Artis. That land was a disused rail yard where the transfer of goods had come to a halt and the hangars and pack-houses were pointless as they had lost their purpose, after the harbor areas had been relocated to the west. This rail yard had not only been a very busy industrious place as the major trans-shipment zone between trains and cargo vessels, it also had gone through a grim period in its existence.

In 1942, the Holland Theatre located at the Plantage Middenlaan, was used as an assembly place for the Jews who were picked up from their homes during the German razzias, often aided by Dutch snitches. That theatre was the stage where the Germans decided which Jew would go to which camp. The thousands and thousands of Jewish people who were assembled there were taken to the rail yard and rudely stowed in the wooden train wagons to be deported to the death camps in Germany.

In the 80s, a period with a huge housing shortage, I am part of a very active politically engaged squatters' movement in Amsterdam, the barren strip of vacated land is being reused by us so-called "city nomads". The city nomads are not necessarily homeless people, but rather, activists and squatters, hippies, punks and other artists. They move their caravans, old busses, transit vans and building sheds on the land and start occupying it. They live between the rails that carry the memories of that dark period in history.

Walking on the land from where so many Jews had been deported, I often sense their spirits, hear their wailing in fear. In the first part there are vegetable gardens that belong to the houseboats. There is only one caravan, collapsed through its frame, supported by wooden poles and with plywood on the walls to the floor, to stop the cold draught under the caravan. It is bitterly cold, and you can tell from the windows that it must be extremely damp inside. The white caravan is covered with algae and other growth, one window with shutters, and curtains of discolored velvet. On both sides of the paving stones, the rough grass reaches up to your knees even in winter. There are homemade mailboxes, dustbins and lots and lots of bicycles, delivery tricycles, transport cycles, worn out city cycles. There are bonfires everywhere, stocks of burning wood and the rails, of course. Further in, it is a bit more populated, more cars, sheds, caravans and old touring buses like mine. Just before I arrive at my new bus, I spot a huge pile of organized branches, two meters above the ground, which is not a normal pile. Pip smirks and says that the "cave man" lives there. The pile of wood is only the tip of a much larger subterranean hut.

Pip opens the bus with a key that is at least 20cm long. The original key is sawn through, and a piece of metal had been welded in between, which made the key much longer. The key goes through the thick hollow steel door of the bus cabin to reach the lock fastened to it on the inside.

The bus has been a 54-passenger touring bus, and all the seats have now been removed, except for the driver's seat with its rusty steel springs. Two pairs of the seat sets stand outside the bus next to the firepit. Pip has some stuff In the bus, but it doesn't exactly look cozy and habited. I buy the bus for 3000 guilders, which is quite a lot, but the whole engine block is fully revised, and all the parts are ready to hit the road. She had the wildest plans for it that never became reality.

I name my bus, "Earthling". It is white and dull moss green. Round aluminum window frames have blue quarter rounded windows above them, in the transition from the sides to the roof. There are small sliding windows above some of the windows. I buy an old pot-bellied stove, install the chimney pipe through one of those sliding windows, and start stocking wood in my long living room. At the back of the bus, I build a wall-to-wall bed with higher parts flanking the bed, the side and back walls. A large second-hand mattress, a duvet and some blankets. It is so cold in the big metal contraption with the wind howling underneath that the lid of the stove glows bright orange, while the temperature barely climbs above freezing point a couple of meters around the stove.

The cold winter in Amsterdam is slowly transitioning to spring, and one by one, I get to know my neighbors who are also coming out of hibernation from the cold winter. I already know my neighbor, Karl, the caveman, well, who I visit often, because his subterranean hut is so fantastical. He is a brilliant man and good company...mad, but brilliant. "Overplayed," as my gran would say—people who are that intelligent they cannot find feedback in their social environment. They then spiral in their own brilliant ideas and become 'overplayed'. Again, my gran had her own vocabulary, she just made up new words if she thought the existing language did not suffice.

The entrance of Karl's hut is a tunnel of intertwined branches that leads me down along beautiful wooden sculptures, which are the steps. Once underground, I can stand fully upright with even a dome of one meter high above my head, the diameter of the dome at least six meters. The whole dome is full of suspended tools, drawing materials, bags with other utensils and food. No cupboards, no other storage space other than the dome roof with endless bags on hooks. It is a round hut and opposite the stairs is a stove, made from clay with the smoke ducts running along the walls! The same system I had invented for the baked house, the smoke ducts through the benches for warmth retention. An ingenious system that I now witness working in real-time! The hut is nice and warm on cold winter days and my buttocks nice and warm on the smoke ducts. I have to put a cushion between my bum and the bench though, in order not to burn my butt.

Tineke lives in the shack opposite me, but I do not have much contact with her. Johanna lives on the second boat and plays trombone, and Teun lives in the caravan behind the cave man. He "dries his underpants on a line to let the skid marks dry properly to then shake them out." Teun is a crazy bloke, with a big beard and a head full of dreadlocks, who thoroughly enjoys making fun of people who are quick with their judgment of the residents of the land. The skid marks story is not true (he says), but he provocatively tells it to journalists who ask preoccupied questions about the habits of the residents.

Lorien lives in the first caravan and pours tea in used jam jars. I never see Lorien without Lolo, her little whippet dog, who will bite if I come up to Lorien too quickly or just because she is a little, grumpy bitch. I only met Lorien when I saw a band play—she was the sax player. Head full of blonde dreadlocks, big breasts that do not know the comfort of a strong bra. She wears 50s dresses with lace and tulle, high patent boots, and all combined with leather and other S&M accessories, as only Lorien can. She has a very striking appearance with an exhibitionist streak.

For water, we the land residents, go to the petrol station on the Sarphatistraat with jerry cans. I build a system with an old foot pump to have running water in my sink, such a half rubber ball that pumps water when you step on it. In the center of the bus, I put a thick tree branch exactly between the ceiling and the floor, right from the center. Hanging from the branch, I build a tabletop with five sides that look as if it is floating in the bus and the branch looks as if a tree grew through the bus, as if the bus was built around it. In the cabin, on the right next to the huge steering wheel, the old radio is connected to eight loudspeakers above the path to the back. I connect my Walkman and am over the moon with my "surround sound" sound system. I often sit in silence because the speakers devour batteries. In less than one hour, the Waterboys wail a bit, then drag and sing out of tune before stopping altogether.

It is a dry, clear and a very cold night when Judith stays with me in the bus. We wake up, I stir up the stove and make coffee. Judith realizes she had done something stupid; she had put her contact lenses in water in the egg cups the night before, but it was freezing like mad. We are swearing and laughing for at least half an hour with each an ice cube in our hands to get Judith's lenses ready for use again. Three spots over is another bus, an old navy blue and white Leyland, a great bus too, but not equipped at all and the bodywork is rusty and rotten. This does not deter Judith from buying the bus, as she's crazy about it. We keep our New Year's resolution, and both now live on the land. Things are not going well between Judith and me though and our seven-year relationship comes to an end. We were too young when we met.

Chapter 18

TOURING WITH ROMANTIC BONES

On International Women's Day, I witness a band play in the street, they're called the Romantic Bones, and I immediately love their music, their own songs, striking women and emotional music. In the evening, they play in the Women's House. I am hooked and want to play with them, be part of that music. I can hear in my head how it will sound with the bassoon. It fits!

After the show, I nervously walk up to the singer called Fish and tell her that I play the bassoon, this is my girlfriend while pointing at Judith, and that I want to play with them, be part of this band. They are four women, all dykes. The fact I introduce Judith is immediately reason enough for them to invite me to the rehearsal room in the Hartenstraat next Thursday.

My life has become rather busy, with the band added (yeah!), because I'm also working fulltime now, with lots of non-negotiable overtime. I had gone to a temping agency on the Rokin and during my intake, the man answered the phone while he was interviewing me. They asked him urgently for a carpenter; he asked if it could be a woman too, while smiling at me. Am I strong? He did not wait for my answer, but said they could judge for themselves. He could see I was in good shape, fit and muscular. When he hung up, he told me that I would be a set builder at the Opera in Amsterdam. I jumped into a coffee shop and celebrated with a latte. I was over the moon.

The next morning, I take the underground to the Bijlmerstation from where I walk. I have butterflies in my stomach. Imagine, making opera and ballet sets! I feel a bit conflicted though, considering the protests around the construction of the Stopera, the ridiculous budget and the scandal around the plans, while the lack of housing is being ignored by the council at the same time. But okay, the Stopera is a 'fait-accompli', and I have a job in the decor center.

I introduce myself as the new carpenter and one of the guys gives me a guided tour of the paint, props, stall and wood departments, the canteen and introduces me to the main colleagues. Straight away, we have to work evenings. Everything is always under huge time pressure because of the maestro's designs, who manages the opera, and the unmovable dates for the dress rehearsal that always comes late. We sit upstairs in the canteen, start eating our sandwiches, and my boss teasingly says to me that I surely do not want to make coffee as the only woman amongst all male colleagues. I reply, as one of the carpenters I will just take my turn, like everybody else. Once we start arm wrestling, I demonstrate that I am in good form and push some men off the table. They quickly start to call me the "woman carpenter", a title I never use myself and I am just annoyed that I always have to prove myself. At least I don't have any aggro anymore and have gained acceptance of my brilliant colleagues.

The first sets I work on are for Rossini's "Barber of Seville", directed by Dario Fo. He is so chaotic that we have to go through multiple iterations of the décor pieces, the stairs, borders and doorsteps before we finally install them on stage for the seven shows. The rest, newly made décor, is useless because the maestro only provided basic sketches of the total set design and then changed his mind all the time, goes straight to the children's village as climbing blocks. It is quite elaborate: stairs, everything in plywood and glued brackets, moulds injected with PU foam, filled columns that look like marble stairs, borders, rails, balconies. Everything looks sculpted in marble.

We have a very gifted painter in the center, who dies young. Harry's death is a huge blow. His talent is irreplaceable, and he is too. Harry could walk on a canvas of twenty by forty meters, with his buckets of paint and a brush on a broomstick and paint a perspective that would amaze us every time, watching it from above in the canteen.

We receive free tickets for the dress rehearsals, and I proudly invite Tonneke to see this first opera, I yearn for her to be proud of me. There is a photo of the decor in the newspaper, and I nick a huge poster for the "Barber of Seville" that will be on Tonneke's wall in the garden room for years.

There are often other activities in the Stopera, while we are installing a set. With different rooms and all the people backstage, the Stopera is an enterprise that is active day and night. Sometimes during the daytime, but also in the evening, after a day's work in the decor center, we go to the Stopera with a group of colleagues to continue working on a set backstage. The props we make in the decor center are transported by truck to the Stopera. For an average opera, this means ten trucks with props. Backstage, it is impressive, an advanced system for the changing of the decors, which continuously keeps people busy. There is a main stage, where the show takes place, and three so-called set-up stages, each seventeen by fourteen meters, four stages plus tow, equally sized empty spaces to slide the stages through. This system enables quick set changes between repetitions and shows. Moving the stages is always stressful for the theatre staff because of the long balloons under the sets to move them like some sort of hovercraft. The balloon sausages are very vulnerable though, and if there is something sharp on the floor like even a grain of sand where the set has to be moved to, one of those balloon sausages can explode and not only are they very expensive, it also means a delay in the schedule that is always under pressure. So, we clean, brush, mop and swear a lot before yet another slide.

It's gala night, and Robert Long and André van Duin, a famous musician and actor, both "gay as a cathedral" (my favorite Dutch gay descriptor), are in attendance. The gala is not in the main room, so we are working on one of the set-up stages and go get a cup of coffee in the canteen from time to time, where the gala guests also have a drink. As I walk through the canteen in my overalls with leather studs and tool belt on my hips, I am suddenly slapped on the bum by André van Duin, who adds "Well fit," and Robert Long winks cheekily. I blush and ask myself with fascination if they think I am a bloke. I have been refused entry at a lesbian dance, because they thought I was a bloke, and there have been occasions where gay dudes tried to chat me up, also thinking I was a bloke, and family, and that's why I am curious what they perceive me as.

"Cinderella" is the second decor I work on, a decor for the National Ballet, then Mozart's "Magic Flute" and finally, "Faustus". "Faustus" has impressive high-tech pneumatic stairs in the center that can reach all the balconies of the facades built in a circle by rotating and moving up and down, the houses with three floors in a semi-circle around the stage.

I can no longer combine the overtime in the evenings with the rehearsals and the increasing number of gigs with the Romantic Bones. I need to quit my job.

I live near the edge of the land. Behind my bus, there is only a group of caravans before you can cross to the birds of prey and the seals over the old railway bridge to the Sarphatistraat. One of the residents in the group of connected caravans is the recently released "Karate Bob", nickname of Slobodan Mitrić, who had served a thirteen-year prison sentence in Scheveningen for the murder of three men who came to assassinate him after he, as a secret Serbian agent, had refused to carry out the order of a liquidation apparently. In 1986, out of prison, he came to live on the land just before I moved there.

There is a strange vibe about him, he is the subject of weird rumors, and you can never really suss him out.

The cave man and I go visit to see what is happening there, but we do not discover a lot, apart from sensing disturbance. He says he only does karate for control and concentration, but after he takes Tineke hostage and threatens her with a knife I no longer feel good on the land. There are other shady characters, and the use of hard drugs increases. We suspect that drugs are dealt from Karate Bob's caravans. The atmosphere quickly changes; it becomes unsafe. Old residents start looking for other places one by one. Some move their caravan or car to the KNSM island; others move to Ruigoord, a free zone outside Amsterdam. Others like me move to a squat or another house. My bus moves with its new owners to the IJ-island while I move to a newly squatted place. I move Lorien's caravan, the old barrel. We hook it to a rented bus and illegally drive through the streets of Amsterdam to bring the algae-covered thing to the KNSM island. We burst a tire on the way and Lorien tells me to stop, I refuse. She will not move that thing ever again and stopping here on a public road in these conditions of transport will lead to nothing but problems. It is already a miracle we are not stopped anywhere. I drive this rented bus without a valid driver's license—the caravan has no registration, it is not fit for the public road and the connection with the bus is improvised. And to top it all, the burst tire! We drive on!

It's 1988, and the authorities order to evacuate the grounds and anything still standing will be demolished. This evacuation order marks the end of a society where not everything has to make room for tidiness yet. It's hard to escape; there are so many rules, rules that squeeze the margin between the establishment and the fringes. Balancing on the edge makes life exciting; in the fringes is where culture happen, where creativity lives, where the fleas live in the fur. We are being conditioned to have our hair shaved off and wear the wig full of chemical substances to ban even the idea of fleas. City nomads, the squatters' movement, hippies, punks, artists and other rebels, have a roof above their heads and a lot is happening in the lively music and arts scene. There is an untainted artistic buzz, but the fringes are getting smaller.

I move to a squat in the Kemperstraat, near the gas factory under a cloud of Maggi smells. Fish lives with Toula, her border collie, on the third floor and Paulien, our drummer, in a squat opposite us on the third floor. Paulien's downstairs neighbor is Marina, a slightly strange Italian woman. There is a rumor that she once took a trip with pulverized scorpion tails in India after which she apparently never was the same again.

Sometimes I visit her and find her in the kitchen, standing on one leg and the other bent like a stork. Motionless like a statue, not a single muscle moving. She holds a spoon horizontally in front of her. She has put an egg upright in the spoon…upright! She negates all the laws of nature. She sometimes stands like this for half an hour, not moving in the slightest, deadly immobile. I sit down at the table, staring at this strange woman and wait until she is ready. Then suddenly she asks me with a heavy Italian accent, "Woulda you like a cappuccino, orrr would you rrathzzerrr scrratchzzze my backa?" I choose the cappuccino and a few minutes later, we sit there drinking the best coffee of my life.

The rehearsal room is in a crouching space under a house in the Hartenstraat, we always meet at Orca before rehearsals, the women's cafe in the NRC squat, on the corner behind the Palace at the Dam. We drink there until everyone is ready to rock, and then we rehearse.

We earn money from the gigs and save for a better PA system. We buy bigger and better speakers and an amplifier that barely fits through the cellar hatchway, it nearly breaks your back. The crouching space is no longer enough, and we start looking for something better, more professional, because we become that too. We find a good rehearsal room on the WG grounds, the former Wilhelmina Guesthouse in Oud West.

The WG grounds houses all sorts of living communes and workshops, spaces for alternative restaurants, it's a bustling place. There are two rehearsal rooms on the third floor, fully sound-proofed with heavy steel doors, and an airlock. Downstairs there is a canteen where everybody gathers for a coffee, read magazines, both people from outside and the residents of the WG grounds, like a mega living room. This canteen is now the meeting point before we go to the rehearsal room to unpack the gear and set it up.

Lorien is generally distracted, chaotic and very endearing. She always does too much at once, which makes her late everywhere. I spot her having a coffee downstairs while we are waiting for her upstairs, everything is set up and ready for rehearsal. Lorien is so honest, she immediately admits it when she has done anything wrong. I can never be angry with her. I burst out laughing and ask her what she is doing here. She says, "Yes, I am on time this time, but then you will think I can be on time, so I decide to drink a cup of coffee and still be a little bit late." Waiting for Lorien quickly becomes a theme and we even write a song about it, "Waiting".

Renee, Paulien, Fish and I stand outside and suddenly, Lorien pulls up in a bright yellow bus. We have no idea she has saved some money, inherited some cash and bought Banana for us to go on tour. Banana is a bright yellow Mercedes 207 bus. Impressive! But this begs the question: Who will drive it, pick up everybody at home, drive to the WG grounds to load the gear, then drive to the gig venue, not to drink all night and then drive back to Amsterdam, unload the gear at the WG grounds, bring everybody home and then go to bed last? Paulien is the only one with a valid driver's license, but she does not want to drive. Lorien does not feel confident enough to drive with everybody on board and I only have my Australian driver's license, which is not valid in the Netherlands. In the first months, we had hired buses and sometimes we used Gineke's old grey ambulance too to drive to gigs. I was always the designated driver. Paulien and I would go to Drive Yourself, rent a bus with her driver's license, and as soon as we turned the corner, we changed places, and I drove.

I love driving, you can wake me up to go for a drive, the bigger and older the car or bus the better. With a car I need to feel I am working, strong engine noises, big diesels, hard gear changes. I like well-made mechanical things that need attention to see how they fit together and to drive with more fun. My mother and father had taught us as children to listen to the sound of the engine, to know when you had to change gears. If the octane level of the petrol was too low you could hear the tingling, the squealing noise of worn brakes or the clutch needed work done. I knew how to change gears, steer, brake and listen to the engine. I had never been behind the wheel, but I could drive before I actually learned to drive in Australia.

Gineke is both the owner of the celebrated Café Quèlle, and the old grey ambulance. She is also a big Bones fan. We regularly play in her pub. In the eighteen eventful months that we are together as the Romantic Bones, we played more than eighty gigs in the Netherlands, England, Austria and Switzerland.

In Zürich, we play to an all-female audience. Lorien, with her slightly exhibitionist streak and original creations, has bought a latex dress for the tour. With Lorien, you always know that nothing will just be normal. Everything she touches becomes different and everything possesses a timeless magic and extraterrestrial peculiarity. She is so unique that everything around her seems to adapt to her indefinable logic. The latex dress is natural matte black rubber, thin, smooth and I understand why the material has a special attraction, it's like a second skin.

Hours in advance, Lorien starts to get nervous, pacing up and down and moving things from left to right, to put them back where they are half an hour later. She usually changes five times before a gig because she has to look perfect in creations no one else could have combined. Now it is the latex dress's turn, and we eagerly wait to see what will happen. Everything Lorien does inevitably involves her whole environment. Not to be the center of attraction, in a domineering way, but Lorien possesses a certain innocence and involves everybody in her situation. She carries talcum powder and increases the suspense. By the time she is finally ready for the latex, everybody surrounds her. The latex is very tight, and she cannot wear a bra and knickers underneath, because the seams would be visible. No, it has to be perfect.

She stands there naked in the center of us all, ready to slide into the latex. Well, that is not an easy task. We cover her in talc powder and pull the latex up but do not get it over her hips. Down again and we try from the top, with arms up and eyes closed. If we would just get to her armpits, we could pull it down to the right place! We're pissing ourselves laughing, Lorien included. Oh shit, she's sweating, making the positioning of the latex even more difficult. ...Finally, it is done!

Lorien poses, critically looking at herself in the mirror from all angles. She is very pleased. I am very pleased, too—that the latex did not rip in the whole process. We tease her and ask if she can still breathe. We have such fun, Lorien does not mind. She is wearing the latex and drapes with lots of accessories over it, which makes it uniquely Lorien. For the occasion, she has a boa of black feathers and fishnet panties with short, high-heeled patent boots, with shiny S&M chains and spikes. We are all excited. Lorien is delicious, with her crazy antics and brilliant dry sense of humor.

When we get on stage, all the time and energy she invests in her outfit are amply rewarded. In her getup, Lorien plays alt- and baritone sax, a wide array of percussion instruments, cow bells, woodblocks, shakers that she grabs every now and to liven up solos or rhythmic breaks with unparalleled rhythms and sounds. The audience has been waiting for months to see us, the act from Amsterdam, and they embrace us. We are flying high on their energy. It feels like my bassoon has a life of its own, we are in flow. We experience a collective adrenaline rush during this concert. I feel altered.

At some point, there is elevated excitement in the audience. I look up and see that everybody is looking at Lorien, who had just gotten up from a long percussion session with the woodblocks on the floor. Their glances are aimed at her sax, or so I thought. I am standing next to Lorien and look down and see what they are actually looking at. A tuft of pubic hair peeps out from under the hitched up latex dress. I have to stop playing and burst out laughing. Lorien knows exactly and smiles, and it feels like she had anticipated this to happen. (Recently, she told me that some decades later, the latex dress had melted in a desert in Arizona.)

We play at the tenth anniversary of *OPZIJ* (first feminist magazine in NL) with Karin Bloemen and Adelheid Roosen as the support act. Hedy d'Ancona, Iteke Weeda, Anja Meulenbelt and Ien Dales, all the big names of feminist Netherlands are there. I invite Tonneke, who is a member of *OPZIJ*. She herself could have easily been one of those feminist leaders.

We play at the Melkweg, Paradiso, Roxy, Tivoli, the Vondelpark, all the women's centers and COCs, benefit gigs and Pink Saturdays. At the opening of the Homomonument next to the Westertoren, we have the great honor to headline at the Maloe Melo, with Rosa King. Rosa King, who can move you to tears with her cutting tenor sax and her rough, husky voice.

Fifi L'Amour and David de Most are our support act for a while and travel with us. They came from Australia to the Netherlands as gender refugees, as they joked; in Australia, you cannot be as openly gay. Fifi is wild, wilder than Lorien, although they are equally extravagant. Fifi is small and has impressive long, black, thick hair always decorated with tulle, bits of fabric, sticks and other bits and pieces, which turn into an unreal masterpiece, almost clownesque make-up on her big round eyes, fishnet panties, pumps, crazy dresses and many accessories in the same style as Lorien's spikes and leather S&M items. Her voice is famous in the gay scene and wherever there is a party they play, the theatrical musical act that never tires. David is a piano virtuoso who creates the craziest music on the piano, dresses in tight, plastic light blue trousers and leather spiked armbands, a top with rushes, and smokes endless fags, chasing them with liters of whisky. The skinny man quietly balances Fifi's extravagance.

Fish, the singer, is a complicated person. One way or the other, she carries tension around her, and if there is none, she will create it. She lives hard and extreme, always balancing on the edge of boundaries. Sometimes it goes well. It goes wrong with drug use, and she became an addict. Fish is half Native American, a stunning woman you cannot overlook. She has to be the centre of attention and if she feels threatened, she becomes nasty. She admits this freely because when you confront her, she says, "Yes, I am a monster," and that makes any discussion where everybody accepts responsibility for their part in an argument impossible. Any discussion with Fish where she is confronted about things she perceives as a criticism is impossible to take further.

Prior to starting the Romantic Bones, Fish had been strong enough to stop taking drugs from one day to the next and set the goal to create a band and become famous—or at least make a living from it in one year. If that failed, she would start using drugs again. Of course, it's very strong to stop drugs like that, but she did not keep it to herself, as the pressure was on us too. If Fish didn't succeed in becoming famous or living from her music, we would be co-responsible for her starting to use again, the message was clear but invisible, an underlying but present pressure.

The Bones existed to save Fish's life. That was pressure, pressure we all unconsciously accepted, because the band would have been impossible otherwise, and we would not have stayed together for the time we existed.

Fish is a passionate woman without limits and writes powerful lyrics, full of melancholy, personal dramas but also interweaving political issues. Songs like "When the Indians Had Gone" and lines like: "When you'll lock your door, I'm on the inside", or "You left your shadow on the table near our bed, you can come and pick it up when the moon turns red" hold such an emotional power that we sometimes play the songs with tears streaming down our faces.

On stage, our love, is palpable. Our music and the magic gives us wings, but we hate each other with the same intensity during conflict. It is never quiet or relaxed and we are always on our guard for the next explosion that usually spawns from nothing, always unexpected. Music is another dimension that exceeds daily life. It is as if everything disappeared and we met each other again in the other dimension, a dimension where only our music counts and that music is drenched in vulnerable emotions. We become soft in our music. The music we make seems to originate from the magical combination of our personalities. Nobody can even imagine that if Renée would stop, for example, we would just look for another bass player. That is unthinkable, as the magic exists in this combination of these five women.

We are not great musicians technically. The Bones are not about fast guitar or drum solos, spiffy riffs or elaborate sax hoops, clever bass lines, but we make our music. Sounds generate and exist in the moment. We improvise a lot and permit the atmosphere of the moment to lead us, and our concerts have an atmosphere where people convert to the emotions present in our music.

Fish and Lorien had started the band together and the name appeared when Lorien played "Lolo's Song" around the campfire, and Fish said: "Lorien, you just have romantic bones". They looked at each other, and knew they had a name for the band. "Lolo's Song" was created from the backing vocals by Lolo, the whippet. When Lorien played, Lolo howled at different tune levels, which made it sound like real melodies. She always sang with Lorien, and this was her song.

The Bones has amassed a big reputation on the Amsterdam music scene. When we arrive somewhere, people seem uneasy, eyeing us in our leather, studs, dogs and chains, but as soon as we start playing at the sound check, people relax, and later at the gig, we're all transported by the magic.

On our English tour, we go to a club Fish knows. The name should ring a bell, but I am blissfully unaware. We enter Chain Reactions, down long dark stairs to the cellar, revealing a huge disco. Paulien, Renée and I are the softies of the band, not dressed in leather with chains, studs, spikes and heavy army boots. We aren't known on the S&M scene that is quite different in London from Amsterdam. Chain Reactions, my God, I should have known....

We walk down the stairs to the dark catacombs filled with suffocating smoke and sweat, slowly realizing where we are. Paulien and I retreat to a corner where we can sit without being seen. Renée tucks in with us but is very curious, so she gets up to stroll around. Plllars tower in the large cellar, holding up the foundation of the building above. One of the pillars is the stage for, as we discover, live sex shows with women only. Famous faces from the music industry grace Chain. I can remember Lesley Woods of the Au Pairs, Yazz, whose only single was "The Only Way Is Up, Baby", but mostly a lot of hardcore women who feel at home here underground.

A short, quite heavy woman is brought in by two butches. Blindfolded, she is dressed in a tight skirt without knickers and a leather bra much too small for her breasts. The butches are wearing leather caps and heavy boots, tight leather trousers and belts with spikes, tight leather tops accenting arms covered in tattoos. They have whips and handcuffs at the ready, while they lead the small woman to the pillar. Their faces express assuredness in this game of domination, but they are not rough with her. In fact, care shows in their gestures. They tie her to the pillar, her hands above her head and legs spread. They stroke her, tease her with the whip. Paulien and I look at each other, giggle and ask ourselves why we're witness to this underground spectacle.

Evidenced by winks and smiles and our earlier shows in the week, everyone knows we belong to the Romantic Bones. We can't really hide. We wait for Fish and Lorien to signal our exit, which will only be when they want to go to sleep.

In Tivoli, Utrecht, we're the last band to play at the Make-up Music Festival, and the welcome is not very warm. An arrogant radio-cow comparing the gigs is not charmed by our look and asks who the hell we are upon our arrival, Renée extends her hand and says: "Bones, Romantic Bones." Priceless, it sets a tone.

A strange atmosphere swelters all night, and the organization is very strict and in favor of Mamma's Got a Brand-new Bag, the sexy, new band with hip musicians and sophisticated riffs. After one hour, we are interrupted in the middle of a song and ordered to leave the stage; our hour is up. Wow, so rude, and we continue to play. When they turn off the power, we play "Lolo's Song" a bit longer without amplifier and the audience encourages us, obviously on our side. Finally, they remove us from the stage by pushing us off it!

At the end of the evening, after the live gigs, the bouncers admit a group of twenty skinheads because they are scared a fight will break out if they deny them entry. While Mamma's Got a Brand-new Bag is playing and we're loading the bus, skirmishes break out in the audience. The skinheads insult women and aggressively provoke them. I stand at the bus with Lorien to take the gear and put it in the bus, when the door that leads to the long corridor of Tivoli suddenly bursts open. Women are screaming and running to escape the skinheads, who me and Lorien try to stop.

Lorien boldly stands in front of them while I try to pull bleeding Mieke and Pink outside. A balled fist pummels Lorien's skull. I hear it crack. People scream, "Run, run!" I pull Lorien outside, as she is completely disorientated after that blow to her head. Fortunately, all instruments and the PA are already in the bus. Everybody flees in the bus as quickly as possible, including the three dogs that are now shaking uncontrollably. I throw the doors shut with the group of skinheads on my heels. I run around the bus to get behind the wheel and drive off as fast as I can. The bus is full of shaken and wounded women.

The moment I open the door and lunge forward to sit down, a fat, short skinhead girl grabs me from behind and pulls me out of the bus. I turn around, grab her by the throat and push her on her back, with my full weight on her and my hands around her neck. I explode. Then as I stare into her eyes and see nothing, blackness, the grip of my hands weakens to match the rest of my body in fear. Her nightmarish void terrifies me. A few seconds later, twenty skinheads start kicking me with their army boots. I roll into a ball, my arms around my head to try and protect my head, anaesthetized by the impact of the hard kicks. They hit my head with their boots. I can only wait. Some bystanders must have inserted themselves, because suddenly I'm being pushed into the bus, I pull the door shut with all the strength I can muster. The bus is pure hysteria.

Paulien, sweet Paulien, sits next to me and whispers, "Babs, turn the engine on, we're going." Everything is buzzing. I groggily push the key in the contact and wait until the light indicator of the diesel bus is unlit. In those seconds, they damaged the bus. We're lucky to get out with our lives.

With my whole body in acute pain, not able to use my left arm or sit upright, we drive straight to the police station. We later heard that the bouncers had immediately phoned the police, who had only arrived when we were sitting battered and bruised in the police station. The skinheads were long gone. They are known in Utrecht, but nobody dared doing anything against them.

The duty officer is not inspired to take statements. "Look here, it is after midnight, come back tomorrow," he says dryly. I lean over his desk and pull him by his shirt over the typewriter towards me with my good arm. With his face 5cm away from mine, I tell him very coldly that he now will start typing because otherwise, I will have a word with his boss. We tell our story one by one, and he types. The rest of the night, we survey mug shots and identify all the skinheads.

I drive to Amsterdam in the early hours of the morning. Lorien has a severe concussion and vomits. Mieke, a fan from Amsterdam, cannot walk, and I have a broken rib, a skull fracture above my left ear, fractured left upper arm, heavy bruises everywhere.

In Sheffield, UK, we play at the university, our biggest concert with an audience of 4,000 women. The next morning, we have breakfast with the women who had organized the concert. Somebody mentions a woman in Leeds, 60km further north, who has a tattoo shop, her name is Babs. A few moments later, we are on our way to Leeds! I have been thinking of a tattoo for years and now, there is a woman called Babs. A sign.

As a child, I drew a tree with a red moon through it. The red moon, the womb where I originated from, my father was the tree. With the Bones, the song, "When the Moon Turns Red" was usually the encore, and I never played it with dry eyes.

The tree with the red moon behind it is on my left upper arm a few hours later. I'm so thrilled to finally have my tattoo. While she was tattooing me, I imagined how that super-fast needle was piercing my flesh. In my mind the needle became increasingly bigger, and my imagination helped me to faint twice, which I obviously attributed to my empty stomach. (Now, twenty years later, the red circle has faded, the red ink has disappeared, the moon is gone, the womb resolved.

130

Only the tree remains, a very pretty tree. It has beautiful symbolism; I have slowly become the tree myself.)

Someone from the audience once shared that we do not have our own aura on stage, but that she saw us in one aura, with all the colors of the rainbow. Our music is magical, but the social life with the Bones is linked to lots of stress and arguments. Fish is a very domineering woman who always argues with Lorien. A push and pull, love-hate relationship. Renée, the bass player, then gets really nervous because she wants to restore the harmony. Paulien gets quiet or enraged, and then Fish must look out. Fish manipulates, has a junkie mentality, licking up, kicking down. I think she sees me as a threat because we fall for the same women, we both are butch-like. After her ex, who teaches me percussion, and I go to a Tina Turner concert, the tension between Fish and me becomes unbearable. She makes snide comments, but makes sure the others do not hear them. I often walk away. I hate the violence of the arguments. They frighten me.

My anger for Fish intensifies, and I have no outlet for it. The social life with the Bones makes me ill and faint often. I've had enough after one and a half years.

The agony of no longer being able to make that music feels like a broken heart for many years afterwards and deep inside.

Chapter 19

THE THING ABOUT GENDERING AND ORIENTATIONS

On Sunday evenings, 'De Trut' (The Bitch) is the spot. The underground, mostly gay club only open on Sundays, is located on the Bilderdijkstraat under an enormous squat building, one of the high-profile squats, like Vrankrijk, Klene and the 'NRC' building. The people occupying these squat buildings are politically motivated squatters, activists against the legislation allowing house owners to leave their properties unrented, vacated and empty while there is, in comparison, such an unacceptable shortage of affordable housing in Amsterdam. The squat scene is closely connected to the gay scene and the alternative vegetarian circuit, as well as the artists, performers and musicians.

I don't like to be exclusively identified with one scene, as it limits me in my social movements, but what I like about De Trut is that different scenes come together there, scenes with different codes and habits, all intertwined and coexisting. Doors open at 10:00 p.m. and then the party thumps till morning. It is an exhilarating place with pulsating cult punk, reggae, rock, avant-garde, deafening music that only leaves you with one option—dance yourself into a pouring sweat, breathing the suffocating smoke of rolies and joints, and drinking lots to get in the flow. Dykes, fags, squatters, musicians, punks, addicts, artists, soul searchers and other hippies all unite in the cacophony of music, alcohol and drugs, then wake up the following afternoon with a hangover and a sore throat. It's also a hot place to meet people outside once you're too late to get in. Fire regulations are strict—full capacity means full capacity. It's worth waiting to get in, especially since the smoke and the loud music inside do not permit any kind of socializing, so standing in line evolved into its own culture.

One evening, while standing in line, a tall, skinny guy approaches me and says in his very distinct accent: "Hey Babs, you remember me, Robbie Bakker from high school?" Before I can answer, he seems very excited to see me. He asks if I ever realized what I had meant for him, that he would never forget what I did for him when I had facilitated the homosexuality awareness classes. That I'm his role model, example and hero. He grabs and hugs me with his clumsy, long, thin arms. I've always liked Robbie because he dared to be himself, different, even though others would make fun of him. In high school, we hung out quite a bit.

Robbie and his brother were identical twins, in high school they were famous for their tap dance acts and rather unusual behavior. They brought their lunch boxes with sandwiches, an egg and a little bit of salt rolled up in tin foil. Each sandwich would disappear at once in their large wide mouths, then they chewed it, swallowed it faster than seemed possible and stuffed the next whole sandwich in. They were from Venezuela and spoke Spanish, so Dutch with their heavy accent made them stand out. Sometimes they dressed up in women's clothes at parties, they were quite flamboyant but closeted. No one even considered them to be gay, just different and fun. Robbie was in my class, so I knew him better then Percy. And now here, outside De Trut, we meet again, I'm so happy to hear that my actions had a positive impact. Once we enter the dance area, we dance the whole evening, and it's glorious to be ourselves together.

Washrooms are my favorite locations to receive abuse based on how people perceive me just being me. It really does not matter in which country I am, statements abound like "Oh, I must have taken the wrong door" or "What are you doing in the women's washroom?" or

"Sir, you are wrong here" or "This is the women's toilet right?" and my favorite, "You pervert!" Plain looks of disapproval are also abundant.

In Portugal, I'm in a camping site and after a whole afternoon reading in my little tent, I go up to go to the sanitation block with twelve toilets opposite twelve sinks and two showers in the back. I enter in my bikini. The two showers clearly not sufficient for the number of women who want to wash, some take off their tops and decide to wash their upper bodies at the sinks on the left side. When I enter, they sweep their arms across their chests to cover their breasts. "I am only going to the toilet." I try and continue to the right, open a toilet door and quickly lock it behind me again. Murmuring outside and some excited voices in Portuguese, then a strange silence. A few minutes later, I flush and open the door to walk out. Two security officers walk quickly towards me and before I realize what's happening, they handcuff me. They do not speak English, and I do not speak Portuguese.

I figure that this has to do with the fact that the women are offended by me using the women's washroom. I am wearing a bikini, clearly showing my breasts and no bulge in my crotch area, but I am not perceived as a woman. Not the first time, so I start dragging the officers into the direction of my tent. Luckily, they do not quite know what to do so they come along. I try to make clear to them that I need to get my passport, which they oblige. My passport says FEMALE, which I point out, hoping gender is, in fact, the whole issue. And so, it is. They unlock my handcuffs while muttering to each other. Then they walk away without a word of apology or whatever. All the people from neighboring tents are gawking at me. I'm embarrassed and mad.

Sometimes I wish I was born in the wrong body; that would be so much simpler, but it is not that. I like my body. I feel comfortable with it and with being a woman. I would not want to be a man. I don't look particularly masculine, I don't look typical feminine, and I dress exactly how I feel, more on comfort than on looks—I just hate having breasts.

But often, I get treated as if I were a man. Nearly daily, I am confronted with reactions from strangers that remind me of being the third sex by being booted out of the female washrooms, scaring women who see me in the washrooms and rush back to the door to look at the sign and confirm they are at least, in the right washrooms. Some of these experiences are truly remarkable.

You know, it really does not seem to make a hell of a difference how I actually look, what I am wearing. My experiences are irrespective of looks; they are based on what people experience around me and that has fascinated me for years now.

Like the late afternoon I was at the beach in Katwijk aan Zee, North Sea Netherlands. It was at the end of the day, a warm day with a bit of a breeze so it wasn't too muggy. Most people had already packed up and headed home. I made a sculpture like I always do when I am at the beach. In fact, I don't like beaches for lying around, sunbathing, which makes me itch. They are no good for reading, too, as you never can seem to find a comfortable position that will not kill your back after each ten minutes.

For me, beaches are only good for kiting, walking and making sand sculptures. I sculpt a pregnant woman, who washed up on shore. Her legs slightly pulled up, her long hair as sun rays around her head and her belly full of expecting new life. She lays on her right hip, her back twisted so that her shoulders are nearly horizontal, her left breast nearly touching the beach. Her right arm stretched along her head, leaning on her left elbow. As the tide swells, the waves come closer to her and she is about to be washed away, wave by wave.

I walk into the waves to wash the sand off my body and wait until she is returned to the sea. The water touches her, eroding the sand from her body. I stand in the waves wearing just my bikini, the water to my knees, observing the slow process that I enjoy so much as an integral part of making the sculpture. I feel the water suck the sand from around and under my feet, trying to keep my balance. The feeling of the late sun on my back and the flow of the waves pushes and pulls. Two little girls come closer. They are enjoying the waves as well, maybe about ten or eleven years old, Dutch, giggling and once they reach me, they are sort of hanging around me. With outflanking movements, they are clearly attracted to the same spot as me, and their giggling is getting more rambunctious. I smile, feeling somewhere between curious and insulted.

"What is so funny, girls?" I ask.

The giggles erupt and one of them chuckles out loud: "We have never seen a man with boobs!" And off they go, running back to their parents further down the beach. I am stunned. The last sand remnants of the pregnant woman surrender to the sea.

The external identifiers are there, but somehow, these girls picked up an energy that overruled the characteristics of the consensus reality of my body in a bikini. So, when we can only believe what we can prove as western science has brainwashed us with, how does that work for a contradicting experience like this?

We are led to believe that there is just one science, but there is, of course, more. Besides the mainstream and indoctrinated western science (you can only believe what you can prove), indigenous sciences are based on natural cycles and connectedness; all living beings are spiritual and connected. Western science is like a religion. Why do we need to believe when we can prove it? Belief is truth. Western science is set up for industries to thrive and people to serve the systems, feeling small and insignificant. Biologist Rupert Sheldrake's famously banned TEDx Whitechapel talk, "The Science Delusion" addresses these concepts and how they relate to traditional gender construct.

Chapter 20

DESIGNING MY ENVIRONMENTS

1989

I live at the Marialaan in Nijmegen, in an old house dating back to 1906.

The neighbor opposite, who has lived there all his life, informs me that you can walk under the other houses from the cellars. The crouching spaces are not closed off by the foundation walls. From the bakery on the corner to approximately fifteen houses in the street, the spaces between the outer walls are connected. My front cellar has a concrete floor; I have a little workshop there where I potter about. Around the corner, there is a trap in the wall. I open it and walk through; I land in grey sand half a meter higher than the cellar's floor. Ancient, grey spider webs everywhere, and I inevitably walk into them with my face. Clumsily, walking stooped through the soft, uneven sand, I can then see under the whole house with a torch. It smells musty and of dry earth. All the dividing, carrying and intermediate walls has arched masonry and space to go to the neighbors. A bit further underneath the house the sand heightens, and I can only see the neighbor's spaces just under the arch. The neighbor says that I might find utensils belonging to the Jews, who had lived in hiding there a few years during the war. I never start digging the sand, I sort of I like the idea of undiscovered memories there. He explained they had made partitions under the arches to flee from one side to the other. If there was a raid where the bakery now is, looking for the Jews in hiding, they would close off the spaces, go further under the other houses and the space under the bakery would look inhabited. The neighbor said the system must have been very effective because the Germans always came back up without Jews. At the end of the war, all the Jewish family members, of four complete families, safely emerged from the cellars.

The house felt good the first time I walked into it. I had come to view a room I could rent. The walls were covered in seventies wallpaper with big brown, purple and bright green patterns, and there were cheap, and by now filthy, carpet tiles on the floor. It smelled musty; the electricity installation looked positively dangerous. There was a big ball of aluminum foil in the hole where it should have a fuse, to prevent the fuse from blowing up every time. The thick layer of paint on the window frames was discolored by smoke and the ceilings decorated with plaster grapes were peeling, but from that first moment, it felt as if the house embraced me. It looked terrible, but I immediately rented the room.

Next to the front room, on the street side, are stairs, and I quickly discover the wallpapered doors that give access the empty space under the stairs. What at first glance appears to be a small room, immediately extends to at least four meters' storage space under the stairs, where I build a sound system and wooden platform to put my double mattress on. The platform is half the surface of the room but diagonally above the square floor surface. From the platform, where the low ceiling requires me to crawl to bed, I can pull wires that are connected to the volume button of the old amplifier and like a remote control, turn music up or down. I also have a bamboo stick through two eyelets to switch the cassette player on or off. The last piece of remote control to reach the on/off button of the amplifier itself is a metal ball on a string, which I have to carefully slide through a PVC slot to turn the amplifier on or off without having to go down the simple stairs steep as a ladder for which I need the handles on the platform to pull me over the center of gravity. My father's old cabinet and the drawing board are under the stairs. I design and carve figures with my father's knife on the desk legs that I built in the other corner attached to the stair posts. An old German piano that I had acquired to study music therapy, stands next to the entrance door. My first year was interrupted because they found out I never earned my secondary education diploma. I later successfully pass the 18+ test, which is equal to a secondary diploma, and I can continue. My fingers tips are too thick to play wide chords on the piano, they pull the black keys down as well. My back is another problem. At home, I sit at the piano with my elbows on my knees because it's too painful to sit upright. That position is not permitted during the training. Besides my spatula fingertips, my back also stops me from achieving tempo in my playing. But I do like the sound of the long, resounding chords, which is why I keep the piano in my little room of only 3 by 3,20m!

I am in bed with high fever and suddenly, it occurs to me that I am fed up with women; I want a guy. The endless dramas and getting under your skin, the emotional trips that hold no truth…over, *done*, let's do this! Wouldn't my life be so much easier with a man? Wow, what revelation, what relief. Imagine living a normal life with a man, not being different anymore, not always having to explain that in fact, my partner is not a man—I'm dating a woman. Always those awkward moments of being confronted with being a lesbian, wouldn't that just be amazing if it disappeared out of my life? My fever is high and my mind delusional although somewhere these thoughts hold some truth. I am tired and frustrated with being a lesbian. I never chose to be one (as if you can) and now I want to choose not to be one anymore. I share my house with Yvette and Cor, who come to check up on me.

With a sudden clarity of mind, I ask for the Saturday paper to go through the personal ads. Yvette storms up the stairs and comes running back with the newspaper, plunges herself onto my bed and together, we sift through all the "man looking for woman" pages. Looking at myself from outside, I can barely imagine what I'm doing, but a high fever is perfect excuse to do something out of the ordinary.

Yvette and I giggle while trying to be serious about this endeavor. Of course, she has witnessed my endless attempts to find the one, which always ends in drama and results in the kind of disappointment that simultaneously feels like a relief. The sense of relief is related to the little voice in the back of my head that persists from the beginning when I am getting involved with someone. The little voice always tells me she is not the one, it's clear in the first days, but I choose to ignore the message. I was raised in a family with my father and mother utterly in love with each other. I naturally believe that one day, I will also be with that one person, my true love; I just need to find her.

Yvette teases, "Babs wants a gu-uy, Babs wants a gu-uy," while contagiously giggling.

Coincidently, I've spent months in bed already, the days with fever unrelated, the first weeks uncontrollably crying myself to sleep and waking up crying at random times through the days. A big blur, a complete burn-out. I barely recognized the severe pain the herniated disks in my lower back caused, the fallout of my legs which had imminently caused the end of my career at the Buitencentrum, a resocialization center for extreme problematic drug users, kind of a last station. The official diagnosis had conveniently provided me with a valid reason to stay in bed. I vaguely remember how it took me nearly an hour to roll over, get one foot on the floor, change the grip of my hand to the armrest of the chair, roll a bit further, get my other leg down, move my weight, get my first hand, then the other to the floor as well, crawl from the side of my bed to the toilet, undress to pee, wipe, pull up my underwear and make the same painstaking exercise back to the mattress. There were times that I half woke up and thought there was another body in my bed, frantically tried to find out who was in my bed, scared, then felt the leg, squeezed it, felt around it and only then realized that they were my own legs that I had my hands on, the nerves in my back so badly jammed that I had no sense in my legs and frankly, nor did I have much sense in my head in those days. The specialist had shared his preference for surgery; though the two locations with herniated disks were not acute so surgery could be avoided. Surgery would be beneficial for a quicker return of the sensation in my legs, but it could possibly heal with resting, it would take time, lots of time and no guarantee. I opted not to have surgery, knowing that I would need lots of time and resting to get that damn sense back into my head anyway. The work at the Buitencentrum had physically and mentally been so hard on me that it had literally floored me.

That afternoon at the Buitencentrum, we were constructing a concrete driveway for the tractor. I had lost some sensation in my legs in the weeks before that day but had ignored the pain associated with the numb feeling. I carried a wheelbarrow piled up with concrete tiles when I suddenly lost all control over my lower body and went down. I laid there and did not have any sensation in my legs. I looked at how the tiles had ripped through the plastic of the greenhouse; Gijs was mad that the greenhouse was damaged, and he stood over me, yelling that I should get up. I could "decide to have pain or the pain to have me, I'm a weakling if I don't get up now!" He went on and on.

Calmness set in. I suddenly saw his weakness. He needed to be so hard for himself to hide his weak side, he was not able to be gentle to himself. In that moment, I understood all the things that had brought me down and didn't want them to have power over me. I was not afraid of Gijs anymore. In fact, I saw how pathetic he was and what a sad man, I even felt sorry for him while I laid there. The year I worked at the Buitencentrum, I wanted Gijs to like me. I would do anything to be in his good books, but the harder I tried the more I failed, till it ultimately snapped my back. While he was yelling at me, I responded quietly, "Gijs, you'd better call an ambulance, yelling isn't going to make me walk now." It felt empowering to address Gijs like that.

During this time, my mother was in Spain, walking part of the pilgrimage to La Compostela, 500 miles by foot. She offered to interrupt her walk and look after me, but I didn't want her to interrupt her noble journey. I said I would be fine. Truth is, I did not know how to handle being looked after by my mum, to be dependent and helpless. Only much later, I realized that Cor and Yvette had looked after me, bringing me food and drinks, changing my bed, feeding Sophie and Freek, my big black cats, doing the laundry, cleaning the room, helping me take a shower (?!), but I remember none of it.

I spent these months imagining myself a few inches tall, going into my spine to plaster, chisel and heal the broken membranes of the bulging disks. I did this many hours per day, escaping from the dire situation, and doing what I love, working with my hands and tapping into the self-healing powers of my body.

As soon as I could stand on my legs again and put one leg in front of the other, I went for small walks, first in my back garden, later to the bakery on the corner. I walked a bit further every day, slowly and conscious of every muscle movement at every step. I walked whenever I could, wherever I could, walking became like a mode, it was all better when I walked. The nerve-wrecking pain from the last months vanished. It felt though as if the slightest wrong move could set me back, so every movement I managed muscle by muscle. All in slow motion, visualizing. Walking was healing for my back and the consciousness of managing every tiniest move, healing for my soul. Walking was peaceful, just me and step by step, just that continuous motion.

The Mets was a small pub downtown that I had heard about, a place that I had never gotten around to visiting. It was owned and operated by two women. Lesbian friends went there regularly, but I am always quite hesitant about "scenes", so I had not been there yet. The months it took before I could walk again had been intensely lonely and social activities right down to zero, so a place like The Mets, an alternative living room, could be just the right place to find new friends, get to know people and start living again. So, the walk downtown to reach The Mets became a goal in itself. At first, I could not even dream about making it there, let alone making it back. It would take a twenty-minute walk for someone healthy, and I still had to make up for lost times and lost muscles, but I was determined to get there. Eventually, I did.

Once I was able to reach The Mets, I made it my daily routine to have Bambu coffee, read the paper, have another Bambu, get familiar with the women working there. After a few weeks, people started greeting me as if I were part of the decor. I had become a regular in a cozy bar downtown where women came to have a coffee on their breaks, a beer after work, new lovers found each other, relationships went on the rocks, where joy was celebrated and sadness covered up with copious amounts of alcohol and friendly gossips abundantly spread to whoever wanted to listen, but it was all friendly and comfortable. The Mets marked my return to life.

Suddenly, bringing me back to the present, where I'm in bed again after that long recovery, Yvette yells, "Here, look at this one! 'Nice guy, 30 years old is looking for a non girly woman, my length 1,85m and just like me you should have no business with ads like these.'" I reply to his ad with 'Non girly woman, 27 years old is looking for a nice guy, my length 1.78cm and indeed should have no business snooping through these ads but I have high fever, so I have an excuse, what's yours?'"

I sign with my phone number and Yvette goes to mail it for me. Yvette is so excited, she keeps repeating, "I can't believe it, this is for you, I just feel it."

I'm not quite sure what to feel and certainly after the fever goes down, I start realizing what I have done. What was I thinking? What would I do if this man called me? It excites as well, the thought that a man could actually be interested in me.

On a rare occasion as mostly a vegetarian, I prepare fresh trout, filled with garlic, thick tomato paste, and thyme, one of my favourite dishes. Cor, Yvette and I are about to start eating when the phone rings.

"Hi, I am Syl," a gentle voice sounds and I jump, realizing that this is the man from the ad! "I received your reply and liked that I could just call you or nothing, nice and direct, no explanations who you are, no nice words but good humor, I liked it, so I thought I'd call." I don't know how to respond, I feel extremely shy, but luckily, Syl proposes to meet the following weekend, so I only need to respond with "yes" or "no".

He would drive a blue Volvo to the parking lot in front of the train station in Nijmegen and meet me on the steps. *Nice, okay, see you next Saturday, okay, yes, bye.* Easeful chat. Then we hang up. I had forgotten to ask for his number in case I wanted to cancel. After all, it's only Monday. I have a whole week to go till I will meet this man or change my mind. It all feels very strange. I am going to meet a man who's looking for a non-girly female partner. What am I looking for?

It is a beautiful, sunny morning, warm and pleasant. The weather isn't helping my anxiety though. Why am I here again? As usual, I arrive ahead of the time of the appointment, I hate being late. A blue Volvo pulls up and parks in front of me. A shabby-looking guy with greasy hair and a cigarette hanging from his lip from under a moustache gets out, looks around and starts walking in the direction of the entrance. I ignore him, pretending to just enjoy the sun when in fact, I'm waiting for the right moment to get up and swiftly head back home. The moment I think it's not too obvious to get up and forget about this whole thing, another blue Volvo enters the parking lot. I'm so relieved to see a gentle-looking, extremely handsome man stepping out of this Volvo that I walk straight at him and greet him. He smiles and introduces himself.

After awkward silence, he suggests going for a walk. We decide on the beaches along the river past the Waalbridge, into the Ooijpolder. We get in the car and a sensation sparks, as if I could see how life with this man could be. I feel nice, but I also feel like a different person. I've entered a life not destined for me, and I hear myself tell him that I've never dated a man before. He laughs, responding that his problem is always falling for lesbians because they tend to be less girly and he likes to do stuff together like fixing his old cars, riding motorbikes and restoring the old farm of his dreams. I confide in him how sick I am of being different, always confronted with what I am because of the responses from the world around me, and now, I've decided to go out with a man and that replying to his ad was my first attempt in this direction. It is a pleasant afternoon and strangely comfortable, not too awkward at all.

The next weekend, I take the train to Ede, where he lives. I find myself, after a coffee and walk through the area, lying under his Volvo to change the brake pads. We joke, get more acquainted and enjoy the rest of the day. He starts cooking and asks if I want to stay for the rest of the weekend and go biking. I still feel as if I have entered a life I'm not supposed to live, but suddenly have access to this wonderful man! I'm in the world of the others, the world where people don't turn around to look at you, a world where you can just answer the question of what the name of your boyfriend is. A world in which I could walk hand in hand without being noticed, where no one yells at you, "Hey dykes", the world where I could relax and not always be on guard.

I'm not fed up with women, but with the never-absent reactions of society on my personal feelings, which feel like abuse to my privacy. The simple fact that I have a girlfriend apparently gives people the right to ask indecent things about my privacy, the ever-returning question how two women do 'it', as if that is the only thing that comes to mind relating to two people who love each other. It forces me in a position of defending myself where I have the feeling there is nothing to defend. The forced unease with myself even though I am not uncomfortable with myself at all, only in relation to the exterior reactions. So now, I'm in the world where all these issues do not exist. Deep down, I do not feel at ease but ignore the inner voice.

When I introduce Syl to my mum, she is so thrilled. She instantly loves Syl and the idea of a potential son-in-law. I'm insulted and weary, well-aware of my mum's taste for much younger men. It hurts like hell, confirming that I cannot make her happier than coming home with a man, her son-in-law. This is pure rejection against who I really am, the part I am passionately trying to ignore. After four months, we are on holiday on Schiermonnikoog, one of the small islands off the North coast of the Netherlands, the inevitable happens. We walk on the beach, a favorite destination for gay couples, and we cross a few lesbian couples.

Normally, I would exchange eye contact, smile, recognize "family" and greet each other, but side by side with Syl, I am ignored, not recognized. A deep sadness grips me, ripping through my heart. I am dying inside, trying to ignore who I really am. There is no choice, and I have to face up to the fact that this life, this comfortable life, the life of the others, is indeed, for the others, not for me. Syl notices. I share my experiences with him. We talk till late that night and Syl stresses that I can't neglect such strong feelings, I have to accept who I am, I can't go on ignoring my own essence.

We decide to break up. He has fallen in love with me over the past months and asks me not to contact him until he potentially contacts me again. Even though I had been upfront with him from the start, it hurts me to see this wonderful man be heartbroken. The mourning and pain I feel in the following weeks are the heartbreak over the life I could never live, the separation from this wonderful man willing to put his own feelings aside to guide me on the way to myself, a woman who loves women.

I am not somebody who, as could be reasonably expected when you accept a job in a strange country, starts reading about the country and gets prepared. Not preparing too much has its advantages and disadvantages. The nice surprises by lack of preparation are sometimes so overwhelming and the disadvantages are that I sometimes pack the wrong clothes. The advantages always outweigh the disadvantages by far because I always wear the same clothes, a pair of jeans and simple, wide cotton shirts with rolled up sleeves, and what I need and forget to take I can buy.

During a week in Florence with Tonneke after my architecture studies, I have one of those experiences, caused by lack of preparation, that I wouldn't have missed for the world. I had just graduated as an architect and I had written my thesis about stairs, the history of stairs in architecture, appearance, and perception of stairs in spaces and how they have defined modern architecture, my architecture.

After visiting the Medici chapels, we continue our trip to the Bibliotheca Laurenziana, where I am unexpectedly overwhelmed by the proximity of the famous stairs of Michelangelo.

In my thesis about stairs, I described these stairs even with an illustration, but I prepare myself so little to a journey, a visit, a holiday or work destination that I didn't even make the link between going to Florence and possibly seeing those perfect stairs. I could have missed them.

In every detail of this city, I feel how this city is an active center in the centuries that have had such a great impact on art and architecture. I virtually see how the city had looked in the period Michelangelo worked there; it was as if I could look back in time. The atmosphere of travelling artists who tried to survive from their art contributes to the dynamics of the city. Painters painting the ceilings of a dome or a chapel on their backs for years. Sculptors who literally worked themselves to death with the marble dust in their lungs.

Everything happened under the reign of the Medici, who governed the city at cultural, political, and social level. With their wealth and ideas about art, artists were able to work with materials and create works of art they could otherwise not even dream of. This did not contribute to the wealth of the artists themselves, but it has definitely contributed to one of the most fabulous periods in the history of art. Art and architecture developed at such speed in Florence that Northern Europe was an area where life was still in the Dark Ages.

Every next project the Medici commissioned had to be bigger and more imposing than the previous. More beautiful and expensive materials had to be used to show off their power and capital. They had to be flaunting works. And it is exactly this that annoys me while standing in the large Medici chapel of San Lorenzo, which is ostentatious, but not because it is beautiful—it shows that no expense or effect was spared to impress.

There are things of absolute quality, whether they are my taste or not, but when I look at them, I know they are good. One cannot deny quality, but taste must be debatable, taste is learned, quality follows universal laws. People have tried to describe those laws throughout the centuries, but without success. Although those laws are not recorded on paper it does not mean that they don't exist. I can think of very different buildings I find breathtaking to look at, fabulous to walk through, that make me silent with their acoustics, make my fingers tingle when I touch the texture of their materials, but you cannot describe my taste by knowing these buildings. The buildings are so varied in color, shape, style, and space that there must be something else that attracts me so much. Their sheer quality fascinates and moves me.

Yesterday, I went to the library with this famous staircase by Michelangelo. An impressive black marble staircase, which has one central walk, flanked by two smaller sidewalks. Towards the bottom it becomes wider, and the shapes start to become rounder. Often, it is compared with lava coming down, slowly but gracefully. I wanted to touch it, but I couldn't; I felt so much respect for it, that I could only look at it and enjoy being in the same room with it.

The following day, my mum and I go to the Medici Chapel. There, a similar experience, this time the small chapel. I stand in the center of it before I realize this is the Medici Chapel, which had been of such great value for the development of Mannerism. It is very austere, a space that makes you quiet and humbles you with its beauty. Again, Michelangelo.

A square chapel, white and grey green, half pillars, arches, very pure. There are four sculptures against the four walls, made by the same artist. It is a masterpiece because of its geometry and its proportions. This was the first time in history that an artist not just copied something old. Michelangelo had used his skills to give a personal interpretation of space. That is the mind-blowing power of Michelangelo.

We stay there for a long time before we move on to the big Medici chapel. What I see around me fills me with all sorts of extreme feelings. It appears as if the walls contain all the possible existing sorts of marble. Big marble statues of the Medici themselves all around. The floor is an amazing mosaic, the variety of marble types from the most remote areas, impressive. High up, where the walls end and the dome begins, there are huge golden ornaments all around and up, dividing the dome in sections. The sections are painted with personifications of Gods, mainly in heavenly blue.

The chapel represents a mirror showing me something important: the reflection of a past repeating itself at this very moment. I have become a part of that process, by working for people with loads of money, spending excessive amounts on their own luxuries. The world of interior architecture in the private sector has a lot to do with the importance of showing off what you can spend. It is not even the money spent that shocks me, but the fact that these people don't even get a smile on their face when the project is finished! My goal is to become a happier person through everything I do. I realize there that my work and the way I am living my life isn't making me happy anymore.

The thought surfaces for me to sell my house, give my belongings away and do something with my skills to contribute to a community instead of individuals. I think of working in Africa as a volunteer, with an organization to be determined later in the process. When we walk out of the chapel, I am relieved, as if a terrible weight had been taken off my shoulders. We drive back to the Netherlands after ten memorable days in Florence—a present from Tonneke, for my graduation as an architect. Back home, I experience a jetlag of a few centuries, as if I had been in a time machine.

PART II.
WHERE AM I?

Chapter 21

COFFINS OF KENYA

January 1999

On my first day in Kenya, I am tired but feel light, I am here, I am in Africa! After I came back from the Florence trip, I started researching ways to get to Africa, get involved in projects, wrote some handwritten letters to random missionaries. Not that I am Catholic or believe in white people going to Africa to convert Africans, but the distant contacts of Tonneke were an entry point without having to commit to the two years with VSO (Voluntary Services Overseas) yet. I quit my job as a restoration architect, sold my house, gave a last supper party with friends. I had one condition for this party: the house had to be empty before they left, with guests taking all my belongings with them.

I sit on the doorstep of one of the buildings in the Pandipieri compound, the project of the missionary who I had sent a letter to, asking if I could come to establish a carpentry training. I just knew the address and had his yes. I look out onto Ring Road, a red dirt track with holes, potholes and lots of dirt whirling around, like plastic bags and the outer leaves of corn cobs. Ring Road is the divider between the city of Kisumu and the slums. This side of Ring Road consists of small huts built from shabby materials, thin branches on the floor, woven branches horizontally placed through them, filled with clay and then often re-used brown, rusty, formerly galvanized sheets as a roof. On the other side of the road is barren land you have to cross to make it to the city, about a half-an-hour walk.

There's hardly any traffic, here and there an old Peugeot 404, doors hanging from the hinges, half open, tires shiny without tread, windows out but with the rubber still in the frames, the bonnet fastened with wires to stop it from opening when driving over the potholes, packed full of people, exceeding the capacity, its belly grinding the sides of the potholes. I wonder how it still moves. But what strikes me most is the pace here. The road is filled with people walking, colorful and packed with big loads on their heads. It's a highway of walking people. Women, tall and slender in very colorful kangas, their heads loaded with baskets, jerrycans and vegetables, or a sheep. They walk to and from the market, to sell their wares or buy essentials. That image is printed in my head forever and will always remain my image of Africa. This walking pace guides me to arrive here, like I am merging into traffic and having to adjust the pace I was used to.

People in Nyalenda, the section of the slum neighborhood where I live, are friendly. Hell, Kenyans are joyful, fun and open. I soon have friends along the road I take every morning to walk to the carpentry workshop, twenty minutes deeper into the slums. They teach me Dholuo greetings, and I discover fourteen greetings with corresponding responses. Practicing them makes the twenty minutes' walk longer and longer. (Dholuo is the language of the Luo population here in western Kenya.)

Women sit outside their huts combing and plaiting each other's hair and decorating it with beads. They roast corn cobs on their jikos (handmade stoves) and sell them to passers-by on wooden tables, along with samosas fried in big handmade thick steel hollow chapati pans. A chapati wrapped in bits of newspaper costs a few *bob*, local slang for the Shilling.

Rattling sawing machines operated with a foot pedal, screws and bolts loose in the holes, make for clattering sounds as I walk along Ring Road. Here and there, I walk past a carpenter and soon, I know them all. I notice how they chisel joints with a sharpened screwdriver, their saw blades rank by the numerous times the teeth have been filed. With everything I observe, I "watch the cat out of the tree", puzzle together all the pieces of where I am. Kids are everywhere, naked with unwashed faces, swollen tummies, but not from overeating. They play with imaginary trucks on wheels created with a milk carton, steel wires and coke bottle tops, running around quickly, which makes the "trucks" tumble on the ground. People are generally happy here, despite their daily concerns about a baby with high malaria fever, a grandmother, who by now, is really dehydrated after four days of diarrhea, somebody killed nearby because they had stolen something, then they've been set on fire atop car tires. Death is part of life.

I remember the most dissatisfied people on the street in the Netherlands. Where people have safe water, good food, good houses, health care, but the capitalistic system thrives when we buy more and more. It needs consumers to thrive. And happy people are a bad business model, so all the advertising is meant to make everyone feel inadequate, not worthy, powerless, if they don't have a bigger car, bigger house, branded clothing and so forth. People get mortgages they can't afford, becoming slaves of their material lives, to make up for feeling not good enough, stuck in jobs they hate, consuming food that makes them sick.

At home, we have a saying, "we watch the cat out of the tree", meaning, we don't jump in before we understand the whole situation, so in these first weeks, I just walk around and take everything in. These are the years of the AIDS epidemic. I witness funerals every day and I notice that people get buried without a coffin. No one dies of AIDS, of course; the stigma is numbing. I witness poor people being wiped out by the disease not to be mentioned, then being buried without a coffin, and witness the shame to the families. The level of injustice activates me; it's my grandma in me. When I look around in the markets, I notice that raw timber is very cheap, planed timber very expensive. No wonder people cannot afford a coffin. But I can plane! I have a plan. I have money from selling my house, so I go to town and buy a bunch of Stanley tools, planes, saws, marking gauges, chisels, pencils, rulers in the hardware shops owned by Muindis, Kenyan Asians. I gather street boys and teach them how to plane. As a woman doing woodwork, I have street girls attracted too. I visit local carpenters to learn how coffins are made, as I did not learn that in carpentry school! We build beautiful coffins, and now, poor people can bury their family members with dignity.

In the compound at Nyalenda, Jackeline is Paul and Lucy's maid, a seventeen-year-old, live-in maid with a family who does not treat her well. She has been taken from the countryside of Nyanza under the false pretense of part-time looking after the kids and being allowed to go to school. Her mother, a widow with too many children to look after, let her go, hoping that an education would help her to earn a living. But there is always too much work in Paul and Lucy's house with their spoiled children, and Jackeline can never go to school. I live on the compound in one of the many houses of the project. I work with Paul in the carpentry workshop I've installed in the past months and teach carpentry to the street kids on Ring Road.

Jackeline is an extremely bright and attractive woman, still young. I wake up every morning to the sound of the brush she uses to swipe the yard between the huts with, all the branches, leaves, and other things. Outside, I see pretty swiping patterns in the red soil. It is a soft and quiet noise, regular and loud enough to wake me every morning. I also wake up because I know Jackeline is swiping. I care about her; her living situation worries me.

Somebody gets confused about whether I am a man or a woman. I point at my breasts and kind of provocatively ask, "What are these then?" He says, "You are just strong, those are muscles." Another man I often see when walking through the slums in Kisumu is constantly drunk on the locally brewed stuff that can kill you easily, or at least make you blind. *Tjangha* is more than 90% alcohol and the big mamas hold competitions about who can produce the strongest, with the base ingredient being kerosene.

I talk to Moses, a friendly carpenter in the proximity of my hut, for whom I file his saw or sharpen his chisels so he can better finish his furniture. That drunk walks past and stops, swaying on his feet. He looks at me and asks, "Are you a boy or a girl?"

I look at him and quip, "Does it really matter?" He is unsteady on his feet and his eyes are rolling in his head. Suddenly he decidedly says, as if he has seen the light, "You are so right, it does not matter, you are so right!"

Every time I see him, he slows down and says, "You are so right." In the neighborhood, it morphs into a catchphrase. People ask, "Have you seen 'You are so right'?" People hate the guy because he manages a few huts, demands much too high rent, and is a bastard to his wife.

He walks past as I am drinking a cup of tea outside with Pamela, opposite his hut. Pamela lives in one of his huts and hates his guts, prompting us to poke fun at him. He asks me if I can forgive him for being drunk. I tell him, "Come back sober tomorrow and ask me again."

The next morning, Pamela runs to my hut in fits of laughter and tells me how last night, the floor of the pit latrine had collapsed, and the guy had fallen in it! He fell in a deep hole filled with shit and maggots. It is a wonder he survived, as those holes are nine meters deep and twenty people, mostly with diarrhea, use those pit latrines, so don't imagine what swims in there. We burst out laughing nearly wetting ourselves. "Serves him right," Pamela says.

He walks straight up to me when he sees me and says full of conviction, "You are so right, you are so right!" He is sober for three weeks, but then he goes back to his old ways.

Before I had left the Netherlands for the three months in Kisumu, I ended the relationship with Mieke. We had met again, years after we met as little girls in Denmark and it felt like a destiny thing, but I didn't think that our relationship would survive the distance. She was entrenched in a dark period governed by past trauma, and I wanted to expand my life, leave the Netherlands. We were in very different phases of our lives. Three months in Kisumu broadened the divide between us, I knew that I would not return to the Netherlands for years…if at all.

I become a VSO volunteer, and during preparatory courses in Birmingham, I meet Marlene, who doesn't have much experience with women. (Okay, one.) And there is a spark.

I move to Rongo, South Kenya, School for the Deaf, to set up vocational training for woodwork. I start writing in the evenings when all the kids are in bed. There are no seasons; along the equator, every day is the same. We barely have electricity and with the battery in my laptop, the "brick", I start writing stories. I think of my dad, and a white butterfly appears. My dad had told me that when people die, white butterflies show up and you just have to re-recognize them. I write the story, my first story, about the death of my father. The next morning, that butterfly lays dead on the ground.

We are called to go to Nairobi for a VSO meeting. All volunteers in Kenya are coming together, we are excited. We catch the Akamba bus at 7:00, but when I grasp the metal rails to walk up the steps, the whole bus says "no" to me. There is a force that pushes me out; I am startled. I tell Marlene that we should take the next bus. We drink a coffee and take the Akamba an hour later. When we drive along the tea fields of Kericho, we get stuck because of a terrible accident; more than seventy people were burnt alive in the flames of the two buses that had a frontal collision, and one of those buses was the Akamba we would have taken. Mark had stayed on the bus; he did not want to wait an hour because he wanted to be early to see his girlfriend before the start of the workshop. His parents had to send his dental records to identify him.

Marlene's VSO placement in Thailand falls through and she joins me in Kenya, but soon falls sick with amoebic dysentery, she nearly dies. It keeps reoccurring, and she needs to leave. My job at the School for the Deaf is more than complete and I do not want people to become dependent on me, so I decide to leave. I hand over three vocational trainings to three deaf teachers who are paid and have a production unit that is linked to customers.

Marlene starts at UVIC in Victoria Canada, and I stay the first three months in Victoria with her, but though I left my placement in Kenya, I am not ready to settle back in a western country yet. While Marlene is contently studying, I find myself applying for jobs overseas. I apply for a job in Kosovo and shortly after, sign a contract.

The agency is Cordaid, Dutch, and I am the manager of a reconstruction project, to get housing materials to 350 families, and provide labor support if needed.

Shortly after I leave Kenya, Tonneke moves to Kenya and starts a project in Dunga, a project that I had developed for VSO. She's even encouraging the locals to call her "Mama Babs", so old wounds of her taking things from me, makes them hers, get triggered.

She writes me a letter informing me that little Babs, Jackoline's baby, died. Jackeline had named her little girl after me, but she died of diarrhea. Tonneke's letter continues that a couple of weeks later, Jackeline also died. Something breaks in me. I do not want to hear that news from Tonneke, who had taken over my whole circle of friends. I cannot talk with them, without hearing about Tonneke.

I am so done, I feel broken and wounded. I write her a very short letter: "Do not contact me anymore, you do you, but I want nothing to do with you or your project in Kenya. Do not contact me until I contact you."

With Jackeline's death, part of me dies too. I am overwhelmed by a wave of mixed emotions. Sad about how cheap life is. I feel a bad omen because the baby had the same name as me and now, she was dead, and I was still alive. I felt guilty because I might have influenced things in her life that made her do other things that led to her death. Maybe if she still had worked with the family who treated her so badly…maybe if she had never gotten pregnant. All pure nonsense generated by the helplessness because a dear friend far away had died. A dear friend who represented a bit of hope for Africa. That bit of hope died in me when she was gone.

Jackeline's death makes me question my presence in Africa, question why and how we insert ourselves in countries with different cultures, we live there, but how much do we actually understand of what is going on, yet we do projects, make assumptions, take actions, often oblivious to the consequences, the changes we initiate. I wonder, trying to figure out who I am in this world.

Chapter 22

MY HAPPY PLACE: AFGHANISTAN

For Cordaid, I operate a separate office in Deçani, half an hour drive north of Gjakova. I build my own team and am as little as possible in the main office—I don't like the atmosphere there. Mone was one of the last prisoners of war in Kosovo and it is national news when they are released. I decide to hire one of them and Mone becomes my driver and confidant. His body is broken, his family smaller, his nights filled with nightmares. Together, we work long days to rebuild 350 war-damaged or destroyed houses for the poorest. He is always positive, sees a solution and uses his great humor to escape from difficult situations.

My project is nearing completion but is cut short due to a disturbing scandal. The country director receives a stolen baby, and she asks me to lie about it to my staff. Yeah, that I cannot do. Instead, I share this with the United Nations, and in no time, an illegal baby trade network gets exposed. They are arrested and I am under police protection. They see how valuable my skills are and transfer me to the UN in Pristina as an architect to refurbish large buildings into the new Ministries since Kosovo is now independent.

On September 11, 2001, the world spins into mayhem while I am in the UN office in Pristina Kosovo, with my colleague, an architect as well, Samer from Amman, who identifies the dancing Palestinians that CNN shows, as footage from a few years ago. Instantly, I get the feeling that there is an intentionality driving the events.

I have medical problems and am repatriated to the Netherlands for a hysterectomy, one of the best things that ever happens to me, as my uterus, an alien who caused me pain and heavy bleeding with fainting every month, is removed. I've never felt I was born in the wrong body, I just never liked my boobs and frankly, hated my menstruation. But then who am I? Why do I feel I don't fit anywhere? Not as a woman, not as a guy, not as a lesbian, gay, queer person, not as a transsexual, nothing feels right. What is my experience of self, gendered anyway? I have no language to describe what I am experiencing, but at least, a part of my physical horror is now gone. In the meantime, my breasts become more and more an obstruction, are a physical barrier I feel every moment of the day.

During my recovery, I look for jobs in Afghanistan now opening up. Afghanistan has always fascinated me. I remember the day the Russians invaded. I get invited to GAA in Bonn, and get the job offer in Jalalabad, Afghanistan, I feel beyond excited.

Only weeks after the surgery, I arrive in Jalalabad. There are no phones or Internet yet, only a satellite phone. Just before landing over Peshawar, I am fascinated by the landscape of flat roofs in the same material as the soil, the same pale red brown color. All small square blocks, varying in size, different in height and could only be distinguished from the roads viewed from the air by the thin, sharp shadows. Some single trees here and there, but mainly red, dry, and dusty.

After a rough landing, bouncing and roaring engines, the plane finally halts to a standstill on the tarmac of the airport and stairs are wheeled to the plane to let us disembark, and then we must walk across the tarmac to the arrival hall. As soon as I step out of the plane, the smoldering heat takes my breath away, it totally takes me by surprise. (Maybe should have prepared for this one!) It's July and around 50 degrees Celsius. I almost panic because it is so much hotter than my body has ever experienced. I try to find ways to

166

breathe without burning my lungs, and flashes of what is waiting for me buzz through my head as panic threatens.

This is my first time in Central Asia. My project aims to build 250 houses for incomplete families returning to their villages. I don't have the slightest idea of what I am getting myself into but feel a strange fascination and hunger for a country that only existed in fairy tales in my head. As a kid, I found out that there is a direct border between China and Afghanistan, and somehow, I knew I would go there one day.

We drive through the Khyber Pass. The heat is excruciating, the wind through the open windows, like some giant hairdryer pointed in my face. The heated tarmac buckles under the weight of the overloaded trucks going into Afghanistan, creating a wavy surface with potholes and cracks, making the road through the pass a treacherous journey. After an hour and a half, winding roads through a much less spectacular pass then I had envisioned, we arrive at the Torkham border, the entry into Afghanistan. I am overcome by a weird emotion, a mix of excitement, shyness, and humility. It is around noon, and a long queue of people is waiting to get into the small office where apparently the passports need to be stamped. This is the busy border, the only crossing between Afghanistan and Pakistan, for the commuters between Jalalabad and Peshawar. The queue consists of only men; the few women turn out to be sitting inside waiting for their turn. The men stand outside in the full sun, neatly lined up and patiently waiting. A long line of men in salwar kameez in white and other monotone colors. I am wearing my green, shiny salwar kameez, which I had tailormade in Pakistan on the recommendation of my office manager. It is not made of cotton, which is exclusively for the comfort of men only. Unusual for me, but I can actually smell my own body odor, the sweat running from my skin, my uncomfortable breasts glued against the suffocating fabric.

As I take in these strong images and imprint them in my memory never to forget, my driver passes me by and gestures to follow him closely. He decisively passes all these men who politely give way to us. I am hesitant to follow him, as all eyes fixate on me and the men in the queue mumble things to each other, but the driver keeps a close eye on me to ensure I am indeed, following him.

We enter a dark room with two big tables occupied by men in old felt uniforms and black caps. Dark green with a black border and military signs, and drops of sweat on their faces, running from under the rims of their caps. There is not a hint of a breeze, the hot air hanging heavy between the walls that surround us. Along the walls, rickety benches are packed with mostly women and elderly or people with disabilities. One woman, whose burqa can't conceal her extremely skinny body, is not alone. Little, brittle crying sounds bubble up from under her lavender blue garment, sounds that her hands under the burqa respond to with gentle moves to calm the baby down.

Next to the two typewriters on the side-by-side desks are piles of passports that keep being added to, passed from the back of the queue by a standing man with the same uniform but with less insignia, clearly a lower rank. The man behind the typewriter on the right is pulling on the ribbon to separate the little hammers with the letters. The fact they are stuck together surely is not due to his typing speed. He gestures to the man in front of his desk to identify his passport and hand it to him. He then painstakingly looks through it, page after page. Then he takes three sheets of paper and places carbon sheets between them that are typed so pale, it seems unlikely they would copy anything. With a great gesture and infuriatingly slowly, he places the bundle in the typewriter and turns the roll, checks if everything is straight and rolls up his sleeves, sips his tea, wipes the sweat flowing from his face with his rolled-up shirt sleeve and asks the waiting man *name, address, reason for returning to Afghanistan, family members* and *profession*. After typing everything, and if the waiting man is lucky, all this will happen without Tipp-Ex. The bundle of paper is rolled out of the machine again and every paper is placed on a different pile. Stamps are checked as if they are inspected for the first time and pressed on an ink pad too dry to be effective. Stamps are violently banged on the papers and finally, one in the passport. Without a word, the man throws the passport on the desk. The owner then picks it up with the same patience and nearly peaceful expression on his face and walks out.

A similar scene transpires at the other typewriter, which is for Afghans who are leaving Afghanistan and want to enter Pakistan. This is six months after the Taliban stopped working, known as the fall of the Taliban and many Afghans still live in the refugee camps in Peshawar but travel in and out of Afghanistan to look for work and possibilities for their families to return.

Once inside that room, I am subjected to the same process of typing, questions, and stamps to get my visa validated in my passport, the triangular stamp banged right next to and half covering the visa I had applied for and received in Bonn.

On the other side of the border, another car is waiting for me because most cars haven't got the papers nor number plates allowing them to cross the border. Everything is extracted from one car and packed in the other, and I say goodbye to the driver who brought me this far. On the Afghan side, I am now ushered in the car by an Afghan driver who cannot speak much English, but his smile is extremely friendly, and I immediately feel more at ease in Afghanistan than during the first days in Pakistan. The journey to Jalalabad from the Torkham border seems to take two hours and because I cannot chat with the driver, I absorb all the first impressions in the silence I feel deep inside.

There is a solid flow of road transport to and from the border with trucks loaded with Afghan families and all their worldly possessions. The trucks are wildly decorated with chains that give the typical rattling noise that will later become so familiar. The metal cabins of the Bedfords are replaced by wooden doors decorated from top to bottom with wood carvings. The jingle trucks are decorated with paintings and bright colors. There is a space of half a meter between the rounded bonnet and the front bumper where often somebody is sleeping, whether the truck is moving or not. They drive on the left in Pakistan, but as soon as we are in Afghanistan, it's back to right. The cars are almost all Pakistani models, steering on the right side, which makes "overtaking" a special experience. My driver cannot see whether he can overtake or not. We are stuck behind a truck and the driver honks at them. All of a sudden, the truck moves to the other side of the road. My driver darts past him, and as I look back, I see that the truck merges behind us again. This is brilliant and almost logical, I am thinking, but it's also rooted in trust and connectedness between these people. I am in awe.

When we arrive in Jalalabad, I hear that the only international colleague who is supposed to welcome me is not here. I stay the first couple of nights in the GAA office, their water and irrigation office. The guards show me a bed in the little room behind the gate. I feel weirdly calm and intensely happy. During the days I sit and observe, have some chats with people and learn my first words of Pashto.

I seem to flow in a sea of happiness that had swamped me as soon as I crossed the border. I experience this for the first time, never in another country than Afghanistan, the feeling that my body is too small to contain that much happiness.

There are no gas stations in town, so the office cars get filled up from large barrels, with a manual pump. The three guards who I stayed with are suddenly fired. Supposedly they had stolen diesel from the barrels. The worst thing that can happen to an Afghan

170

is to be called a "thief" because his status, his life and family are then dishonored.

I post advertisements for jobs I want to interview people for at the United Nations (UN) and in another coordination office. I'm seeking engineers, architects, a logistics coordinator, guards, and a driver with a car.

I follow the situation with the three guards in the office and I suspect that the head of the logistics unit is behind the disappearing diesel. I ask Malyar, one of the sacked guards, if I can please interview him for the position of guard in the new office of my project. He says, amazed, "But Babs, I am a thief, how can you interview me?"

I reply, "I'm not convinced that you are. I will only believe it when you prove to me that you are a thief." I hire the three guards and unknowingly, save their reputation, reinstating the honor of their family and their place in the community. This starts my unusual reputation in town.

During the nights, I drink three liters of water and do not need to pee because I immediately sweat it out. I do not sleep more than one or two hours per night, get up at 5:00 a.m. to go to the office and start the day. I've already rented a few cars, hired staff and set up an office in no time, and am just floating.

I hire Shamsul to be my translator, and his first task is to find a female translator for me, too, for when I am in meetings with women only. We start the assessments of all the villages where we are supposed to work. In these first weeks, the woman in Samarkhyel asks me to close my eyes and it changes my presence in Afghanistan. I am tuned in.

I quickly understand that I should eat with my staff in the office, as it relaxes people and other conversations start. I ask Noorzia, my female translator, to find a woman who urgently needs money, preferably a woman alone with little opportunity to earn money.

Noorzia arrives with Qader, a small woman with bent legs and rough hands, beautiful hands, tanned by the sun, damaged, muscular, the history books of her life. Her eyes immediately strike me, light green, grey-blue, very clear. They are shining and surrounded by deep wrinkles that mark her whole face. I employ her and she brings me endless cups of green tea, kisses me every time she enters the room, smiles her toothless smile, chatters away in Pashtu. I reply in my Dutch dialect, and we seem to understand each other. She laughs a lot and makes jokes. I am always pleased when she is around. Qader is a terrible cook, roasting or frying everything for hours in too much animal fat. But I love her and because I love her, everybody eats her food without comment.

Qader Bibi, now my Afghan mother, has a belly like a book of scars of shrapnel that had ripped her belly open, her mouth full of rotting stumps by the lack of vitamins and excess sugar during the war years in Afghanistan. She has lost her children, at least eight of the thirteen she sometimes speaks about. Her husband was beaten to death in jail by the Taliban. As the lowest ranking in the community, she lives in the slums of Samarkhyel, a ruin of a village where those returning to Afghanistan find temporary shelter.

Our project description is to rebuild 350 houses, and during the first weeks, we meet with the men and women shuras, separately. When I meet with the men, Shamsul is my translator; when we meet with the women shuras, Noorzia translates. These meetings serve to determine together with the communities who the most "deserving" families are that need to be included in our program.

Later in the first year, I fly from a newly post-Taliban Afghanistan to Sydney for a short holiday where Marlene is doing her master's in public health. Post-Taliban Afghanistan, in early November, means the following: no Internet, I have a satellite phone I can retrieve emails with via France telecom at $5 per minute. In my simple mud stone house, we have a generator that switches off at night for the neighbors because of the noise. There is hardly any alcohol available and the rare occasion that the International Committee of the Red Cross (ICRC) manages to get their hands on a bottle of red wine, we share it amongst six people with our meal. There are still few signs of westernization, something that unfortunately, becomes increasingly prevalent in the following years. At the beginning, Afghanistan is still fragile, naive, and splendid.

From that Afghanistan, I arrive in Sydney and in less than twenty-four hours, find myself amongst thousands of gays who, because of the heat, are scantily clad and celebrating the final day of the Gay Games. Beer bottles everywhere, naked body parts like arms and legs, not to mention bellies and backs, seem brazen and shameless after where I've just come from.

Upon my return, I am more than happy to be back in Afghanistan, home again, understood. It probably sounds odd that a Dutch woman who loves women, feels so at home in Afghanistan, vilified as backwards by the media.

I had flown via Karachi and Quetta to Peshawar from where I took the now familiar route through the Khyber Pass. The pass itself is only 1070 meters high and not extremely spectacular, but you can feel the loaded history; Alexander the Great who marched through it in 326 B.C. and traveled on to Southern Asia. In the 16th century, the followers of Genghis Khan went through this pass to build the Moghul dynasty on the other side. The pass has been used for centuries

by caravans with loaded yaks, donkeys, elephants and camels, the famous silk route.

Night falls as I arrive at my house. One of my guards opens the fence, and he's so thrilled to see me again. In the moment we greet each other, I smell Fahrenheit, my perfume! I immediately swallow my acute anger and continue with the greetings, then unpack my things from the car to bring them inside. The fact he is wearing my scent means he has been in the house, in my bedroom, going through my things and actually spraying it on! I feel violated.

I suppress my first reaction until finally lying on my bed and thinking about the incident. I instinctively know that you don't immediately jump to conclusions in Afghanistan. My conclusions are typical for my own culture, for what I'm used to. In a country that is so different, I can say with great certainty that I don't understand many things that happen. But I do feel violated in my privacy. I try to imagine why he stole the perfume. Maybe respect? By smelling like me, he wanted to show that he respects me? It is clearly not stealing in his mind, because he was clearly not hiding it!

I have to think of something to reclaim my privacy though, which is vital to my situation, as Marlene will join me here shortly. Two women who sleep in the same bed is not something I want to attract attention to in Afghanistan.

After an almost sleepless night, I ask the guard, as I get into the car, to come to my office at 8:00 a.m. He nods pleasantly, still surrounded by a cloud of Fahrenheit. As soon as I am in my office, I ask Shamsul to come in and close the door. I explain what happened and ask him not to tell anyone else. I ask him to translate accurately, word for word, as soon as the guard shows up. He nods in agreement. At village meetings, for example, people will talk for a while and Shamsul will then briefly summarize what had been said, but now, I've asked him to translate word for word and then never mention this conversation ever again.

The guard walks in. It is really such a potent perfume, I muse, as scent particles remind me of the invasion. I start to tell my guard of the importance of my little 3 x 4-meter bedroom in that mud brick house, the only place in Afghanistan where I can be myself. I continue, I am not Afghan and never will be, that I never truly will understand Afghan culture, but I'm doing the work I believe in, with the people who are part of our team, and many people will benefit from our project.

Finally, all I need to do my job and deal with the difficult circumstances in Jalalabad is my *privacy* in that one little room. Shamsul translates everything word for word and the guard listens attentively. I go on for twenty minutes about the importance of that room, and then signal that I'm finished. He leaves my office slightly confused.

Usually, we lunch together with the whole staff at the office, but Qader Bibi is ill, so I go home for lunch. I sit outside on the veranda while the cook brings the meal. The cook turns up—surprisingly, along with the boy who cleans the house, the three guards and one of the drivers who speaks a little English. They all stand around me, and I ask them what's up. "Ms Babs, we promise you that this will never happen again," the cook stumbles. They tell me that I can be sure no one will go into my room again, except for the cleaner. I look at one to another in astonishment, pretending not to understand what they are talking about but thank them for what they said.

Nothing was ever spelled out, nobody had to feel ashamed, nobody lost face, and all of this further consolidates my reputation in Jalalabad. By showing my loyalty and willingness not to judge them in these situations, I have become family. In Afghanistan, you do not make friends. You either don't like the country and leave, or you become family.

Afghans have a sixth sense but never talk about it because they all have it, and it is nothing special to them. They live with it; they don't look but feel. They don't look if you wear your head scarf, but they feel how you are and if that is good, everything is good.

We are in Balabagh, one of my favorite villages, which has an old hammam ruin and other signs of ancient history. We are meeting with the women, and it is around 50 degrees Celsius.

Noorzia says, "She is asking if you have children."

I respond, "No, I don't, I had to make a choice between having children and doing this work, I cannot combine it."

Then, "Are you married, and what does your husband think of you here?"

I say, "He's afraid of flying." I chuckle a bit inside myself. This is not the place or country to say that I love women. I do not want to lie, and I want to avoid that conversation as much as possible. Light jokes help.

The wound from my all-too-recent hysterectomy is still very present. When I need to pee, it hurts. I do have to pee, given an hour in the car over rough roads and a few cups of green tea here with the women. I lean over to Noorzia and ask her if she can ask where I can find the toilet. Her whole face shoots into a panic and she whispers, "That is not possible, you cannot go to the toilet here!" Noorzia acts like I did her an indecent proposal, and her whole composure is so tense, that the women ask her what is going on.

I ask, "That's impossible, what do you mean?" There is no toilet, she repeats. I tell her, "It is not an option not to pee. My surgery hurts and you must help me find a way. We all drink tea, we all need to pee at some time, what is the big deal?"

Noorzia looks at me and says, "Are they drinking?" I glance to see all the full cups. Am I the only one who had tea? Some might have taken a tiny sip, but I realize that none of them actually drank their tea.

I recover from that discovery and say, "I don't care what you do Noorzia, but I need a solution." It feels like I am forcing her arm to just get me to a toilet, but the amount of stress, panic, and sheer embarrassment my question has caused, makes it clear that there is a bigger issue here, leaving me wondering.

The elder women ask Noorzia what is going on. I stress to her that she must ask, and Noorzia panics. Clearly ashamed, Noorzia shares my needs, whispering. A sudden cacophony of voices erupts, all the women chime in. Some of them jump up and two of the younger women wave their hands at me to get up and follow them. We walk outside, exit the meeting room that is sitting on top of the big house of the Malik (village leader) and his wife.

The room opens to a large flat roof from where we overlook the whole village. A stunning view with the mountains and the dry plains siding the river. The green trees in sharp contrast with the dry mud. Typically, in hot places like this, the kitchen is upstairs, so no additional heat is added to the downstairs rooms. The "kitchen" here is opposite the door of the meeting room; three little walls, with a bunch of pots. They point at the pots, and I look at them to get confirmation that they in fact, mean that I go pee in this tiny cooking place. They nod and disappear back into the meeting room.

Seriously? I think. *Okay, whatever. I have one painful bladder and at this point anything will do!*

As I take down my pants, I realize that the beautiful view over the village I have, is giving people outside the home a view of me. So, I need to squat down first, and then remove my pants—it's a challenge, but I manage. From behind the pots, I can still see the kids play outside. I am behind the stack of aluminum pots in the corner, the sun burning on my head.

While I am slowly getting a feeling of blissful relief, my thoughts turn to the problems these women face. The puddle of my pee is immediately absorbed by the dry clay of the floor and virtually evaporates instantly. While still squatting, and no tissues to wipe myself, I must pull up my trousers. I am so relieved!

I walk back in the room, and the women seem as relieved as I am. A bit of an uncomfortable silence, which I break with a question. "Noorzia, can you ask them, with all the tea they are drinking in this heat, where they go pee?" Noorzia...oh, if her eyes could kill me now... But the reality is, if they do not have a place to go, the consequences for their health are dramatic. It starts making sense in my head that the mortality rate of women here is the highest in the world. If they cannot drink while it is so hot, because they cannot go to the toilet, their kidneys and bladders are fucked!

Nadia, my architect who is here as well, has been quiet so far. She is not a Pashtun and generally holds back a bit, but she positions herself next to me and says, "Babs, what do you want to ask?"

"Thank you, Nadia. Ask them where they go if they need to pee or poo." Nadia turns to them and asks. The women have lively conversations, and there is some laughing, unease but also, eagerness, I sense.

Nadia reveals the much-anticipated secret: "They wait till the evening, and then they can go out the huge walled compound and squat. During the day, they are not allowed outside."

I boldly ask, "What would it mean if we were to build latrines next to each house that we are building?" Nadia translates and the women's faces change; they move closer, lean in for more conversations. *I am onto something*, I'm thinking. Nadia translates in a kind of summarizing way what they are talking about. "They can never really explore possible solutions, because they never have the means to do it, so why ask questions, if you know it is not possible? Pregnant women cannot hold it up and pee behind the pots as well; they talk about the pains in their bodies, especially during pregnancy and delivery; they share that many women die during delivery and that they are scared to become pregnant." This is my glimpse into the intimate lives of these women, who live within the confines of these walls.

On the way back, Noorzia and Nadia are excited. Nadia says, "Babs, how are we going to build the tashnabs (toilets)? The health of the women is such an issue, because they cannot talk about it…" She pauses. "So, *we* need to talk about it."

I reply, "Yes, we do need to talk about it. By talking about it and building tashnabs, we can prevent a lot of suffering and death." Noorzia looks quite worried, realizing what we are saying.

Back in the office, I call the team together and share the plan of building tashnabs next to every house we are building. The original project budget (developed behind a desk in Germany) is based on buying all the mud bricks and fired bricks in Jalalabad and trucking them to all the villages. The budget line for transportation, truck rental, is quite large. We brainstorm, we bounce ideas around. What if… "people in the villages produce the mudbricks, we can organize mudbrick production is each village. We can pay them the same as that we pay here in town. The villagers have income, and we save the transportation costs. With these savings, we can build the toilets." Can we do that? We name our team the shitty team, and I am the shithead. If talking can lift the stigma, let's talk shit. We all laugh.

This is one of the reasons I am in love with Afghanistan; nothing is ever impossible. Working in Afghanistan feels like being in an ongoing improv, always "yes, and…" Literally within an hour, we have a plan!

The team arrives early. Qader makes tea, and we check in where everybody is going that day. Nadia says, "We will need a team to choose the best location for all the tashnabs, so that it does not cause hygiene problems, they cannot be oriented towards Makkah (the city in Islam where the Prophet Muhammad was born and the Quran was revealed), and it needs to be safe and accessible for women and not too close to the kitchen for hygiene purposes." The team needs to inform people how to properly use and maintain the latrines. A holistic project is forming, I am so excited, and that excitement is translating among the whole team. I dive into the history of Afghan latrines and discover an ancient system whereby urine and solids are separated. Urine runs into a pit with pebbles and lime to neutralize the ammoniac, the solids are mixed with ashes and used as manure on the land.

To determine what the location for the tashnabs will be, we create a hygiene promotion team of one man and eight women. Marlene works with them to efficiently inform people how to use such a dry latrine, how to clean it, and other personal hygiene subjects.

Since we are liberated, and everything has a name in the Netherlands, language becomes simultaneously a restriction. In a country like Afghanistan, for example, I can't talk about certain things, and it has to remain an absolute secret that me and my partner are more than friends. If I don't give it a name, I don't force them to have an opinion. We live two months in the same house in Jalalabad, share the room and work in the same office as she helps with the toilet project.

Marlene has come to Afghanistan for a short stint, so we are together, and it is clear she is an important person in my life, but nothing has a name. In the Afghan culture, a young woman always must be accompanied by a so-called Muharram, a close male family member to accompany and protect her. I am neither man nor woman, I just am in Afghanistan, but my status is of a man. They joke that I am Marlene's Muharram. As a result, every e-mail from Afghan friends when I'm not in Afghanistan always starts with the question: "How is Miss Marlene?"

I only wear a head scarf if Shamsul tells me to. It's not in my best interest to walk around without it, but the opposite happens too. When I first start driving a pick-up truck, Shamsul tells me shyly, but with a big grin, "Babs, don't wear a head scarf behind the wheel, you will confuse people." Having been the first Afghan I hired during the first week in Jalalabad, with his shaky English, but unrelenting reliability and commitment as my translator and right hand, he became a dear friend over the years, and I became part of his family.

The sixth sense, Afghans live with it, and I understand that. I live like that myself and in a country that's so different, like Afghanistan, I trust it blindly.

As much as I want to stay in my happy place, the threat of an upcoming war in Iraq results in no extension of my project and I must leave.

Chapter 23
BAD DETOUR

2003, Ethiopia

It takes me years to get some images out of my system.

The Derg regime (1974-1991) had started relocating farmers to land where they didn't understand how to farm since intergenerational knowledge had been lost. The rain season is short, so if farmers plant after the rains start, there is not enough time for the crop to mature and come to a harvest. That is not a drought, that is farmers not understanding the land they are on. I was sent to Ethiopia to do a photo report on a food distribution program. When I arrive, I learn that the food was meant for 40,000 people who were recently relocated to so-called fertile land. What I find is a situation I wish for no one to witness. I entered swampland without sanitation or water provisions. The deeply corrupted government forcefully relocated 40,000 people into their death, less than half of them maybe still alive. I witnessed piles of rotting people. The stench will never leave me. A government doing that to their own people!

Marlene and I travel to various villages to measure the level of malnutrition in children. We are in Oromia, in the south and the environment crying underneath all the suffering is vivid, stunning, lush greenery. No drought here, but farmers planting root vegetables at the bottom of the hill, where they rot in the ground soonest the rain runs down. We arrive in a village, and we spot a group of men just sitting under a central tree. We notice that kids above four or five years old are well-fed and healthy, but then all the younger children are profoundly malnourished. We learn that the fields to harvest are a day's walk away. The women trek the whole way to work these fields with babies still breastfeeding. The age group of children in between is outright being desecrated by starvation, while the men sit under the tree doing nothing all day, waiting for foreign aid to feed their children. I get so mad after having seen the desperation of the people in the swamp.

I am dying to leave Ethiopia and write a ballsy letter to Nigel Fisher, head of UNOPS in New York, who I had met once in Kabul but would miss him if he were to pass me by in the street. I write: "Hi Nigel, remember me, we met in Kabul. I saw the job posting for basic infrastructure specialist for Afghanistan, do you think you can introduce me to the right person?"

Chapter 24

LAND OF FAIRIES AND GODDESSES

2004

I am on my way back to Afghanistan, and Gary Helseth, the country director for UNOPS, picks me up in Dubai, thinking I am a high-ranking UN person, because Nigel had forwarded my info directly to him, embarrassed he did not remember me. When I arrive in Kabul, colleagues ask me if I can help them get a job in New York and I start to understand what happened. Without a question, I become one of the senior project managers and get to manage a school reconstruction project for UNICEF, which I have to pull out of the mud, retender and add compensations. Then I get the USAID school reconstruction project based on the success of the previous one. USAID tells me to use international contractors, but I refuse. You ask me to build schools; to me, that means you don't know how to do it, but then you tell me how to do it? No, I am here because Afghan men need jobs, and their children need to go to school, so I work with local contractors only. "If you don't agree, you can find another project manager," I tell them. They cave to my approach, but there is immediate tension.

Schools and clinics in Nuristan are on the list and I am told by international colleagues, that that is a lost cause, I'll never be able to build there, no one has for decades.

Previously it was called Kafiristan, the land of the infidels, the Kafirs. (كافر kāfir; plural كفّار kuffār) is an Arabic word meaning "rejecter" or "ingrate"). The name *Nuristan* means Land of Light, the light of true faith since the rebellious infidels were finally converted. Only in 2001, the official administrative province Nuristan was formed from the Northern parts of the Laghman and Kunar provinces. A province on the border with Pakistan, just across the border of the Northern Kalasha valley and the village of Chitral, one of the last remaining non-Islamic pockets. A village in an area where the last remaining heathens live who celebrate exuberant festivals for fire, earth, water, and air, who believe in fairies and live with the seasons, who believe that animals and plants have souls. The Kafirs of Nuristan used to practice the same beliefs and celebrated the elements and the seasons. Only in 1895, Nuristan was given its current name when King Amir Abdus Rahman violently converted these Kafirs to Islam.

Nuristan is the remotest of provinces in eastern Afghanistan, below Badakhshan and north of Kunar province, the famous tribal zones, the North-Western Frontier Border, Nangarhar province south with its capital Jalalabad, the famous border region, the area where Bin Laden was hiding in the inhospitable Tora Bora mountains.

I often wonder when passing through these mountains on the Afghan side of the border, how any foreign invader could have ever even suggested they could track down or defeat the local guerrillas, Osama Bin Laden's comrades here in this region. Local Pashtuns, generations of people who grew up on these slopes, who read the sky and predict all movements beyond the visible world. These isolated mountains, these barren slopes full of caves and tunnels, this indefensible land, these deserts of black rocks only accessible to the people who are raised here, and I often wonder how anyone survives there.

No foreign army has ever defeated the people of this region and there is a good reason for it. Osama Bin Laden chose well; its location, for one thing, but also the country, Afghanistan where the local customs are to honor your guest, whoever they are. Afghans would never hand over a guest to a foreign nation, which would be against their tradition of hospitality to the guests to their country. Hosting Osama Bin Laden was the misunderstood Afghan custom of hospitality, interpreted as support to his involvement in the attack on the Twin Towers.

The border between Afghanistan and Pakistan was only established in the late 40s after the Brits had lost two wars against the Wazir, the most famous tribe of the greater Pashtun tribe, the same people that Alexander had lost much of his soldiers to. When the Brits lost their second war against the Wazir in 1893, they withdrew behind the Durand line, the line they had purposely drawn through the heart of this Pashtun tribe in an attempt to divide them, weaken them and possibly defeat them, but the Wazir had an infamous reputation regarding their resistance against foreign invaders. No one has ever defeated them.

The people of Waziristan, since 1947 officially part of Pakistan, were Pashtuns first, then they identified as Afghans but certainly never became Pakistanis at heart. They were no longer part of Afghanistan, and Islamabad never managed to get control over this region. The Wazir, as well as the other Pashtun tribes in this North-Western Frontier Border region, were even more isolated now that they were part of Pakistan. The administration of Pakistan had no business with those Pashtuns, they only exploited them for their resources and talents and in return, the Wazir got deprived from the most basic needs like basic infrastructure, education, health care, access.

The Pakistani government did not even allow them to vote. The divide that the Brits had planned so carefully when establishing the Durand line has resulted in an isolated area with people that have ultimately nothing to lose and are willing to die to defend their culture and pride. In effect, this is where the root cause of the Taliban movement stems from, these Pashtuns, not liked by Pakistan, to date, still identify as Afghans, but as Pashtuns first. They have nothing to lose and are full of hate against the foreigners who come and occupy the country they belong to and support the country they live in, polarizing the whole area.

When people have no jobs, no education, no future then to be treated as the lowest on the social ladder, they have nothing to lose and are cheap labor for any cause. The U.S. recruited the young Talibs from the Saudi-funded madrassas and training centers just over the border in Pakistan to be the foot soldiers to chase the Russians out of Afghanistan and bring a new regime to Afghanistan. This became the Taliban regime, supported and paid for by the U.S.

Since I live in Afghanistan, I hear stories about Nuristan. The first year my project was only in Nangarhar province; Jalalabad, its capital. For my work I had nothing to do with Nuristan, but the stories made me curious, it held a huge attraction for me, and I wanted to get to know the people. The same kind of attraction like when my father told me about people who were so different, people who are born from a tree and are buried under it after their death.

The storytellers spoke with respect about these people who had reddish hair and blue eyes. The stories spoke of the ruggedness, the steep mountains, and the harshness of life. How tough the Nuristanis are, yet believed in fairies; that the women do all the heavy work in the fields, while the men tend the cattle; about the women who never wore a chador and the nubile age for women is around twenty; about an old caste system with slaves (baris), to which the current name for artisans still refers. About their woodcutting art and typical wooden buildings, where they had Goddesses in the past and today still have customs, integrated in their current Islamic faith, though they still refer to the old Goddesses, fairies, seasons, and elements amongst themselves. The Nuristanis are also heavily superstitious, whereas superstition is considered evil by the rest of the Afghans and the Muslim faith in general. I wanted to know them.

When I am asked to be the manager of the USAID schools and hospitals project, I receive a list with the locations where the schools and hospitals had to be built. There are nine schools and hospitals on the list for Nuristan. It seems a dream come true! I employ the same people who were part of my staff during my first project in Jalalabad. Shamsul, Sabir, Azim, the guards, two drivers and of course Qader Bibi, my happy team. Noorzia is studying to become a doctor, Nadia is with her family, both in Kabul.

We set up eight regional offices all over Afghanistan, employ a lot more people for seventy schools and hospitals in total, which almost all have to be built from scratch, virtually no rehabilitations. The indicated provinces for this project are four provinces around Herat in the west and four provinces around Jalalabad in the southeast. In that time, I also must make the last visits to regional offices to finalize the project for UNICEF in which we had newly built or rehabilitated more than 200 schools and hospitals. In the meantime, I had traveled to all corners of Afghanistan and the more I saw, the deeper my love for this country and its people grew.

With Gul, my translator and guide everywhere I go. I am checked in to visit Herat to see the progress of the building of the schools with the staff. Gul has never flown before and has never been further than Kabul in his own country. We board a UN beach craft that transports twelve passengers. He sits quite frightened in the seat on the other side of the central path, hands clenched on the arm rests, and the rest of the small plane only has three other passengers.

We fly to Herat via Badghis. After take-off, he relaxes a bit and looks out the window. After ten minutes, he points out the white mountain tops of the central highlands of Afghanistan, flying over Bamiyan. He says this must be Bamiyan where the Buddhas were blown to bits. I am amazed he recognizes it. I have always wondered about how fast Afghans adapt and settle in a new situation. How could he know that we already were above Bamiyan only ten minutes after Kabul? How could he recognize it without ever being there, and it takes at least eight hours by road? How could he recognize this land from a perspective he had never experienced before?

When we land in Badghis, we are told we are not allowed to get out in Herat due to unrest in the city. The governor of Herat has been replaced by another by Karzai and the new governor had been welcomed by the head of the UN. The supporters of the sacked governor are now attacking all UN buildings, and there are riots in the streets. We stop in Herat to refuel and then fly to Kandahar and adjust our program.

We have to be flexible in Afghanistan because something always happens to screw up the planning. In Kandahar we visit schools in the last stage of construction, the last schools of UNICEF. We also arrange with the senior engineer to meet us in Zaranj. He will go by car, but that is excluded for me as a non-Afghan. The road passes through the notorious Kandahar and Helmand provinces and with elections imminent, there are stories about hundreds of infiltrators left, right and center. I never believe those stories because they are spread with a purpose, a purpose that serves some, but certainly not the projects.

Gul and I book a flight to Zaranj, the capital of the Nimroz province in the extreme southwest of Afghanistan, near the border of Iran. We land in a sandstorm, as they continuously rage in Nimroz for three months per year. The pilot nervously asks if we mind looking for the landing strip too because there is no visibility at all. A few seconds before we land, we see children run away from the landing strip that appears to be more like a gravel tennis court than an airport. The plane rattles and shakes and after some heavy braking, we stop. The pilots look so relieved to come to a standstill. Gul and I explore Zaranj to search for the engineer from Kandahar.

Afghans do something we used to do, something my grandma always did, a habit that has mostly become obsolete by other types of communication we now have. If an Afghan leaves his familiar area and meets people in the new area, he immediately asks questions and tries to find links to his own community. Find connections, family or other relations that link the new community to home. As soon as those connections are found, everybody there becomes family, and you are at home again. The relation ties are found, and you are no longer a stranger. Afghans are hospitable by nature and welcome their guests, but if you also found how your families are connected you are invited for a meal and a bed for the night and you are safe. With Gul by my side, I have experienced this several times and looked on in amazement. How marvelous that an outsider, a newcomer, becomes family in a few minutes. The whole of Afghanistan is in fact, one big family, you only need to know the links. I am considered as part of their family by my Afghan friends I have known since my first project in Jalalabad and am subject to the expansion of the family ties wherever we travel.

Zaranj is located on the border with Iran, and the bridge across the river marks the border. Only the river is not there anymore, it redirected deeper in Iran, which caused a dispute about the actual location of the border. The bridge, now in the middle of the desert or the river a few miles further.

A day later, we travel into the desert by jeep to search for the four schools. We drive out of Zaranj towards the north. I often wonder how the drivers know where they are heading because the sand dunes move with the wind and there are no roads. The only marks are village ruins that remind of a time, no longer than ten years ago, that there were still settlements here, water. Now everything is desert, dry and dusty.

The water in the shower in the guest house is salty. We drive through places where smuggling is thriving, thousands of oil barrels and shady characters who don't invite us to stop. Don't even think of taking photos here.

At one point, I see a border checkpoint on the right and see us on the map in my head. If we are driving north and this is an Afghan border control post on the right, it can only mean we are driving in Iran. The drivers know less clearly where they are going than I thought. Gul and I laugh about it but ask them to hang a right a bit. I have no passport or any identification with me. It is safer to travel without it.

We stop in the middle of the desert for a drink of water and to stretch our legs. The horizontal winds continue to rage undiminished. I, of course, wear my green salwar kameez on this type of trip inland, to attract less attention. I get out and stand there facing Gul. He looks at me with a telling face and a held-in smirk. He gestures with his hand, *up, up.* He moves his hand, palm upwards, up and down while looking at my ankles. I look down and see my trousers hanging on my ankles. With the wind I had not felt them coming down! I pull them up and Gul has a fit of laughter. Once I have them up and secured, I crack up laughing as well. I am a white woman, standing half naked in the desert, illegally in Iran, in a region where I can't even roll up my sleeves because skin cannot be revealed. The drivers have turned away and pretended they had not seen anything. In the car though, soonest we are moving again, Gul relives the event with the drivers laughing so hard, it's contagious; we all cry laughing.

In the evening, in the UNOPS office, Gul enters my room, no knocking, nothing. He smirks, walks to the chair where I hang my trousers after I change back in more comfortable jeans. He takes the trousers. His eyes twinkle. I am working on my laptop, and just witness him doing what he does.

He plonks down in the middle of my room, on the carpet. He crosses his legs and pulls the polyester cord out of my baggy trousers. He looks at me, confirming what he just did. Oh, that smirk! He puts a cotton cord on a safety pin and pulls the cotton-woven cord through the seam where he has removed the nylon cord from. He demonstratively stands up, puts the trousers back on the chair and says, "There." We burst out laughing. The same Gul would later, on a journey through Nuristan, place his mattress close to me in the room where at least ten other Afghan men were sleeping, with the words: "I'll protect you, you can't trust those Afghan men," again laughing out loud and that's how we slept, Gul close to me. But never, ever has there been a time I thought oh, this is too close, a bit too far, nothing, Gul is loyal and pure, and we laugh an awful lot on our travels together.

Often, when I am at my computer for too long, I feel the hands of Qader Bibi massaging my shoulders and neck, and I leave the keyboard and give in to her hands that seem to know exactly where the knots are. After a while, it stops, and I continue. Sometimes I hear a light snoring behind me, and she has fallen asleep on the floor behind my chair.

I hear some commotion downstairs and soon after, Shamsul walks in, with a slight sense of panic on his face; an imposing man with a large black turban and a huge beard, right behind him. The tall man walks in, passing Shamsul in the doorway, walking right up to my desk.

I stand up, put my right hand on my heart, bow lightly, and say, "A-salaamu alaykum" (peace be upon you) and to Shamsul, "Would you mind getting us some tea and biscuits?" Gul, who has heard about the visitor and translations are possibly needed, sees Shamsul leave. Gul comes behind my desk to be close for translations, and whispers at me, "Governor of Nuristan."

The man stands in front of my desk and says rather sternly, "I am the governor of Nuristan, and I am here to find out what you are going to do in Nuristan." He pauses, distracted by the soft snoring sounds behind me. He leans over a bit and sees Qader Bibi. I bring my index finger to my mouth, indicating that we better keep our voices down a bit. His face changes, relaxes, becomes softer, and he smiles.

Gul always knows everyone, always knows the latest news, arranges everything; he organizes the office, the drivers, the field trips, everything. I never had to tell Gul anything, he would have done it before I thought about it.

I ask the governor to take a seat, and that tea is on its way. He crosses his arms, sits his back straight, his black turban slightly tilted on his forehead, his white beard clearly dyed black and his hands and face tawny and weathered. His presence feels right, and I quietly wait, as it would have been impolite to start talking to him, he came here to tell me something. Shamsul comes in with the tea, the endlessly delicious green tea with cardamom seeds that we drink by the gallon when it is so hot. Around and above fifty degrees Celsius in the summer months in Jalalabad, at night not cooler than thirty-five, but okay, this time, I have an office with air-conditioning and the governor clearly enjoys it too.

Suddenly, he repositions himself and says: "So, what are you going to do in Nuristan? Will you also make me promises like all those others who never followed up on their promises and beautiful words?"

I take a moment and open by saying, "Thank you, governor, for coming all the way to meet me, and for being frank with me, I appreciate that. When we know each other's positions, it is easier to work together. As you know, USAID asked me to manage the schools' reconstructions in the Eastern provinces, Nuristan being one of them." He listens attentively and Gul translates respectfully.

I continue, "At this moment, all I have is the list of 167 schools, and nine of them are in villages in Nuristan. Many people, including USAID themselves, have already told me that I will not be able to build these schools, because so they tell me, it is too remote and too unsafe. So, I am not promising you that I am building these schools, but…I am giving you my word, that I will leave no stone unturned to make sure Nuristan gets these schools." He repositions again and before he can say anything, I say, "But…I need your help to travel through Nuristan, so people know who I am, who my engineers are. It would be my honor to come and visit your amazing province and work with the people of Nuristan."

He stands up, his face open. He gives me a firm nod while he smiles and lightly bows. I do the same, and we say our goodbyes. And there, he walks out the door.

Qader gets up behind me and apologizes. She had woken up but kept quiet until he was gone. I laugh, grab her hand and say, "It's all good, I am glad you had a good nap. I made the governor talk quietly not to wake you." She bursts out laughing, her hand on her mouth, ashamed of her toothless mouth. We all laugh, relieved too.

In the next weeks, I send some of my engineers to Nuristan to identify local men who can build, experienced in the traditional building methods. We do workshops with them, training about safe building with these traditional methods, how to run a project and in fact, how to be a contractor we can work with in Nuristan, people in their own communities, people who will build the schools for their own children, but of good quality.

I design the Nuristan consortium, a way to get around the USAID requirements stipulating that I can only direct contract construction companies. The entire "happy team", named by Shamsul, is passionate about building the schools and hospitals there. In the meantime, most schools and hospitals are already under construction in the other provinces, but Nuristan takes more time. The Nuristan consortium consists of two contractors from Jalalabad who are known in Nuristan. Nuristan is such a close-knit and closed community of only 60,000 Nuristanis in the whole province that outsiders are shunned, especially foreigners, and certainly if they travel with weapons.

These two contractors, we called the "umbrella organizations" in the consortium, will both manage the construction of several schools and hospitals being built by the new contractors from Nuristan. They will help them with the administration of their project and ensure that I regularly receive reports about the progress of the work or the problems that need to be resolved. In the meantime, we are already busy with drawings and building plans in the design department to make an evaluation of the costs. As the schools are budgeted, they are based on concrete buildings, American standard, but because Nuristan is such a difficult area, that isn't possible. The slopes of the high mountains with deep valleys are inaccessible and steep and there is little flat land available. There are barely any roads, and the transport of heavy materials to Nuristan is virtually impossible.

The traditional wooden building method, developed hundreds of years ago and suitable for this inhospitable region prone to earthquakes, demonstrates its suitability for this region. Many buildings, two or three stories high, have been standing here more than a hundred years, safe and still solidly attached to the steep slopes. Nuristan's surface mainly consists of forests with huge trees, Himalayan Cedars that traditionally only get felled if the community decides to use a certain number of trees for a building. The trees are felled here and there, not a clear cutting of one single part of the forest. New trees are planted to compensate the felled trees, and the structure of Nuristan is thus, a well-balanced system where the woods are not emptied.

In the last few decades though, with the wars and the wood shortage in the rest of Afghanistan, it has changed, these majestic trees are more frequently illegally logged by people from the outside who carry the huge logs over the border with Pakistan to sell them there. The control of the communities has disappeared. Only 3% of Afghanistan's landmass is still covered by forest, and most of that is in Nuristan. In my opinion, this is a factor in the artificial insecurity of Nuristan; there are big profits to those who cut the forests and they do not want the control of the government to oppose the clear cutting.

They benefit from the insecurity, and I could go on speculating, but I know too little about what lies behind it. But one plus one is still two.

In the consortium, we bring an element of the old structure back by setting up tree nurseries and re-planting trees for the wood we use for every building. Because of organizing these workshops where I register the Nuristanis as contractors of UNOPS, I am now able to give those new contractors their own contracts for the building of the school or hospital in their village. It provides a direct contract in accordance with the donor's stipulations.

Because we now construct the traditional buildings and hardly have to transport materials to Nuristan, we can build nineteen buildings for the budget of the nine on the list and select the additional ten villages with the Ministry of Education.

Still under contract with the UN, I must comply with the safety instructions that make it impossible to go to Nuristan. Nuristan is labeled a "no-go" zone. The role of the safety coordinators of the UN should be to make sure that I can do my work as safely as possible, but after the great attack on the UN in Iraq, their mission has changed. They are no longer there to enable me to do my job as safely as possible; now, they simply blanket restrict access to some areas, because then nothing can happen to you. Liability drives the agenda, not the purpose of the work we are supposed to do here.

The UN is liable if something happens with fatalities. Prevention has become the strategy to avoid problems, but also made it virtually impossible to be in the field. This is not a big problem for most UN organizations because many are active in administration and policy making, and those activities are possible to be managed from inside their offices. But UNOPS, the implementing branch under the UNDP, is specifically in the field to work with contractors, supervise the building sites, meet communities and work directly with them.

Gary fights big battles for access and invents creative solutions, which means that he and the UN security are not great allies. He wants all areas to be accessible in principle unless there are clear indications of danger, instead of the UN defining total no-go zones that are non-negotiable.

The preparations for the presidential elections are in full swing and the UN manages to get me a seat in a helicopter and finally fly to Nuristan. The helicopter will land on the governor's grounds, in Parun, central Nuristan. I am only allowed three hours on the ground, not a lot of time, but better than nothing. All nineteen buildings are already in the foundation-digging phase, and the beautiful stone masonry is progressing.

I have $25,000 on me for the first payments to the Nuristan contractors, they know I am coming. When we step out of the old, rattling Russian MI6 after a one-hour flight, a large group of people is waiting for us. The governor and forty Afghan policemen wearing the infamous felt, dark green uniforms, many with just that little bit too-short trouser legs. The Nuristani consortium contractors are there, too, and stand behind the dignitaries in anticipation.

The governor, the imposing, tall man who came to my office, resolutely walks towards me, spreads his arms, and hugs me fully, chest to chest, and greets me. I am completely taken aback by his intimate display of welcoming. Only men greet each other like this, and international women get a handshake at best. While he greets me, Gul translates: "He says, 'I greet you like a man because you kept your word like a man'." I am touched, it feels like a public initiation. *Now we can do anything here in Nuristan.*

Gary arranges for me to be on a contract as consultant of an external organization, which means I no longer have to comply with the UN safety measures. I am now a subcontractor to UNOPS and can follow my own gut feeling and trust my dear staff to assess our safety and the risks and invent ways to travel.

There are other reasons to think of such a contract. In the UN guesthouse where UN staff must stay, houses currently seventeen men, with the imminent elections, most are ex-soldiers who now handle the election logistics or security. Not an environment I like to stay in. The one responsible for my safety doesn't like me and that is mutual.

A minibus with women working for the elections had been blown up. Women who risked their lives travelling around to inform communities about the elections. The driver had flicked a switch under his seat and then ran away. The bus was blown to pieces seconds later. Three women and a ten-year-old girl were killed. The others had severe burns, and one woman lost her legs.

My security coordinator refers to those women as "burqa-babes" over dinner. I am sick with anger and disgust about this colleague but swallow the comments until the next morning. He does not handle criticism well.

The next morning, I drive to the office with him, I have arranged to be his only passenger. "You know Bruce, it is very denigrating and inappropriate to call the women who risked their lives 'burqa babes'." He hits the roof and shouts that if I had my way, he wouldn't be able to say anything anymore, that I have a problem with men and that he is fed up with my comments. Shouting and raging, we get to the office. The slanging match continues in the parking lot, and I insult him in public—something I had never done before. I never swear around Afghans because they experience it as very offending. The tensions between Bruce and I had built up over such a long time that I swore out all my frustrations and he did the same. I storm up the stairs and run into my office, fuming. I bang the door shut behind me and sit breathlessly at my desk. Suddenly, the door opens. I think, *very brave to walk in now!*

Shamsul stands in front of me, seconds after slamming the door so hard that I assume it is clear I want to be alone. Shamsul

197

hums and errs, looking extremely serious and then says, eyes to the ground, "Babs…we have decided…that we would do anything for you, anything, but please never get angry with us." Then he can't keep serious any longer and bursts out laughing. He brings me back.

Shamsul always makes such dry comments; he has a serious demeanor that does not betray his sense of humor. Another time, he comments to a much-loved Australian colleague, who says "fuck" every other word, "Mister Brett, it doesn't matter if we speak English or not, we always at least understand half of what you say." We howl with laughter; Shamsul is precious!

The schools and hospitals are all under construction and we organize a long trip to Nuristan in secret; nobody apart from the people going know about our plans. We hire two old taxis, two worn out Toyota Corollas that will not stand out on the way from Kunar to Nuristan, and we leave very early. Gul has prepared the trip and had two big salwar kameezes made for me, big enough to wear over my normal clothes so I can at least use the pockets of my jeans, and I will be warm enough in the coming winter.

The road is bad, and it will take the whole day to reach the south border of Eastern Nuristan. Nuristan is divided in three parts, east, central, and west. There are no roads between these districts; from the east you can only go to the center if you go back to Kunar and go back north via the Pech Valley in the direction of Parun, where the governor's home is. The mountains are so steep, and the river valleys run from north to south where the access roads are. It is mid-November, and we can just make a trip to all the building spots before winter. The winters are long and harsh in Nuristan, the roads are blocked by huge snow loads that slide down and make the already bad access to the valleys absolutely impossible for months.

I sit in the back of the first Corolla with a headscarf on my head, which also hides my face; it's better nobody suspects a non-Afghan woman on the way to Nuristan via Kunar. After fourteen hours of navigating extremely bad roads, four flat tires and with just one car, we finally reach Bari Cod in the dark. We have to leave one car behind because it broke an axle, the suspension had given the ghost, and the good tires were finished too. We all squeeze into the one car and continue driving, as if it were perfectly normal. A few hours later, we get a flat tire again. It is the fifth and already late at night and dark in the bleakness of north Kunar. The weird thing is that Afghans don't get stressed if something like this happens. There is always a solution. Even if you can't see a logical solution to the problem, even if everything seems lost, in Afghanistan there is always a way. I learned that.

There is a house nearby with lights on and Gul walks to it. The owner sees us and puts the kettle on the fire. A few minutes later, we are sipping tea, and I think nobody is doing anything to solve the problem. *Just wait*, I reassure myself, *and warm up with a cuppa.* We drink tea and chat with the man for at least an hour. How cozy, but it is getting later and later. Only two cars drive past in that hour. In both cases, Gul walks up to the road for a chat and returns, sits down again and we continue to chat, and nothing else happens. A third car arrives in the dark, and Gul doesn't even get up. The car stops and a man gets out. Gul seems to inspect the scene only when the man walks our way and sits with us to drink tea. *Nobody is in a hurry and oh, why would we be? We're only in north Kunar, completely cut off from the world, with that one car on only three tires, it's gets later and later, we still have to eat, and we are at least one hour's drive away from the place we've planned to sleep!*

After a cup of tea, the man stands up. *Now what?* Gul and Haji Blue say their goodbyes to the man and thank him. They walk to our car, place a jack under it, and I see that the man who came to drink tea had put a tire next to our car, a tire he retrieved for us from the next village. He had driven by earlier. Tire on, we're ready to roll, and as if nothing had happened, we get back in the car and continue our journey in the ink-dark night. This type of situations changed my life perception, a change linked to trust and serenity of the moment. No panic, there is a way, maybe from an unexpected or unimaginable side, but there always is one, splendid.

Haji Blue is at the wheel, the Nuristani contractor who will put us up the first night in the front, and me, Gul, Qahar in the back. Qahar is one of two "umbrella" contractors. We call Haji, Haji Blue because of his bright blue eyes and to make the difference with the other Haji in the happy team, called Haji Moon, because his car is named Moon. Bari Cod is a village consisting of just a few houses next to the river on the border of Pakistan and Afghanistan right across the border of Kunar and Nuristan.

Alas, we are finally in Nuristan…*Nuristan*! We are welcomed by the contractor's whole family waiting for us, with a meal, black tea with full fat milk and lots of sugar. Bliss. At the same time, when I make these trips, I learned that I need to train my bladder on the very limited possibilities to empty it, I place my whole body in survival mode. No joke. That first night in Bari Cod, it had been at least sixteen hours since I last went to the toilet, in the office, just before we left. But nature calls mercilessly. Gul has packed toilet paper in the car but finding a place where you can use it is a problem…again.

Gul goes investigating and returns later with a woman. He tells me to follow her, armed with my toilet paper. The house is an authentic Nuristani house with two floors. Thick, horizontal, wooden beams, the spaces filled with rough mountain stones and clay, the whole walls smeared with a mix of clay and straw. The woman and I walk down the stairs of the upper floor where the men and I stay, to the women's room down in the dark, filled with the smoke of leaking pipes of the wood stove and the women with many children. Four brothers and their whole families live in the house that consists of the one large men's room upstairs and the two smaller women and children's rooms downstairs, where the cooking is done too.

When my eyes adjust to the dark, I also see two very old people. A granddad, even though he is a man, joins his wife and children in the women's room. Being that old has its advantages, and certain rules become a bit vaguer. An old woman is sitting on one of the beds, her body just a stump, her legs missing, ripped to shreds by grenades. She manages the household, the whole room, as if she is a remote control; she might be disabled, but she has a clear position in the family. We are on our way to the toilets, but we have to make a stop in the women's room, and I am shown a place on a bed.

I sit next to the grandmother who seems blind, and her skin hangs loosely from her bones. She looks more than hundred years old, but based on her children's age, she is probably no older than sixty-five. She moves closer to me and takes my hand. Her hands are cold, and I fold them in mine to give her some warmth. I lose count a few times when I try to count the children running around, but there are more than fifteen, only dressed in tops and with bare bottoms. Every now and then, one will squat and let run what needs to come out. I am jealous; my bladder gives me cramps and stitches in my whole lower belly.

The younger women start organizing water, kettle, wood, fire, food, plates and cups as soon as I walk in. I am amazed how quickly these women have tea and food ready. They do wonders with the very limited means, only I can't stomach the idea or the sustenance of more tea! The woman who had left me with the other women returns and gestures me to follow her. There is much hilarity when I get up and the woman seems to announce something to the others. Except for the blind grandmother, the granddad maintains his place by the grandmother and aunt sitting on the bed. Everybody gets up and follows me.

We walk into the darkness, following the woman at the front carrying the one coveted oil lamp. We walk through an alleyway and reach the animals. I notice goats, sheep and a few cows, first their smell, then their noises and finally, I make out their shapes in the weak light. With that many people around, they're restless and start to get up. I am pushed through an opening in a clay wall, past an old rag that hangs diagonally in the opening. I feel under my shoes that I'm standing in a layer of shit at least five centimeters thick. The woman quickly walks in to hang the oil lamp on a nail in the wall. Eh, an oil lamp with all the biofuel, I quickly let the thought go. Now, I can see. Yep, it's all shit.

A hole in the floor looks like it was once intended as a toilet. It's a huge performance to lower my salwar kameez trousers without dropping them on the floor, and then, when I carefully open my jeans and lower them, I must make sure the long upper of the salwar kameez remains above the excrement. Finally, squatting, I manage to keep everything above the floor. Outside, twenty people are chattering about my every move. Meantime, my bladder is so full that it takes a while before the first drop appears. No cooperation down there. It can be another long trek to the next place before I can relieve myself again, so I am fixed in place to squeeze out everything I can. No more tea, I decide, no food and no drink, only the strict necessary, just like the women in Balabagh. *Prevent the problem*. Now, my reinforced motto.

Back in the men's quarters, where at least twelve men sleep, they have already installed the mattresses. Mine is in the furthest corner. I lay down under the covers fully clothed and Gul moves close to me. With a wide grin on his face, he says, "You can't trust those Afghan men, I will protect you." We roll about laughing. God, I love this man! There is never a moment that I do not feel safe with him. Soon, we fall asleep.

Chapter 25

GUEST IN KABUL'S UNDERWORLD

It's bitterly cold. Persistent biting winds howl around the old Russian buildings when I enter the dark staircase. The wind whirls into the stairwell through the windows where the glass is missing. The air is so dry that my nose has painful scabs inside. When I blow my nose, there is blood in the tissue. The Ministry of Public Works is situated on the outskirts of Kabul, in Mikrorayon, next to the Kabul River close to the roundabout where the dangerous Jalalabad Road leaves Kabul heading for the Mahipar pass through the Hindu Kush to reach Jalalabad only 150 km closer towards Peshawar.

Our flight from Herat is delayed. We arrive back in Kabul much later than expected. Gul is exhausted. I thank him for all his work under the extreme circumstances of the last days, hug him and ask him to pass my greetings to his family. "De Khudai Paman" (go with God), we bid each other and off he goes. I'm here to pick up my stuff.

Earlier, I had called Hafiz, one of my engineers, to leave the key to the office for me because they would have left by the time I got there. I walk into the numb darkness up the staircases to the third floor. Uninspiring, old Russian concrete staircases with two flights and a landing to reach each next floor. Cheap grey carpets cover the old concrete surfaces. A musty smell lingers in the stairwells; the carpets are always moist. Three times a day, the cleaners sprinkle the carpets so the dust will not infiltrate the air when hand-sweeping them.

Only in the evenings, I do not find a cleaner on those stairs. At any other time of the day, a bent over man with a hand broom, in a salwar kameez as sprinkled as the carpets, greets me in response to my "salaam alaykum" (hello), back "wa-alaykum salaam (hello to you), Babs."

I arrive at the third floor, and the guards are sitting with one of those godawful pressure lamps that can explode anytime. An electric stove does not work because the generator operates only during office hours, and it is well past 8:00 p.m. Instead, they have a kerosene stove, which fumes more than it should. Greetings abound before I take a left into the long hallway.

One of the guards comes running after me with a torch and smiles. I put a hand on his shoulder. "Tashakor." I grab the handle of the door to my office and find it locked. I look under the mat hoping to find the key, which I asked Eng. Hafiz to leave for me so I could access my belongings. I've moved my belongings from Jalalabad to Kabul to live with Jan, my boss, as a result of being summoned to Kabul, separated from my Jalalabad staff so USAID can do their investigations. They've accused me and my team of corruption. But events have been wildly overblown.

Before I have time to even think about preparing, I have to go on an emergency flight to Herat to take care of things that have gotten beyond the control of the regional team there. The provincial minister of education is not willing to confirm the sites for the schools with us and the team is unable to convince him; he will not budge. The minister of education needs to confirm the sites for the schools because the Ministry owns the land on which the schools are constructed. As soon as the schools are completed, the Ministry of Education becomes also responsible for providing teachers in the school and paying their salaries. Every further activity hinges on the approval of this provincial minister of education. There is a history of promises about acquiring the sites but equally many cancellations and excuses not to confirm the sites with us. I had decided to fly here myself, as time has run out. The project is behind schedule while I'm getting bombarded with pressure by the donor.

I step into his office, and they expect me because my staff had managed to get an appointment. "Salaam alaykum", "wa-alaykum salaam", and the whole ritual of greetings and welcoming words. An impressive large man sits behind his equally impressive desk, a framed photograph of Karzai behind him on the wall, the flag of Afghanistan on a fake golden console in front of him.

His desk is empty except for a small pile of papers, a tray with cups and a thermos with a bowl of nuts and sweets. His desk is covered with a sheet of glass. Under the glass, I can see a poster-sized calendar, a cheap print with bad colors, all too purplish and greenish. The border is full of advertisements for car tires, jeeps, 4-wheel drives, spare parts and welding equipment. Next to the calendar are two postcard-sized prints of female Bollywood stars, with much more skin exposed than any woman in Afghanistan would ever be allowed to reveal. He waves his hand at one of his staff to bring tea and gestures for me to have a seat.

I sink in a chair with way collapsed cushioning, upholstery that is useless. I reflect on Roger Bus and how he hammered the little nails in the ties and fabric of the layered upholstery. It is an art, and with these chairs here, an art that had failed to be understood! I sit with my elbows too high up on the arm rests. He asks how my trip to Herat had been, when I arrived and where I am staying. I answer his questions, and we wait for the tea.

"So, what is your name again? Babs, right...so Babs, why did you want to meet me?" he inquires as soon as the man pouring the tea is not blocking the view. I try to sit up straighter, move a bit forward, out of the deep seat of the uncomfortable chair. More composed, I say, "Thank you for welcoming me to your office, I am sorry to take your time, I know how busy you must be, but I am here to discuss our schools-reconstruction project with you." He nods his head and waits for me to continue. "I am here because I understood from my staff that there are some problems with getting the sites confirmed with you, for us to build the schools. I would like to discuss with you what we could possibly do to help you speed up this process, as the project is lagging here in Herat. In the four provinces around Jalalabad, we already have all the schools under construction and in Ghor, Badghis and even Farah, we have activity on each of the sites. Just here in Herat we are behind." He shuffles on his chair, sips his tea. I reach for my tea, waiting for his response.

Other people in the room do not look directly at him nor me. Heads are down into the tea. The atmosphere is quite tense, but I am adamant about unlocking this situation today. He attempts to promise me the sites, the kind of promises that my staff had received over the past months, which never resulted in anything. I need to find out what is going on and decide to go on the offensive.

"Look," I say, "I have the money to build fourteen schools in Herat province, all I need is the sites signed off and I can start work." He leans forward and responds to my change of approach. He looks me straight in the eyes and challenges, "Do you think we need your money?" I'm taken aback and fall quiet for a minute. My brain works hard in finding the right words, going over various strategies. I won't give up. I meet his eyes and say, "Are you trying to tell me something?" A smile appears on his face. I think we like each other. I presume that we are closer towards a solution. He says, "Yes, I do have something to tell you, and I will show you."

There is silence. Mystery stirring. Maybe reconciliation. He asks the other men to leave the room and in a blink of an eye, it's just him, his deputy, Gul and me remaining. "I will only show you, but," the man wielding the power here says, nodding in Gul's direction, "he has to stay here. We need to blindfold you while we drive outside Herat where we need to go. If that is okay with you, inshallah?" I feel the blood pumping in my temples. I think to myself that I'm either completely nuts to go along with this or I will have a hell of a story after I return.

Gul manages a shimmer of a smile, enough to ease my raging thoughts. We don't need words. We know the gravity of our situation that needs resolution. I give my phone and bag to Gul to take to the office. No need to tell Gul to make up an excuse for my whereabouts for the remainder of the morning, possibly well into the afternoon. I wink at Gul, then turn to the director and say a little too confidently, "Okay, we can go."

It's still early morning when we drive out of town. My hands are tied behind my back, he assures me, so I don't know the location he's about to show me, nor can I report to anyone what I see. A white scarf with a black grid of little blocks is wrapped around my head gently, tight enough to ensure I cannot see a thing. I feel someone sitting beside me in the back of the big Land Cruiser. The deputy? The radio is blaring traditional Afghan music, making it next to impossible to talk even if we wanted to.

I smell a cigarette being lit. I've not smoked for years but if they offer me a smoke now, I wouldn't say no!

We drive for hours, it seems, on the bumpy roads, and I'm increasingly uncomfortable with my hands tied behind me. The roads are progressively worse with big potholes. We drive on dirt roads, loose gravel, the car skidding regularly. The driver honks at everything and nothing. After an agonizing hour or so, the car stops. I hear them get out and slam the doors. Then someone opens my door and gently grabs my arm to guide me to step out of the car. Somewhere ahead of me I hear large steel doors opening, and we're walking towards the sounds. The hand holding my arm guides me gently down some stairs, sandy steps, irregular, then a turn to the right and more steps, further down. It smells dusty and rural; we are far outside town.

The wind blows and it is rather cold. I do not see anything but the vague light the white scarf lets through for a brief reprieve, then darkness. Heavy metal doors close behind me, a squeak, a sliding lock, and silence. The hand lets go of my arm and unties my hands. I can now take off my blindfold. Stinging cold on my eyes. I almost want the scarf on again for warmth.

I need time to adjust my eyes to the dark place. Vague light bulbs become visible on the metal ceiling. I stand in a narrow path, no more than 60cm wide, between stacks of pallets with small paper bundles. We're in a container, and the minister is closely watching me and my response. Then suddenly, he waves his hand for me to follow him and gradually, it's clear that we're stepping through interconnected twelve 40-foot containers jam packed with American money and weapons. From the number of steps that we took to descend, this is an underground location.

I look at him and say with an approving smile, "So, now that we are here, you wanted to tell me something?" He smiles back and started describing what I am looking at. Bundles of new 100-dollar notes, saran wrapped. He's confident and pleased to say, "This pallet here is $43 million the U.S. government paid us only two months before 9/11, when we were still under Taliban rule." He stretches his back and quips, "So, now, I ask you again, do you think we need your money?"

I weigh my response. I weigh every word, knowing I could say something stupid or perfect in his eyes. I look at him, stretch my back as well and reply, "Well, are you using this money to build schools for the children?" He cracks an open smile at me and says, "Fair enough," he chuckles. "No, I am not using this money to build schools. Let's go back to the office."

As this little trip underground winds down with a hellacious return on the same bumpy roads, blindfolded with hands tied behind my back, I have my fourteen sites in Herat province confirmed and signed off that same afternoon. The engineers will start tendering the next morning. And I'm safe!

I still need my stuff behind the closed door in my office in Kabul. My base, my main office and team are in Jalalabad, which I had requested when I became the project manager for the schools and clinics. Jalalabad and the four provinces are a large part of the project with UNOPS, and I have my friends and family there, where I feel most at home. Gary had obliged. Gary practically grew up in Afghanistan and understands that you become family here and then you need to be close, live and drink tea with them.

But the project stretches over eight regions over the whole of Afghanistan, and Kabul is the hub I transferred through every time I go to another regional office for a visit. In Kabul, I also have to do the budget, procurement, paperwork.

Where is the damned key?

I am filthy from the days in Herat, crappy airports and delayed planes. I am exhausted and want to go home, have a glass of wine with Jan and chill out.

The guards don't not know where the key is either. I'm done. I ask them to step back. I take a good swing and kick in the door. The guards jump nervously. I assure them that I will replace the lock and leave a note so that everyone knows that it was me who kicked in the door.

So, I enter and on my desk is the damned key next to a note from Eng. Hafiz. The note reads, "Dear Babs, welcome back to Kabul. Hope you had a successful journey; may peace be with you. How is your health. Greetings to your family. Khoda Hafez (may God be with you), see you tomorrow, inshallah (God willing). Yours truly, Eng. Hafiz."

We organize another secret trip to Nuristan. IRD has sent some people to Nuristan to produce made-up reports about the poor quality and mismanagement of the sites. I know this is not true following the reporting of my own field engineers, but IRD and USAID discredit the trustworthiness of them, accusing them of bribery and corruption. I know my team, and I would jump in front of a bullet for them, as they would do for me.

With the schools well underway, but increasing pressure of IRD and USAID, I need to see it for myself, maintain our good relationships and get firsthand conversations with the contractors, to make detailed photo reports.

We leave super early without anyone knowing. We drive in two old Corollas hours and hours over the dusty roads, our speed leaving big dust clouds behind us. After a long day, we pass through North Kunar to enter the eastern valley of Nuristan. It is a spectacularly beautiful landscape, wide fields on each side of the infamous Kunar River, known to be rather dangerous. The melting water comes from the high mountains of Nuristan and feeds the whole valley, all the way to Jalalabad, with crystal clear water.

The road surface is now just loose gravel on compacted fine mud, dry as a rock. The car skids now and then as Haji speeds through the curves. On this part of the road, you do not want to slow down. Suddenly, Haji slams on the brake; we fly forward in our seatbelts. Loud screaming all around the car. My heart pounds in my throat. *What the hell?* Some twenty young men had jumped in front of the car, all carrying AK47s and Kalashnikovs pointed at us. The guys have their faces covered with their black and white scarfs and scream and run around the car.

They rip open the doors and demand with loud yelling that we get out. I have my black and white scarf wrapped around my head, and they are asking questions, yelling at Gul for answers. Gul says, "They ask if you are an American, they ask if we carry guns." In the sheer panic of the moment, I crap my pants. As I feel the poop hang in my underwear and stick between the cheeks of my bum, all my panic disappears.

They might as well kill me, I am thinking, *it doesn't get worse than this.*

We are on our way to Nuristan, and I know from my latest experiences that there are no toilets for me, let alone a shower or the chance to get changed. I am done. I say out loud, "Shit, Gul, what do they want?" I'm looking at Gul and feeling ridiculously calm. I am not afraid, I feel no panic, I am just mad, mad that my body betrayed me. I say to Gul, "They might as well kill me, can we get this over with?"

Gul looks confused and asks, "Babs, what is going on?" I look at the guys standing in front of me, not screaming anymore, because they sense the shift in me too. I say out loud, "Ask them what they want, I just shit myself, so are they going to kill us or what?"

The guys are completely taken aback by my tone and lower their weapons. They start asking Gul questions, and suddenly, he's walking away alongside them calmly. One of them makes a phone call. In no time, a rickety Toyota pickup arrives, and Gul tells me to get on the open back, he joins me, and so do a few guys who had ambushed us. I think, *smart to put me in the wind, I probably smell.*

Our drivers follow us, and we drive twenty minutes into the first village of Nuristan. They load us to a house, and I am held at the door. At this moment, I am really curious what the heck is happening. One of the guys is talking to women inside, and two come out. They take my hands and guide me to a room in the back, some kind of storage room. Soon after, two men come in with a galvanized tub, and two others with jerrycans with water, a kettle with hot water, and one carries a pile of clothes.

From their gestures I understand that I should take my clothes off and take a bath. Seriously? They leave an oil lamp, as evening has fallen, and exit the room. I kind of chuckle to myself, not quite understanding what the fuck just happened, but I am grateful that I can take off my crap-pants and wash up a bit. I change into the clothes they left for me, a shirt and long underwear, and a salwar kameez for a man. What a relief! I leave my dirty clothes in a pile. I'll deal with that tomorrow.

I leave the room and follow the sound of many voices, weirdly sounding like a friendly gathering. One of the women sees me, takes my hand, and guides me to the room where all the men are now together. I enter and all of them look at me, get up fast and make a little bow to me, each with the right hand on their hearts. Gul laughs at me and says, "I told them who you are, that you are Babs who builds the schools in Nuristan. They are so sorry!" I look at the room filled with guys, put my hand on my heart, bow to them and say, "Moshkel nes, dera manana" (no problem, thank you).

The women bring in big platters of food and nan. I can barely believe what is happening, but here I am, in a room full of Nuristanis who nearly killed us, now in male clothing, having a feast. Gul is so happy and says that he was "never afraid", with that big smile. I love his humor. After the meal, the women and some children bring in tea and sweets, which I eat heartily. I feel like celebrating that we are alive.

The men talk to me, and Gul translates, "They say that they will come with us to all the sites of the schools to make sure that we are safe while traveling through Nuristan." What a blessing.

After the feast, I hear snoring all around me, and stare at the ceiling. I cannot catch any sleep, the scenes of that day playing through my head.

In the morning, I hear pots and pans outside and I get up and see the women prepare pancakes, whipped cream, and blackberry jam. I greet them with warm smiles. I help carry a plate with pancakes in, and they just smile. Normally it would be insulting to the host when a guest offers a hand; a guest is expected to sit and receive the hospitality, but this is different, like I am one of them.

For eight days, we visit all the school sites and meet the communities, watch the progress, and discuss the challenges and changes. There are problems at some of the sites. Nuristan has steep mountain slopes, and it is hard to find flat pieces of land to build a new construction. Some of the sites are simply not feasible to build. We discuss ways forward and agree on next steps.

It is a few weeks after our last trip to Nuristan. The reports from my field engineers indicate that most of the constructions are now between 60 and 90% completed, but some sites continue to be problematic. I have to investigate further because I'm determined to get these schools built. Besides the work, I absolutely love being in Nuristan—the people, forests, mountains, and the magical feeling of traveling to a time 300 years ago. I feel so connected and so alive. My father's bedtime stories about these tree people in that landlocked country echo in my mind. How did he know of these people?

Around the same goddamn place in North Kunar, again, Haji slams the brake, and screaming guys stop the car. Fuck, we're getting ambushed again. I am not afraid this time, and rather boldly, I get out the car and say, while pointing at my chest, "Zma Babs." Immediately the guys lower their guns, and say, "Wabakhai (sorry) Babs," and come and shake my hand. Warm greetings and laughs. It is getting late; we say goodbye and continue on our way.

We hire local cars to go up the valleys, ride horses through the eastern valley. First, we go up to Bargi Matal, the furthest northern village up the river in the eastern valley of Nuristan. We visit two schools and a hospital showing good progress. We go down south again. It is the end of a long day, and it already dark again; we are still at the river.

We had planned to sleep that night in Kamdesh, but the day trip is taking a lot longer than we thought. This trip we travel by ourselves, and do not have our escorts with us. They had local cars. Now it takes us much longer to get from village to village.

We are still down at the river, it is getting dark, and Kamdesh is high up the mountain, at least 2,5 km steep up. We have no option though but to take a break, scoop some water from the river to drink, and start climbing. The clear moon lights up the path a bit, but it is still hard to see where we are going. I am sweating profusely, and I often stop to catch my breath.

It takes us more than three hours of steep climbing, through brush, rather dense forest, and thorny bushes. All scratched up and exhausted, we arrive in this beautiful village and walk towards the large house in the center where the most important man of the village lives. We all lay down around a little wooden stove and fall asleep instantly.

I wake up and the sun is out. We are so high up the mountain that the river down in the valley is but a shiny sliver of silver. The man who greeted us last night, speaks English, and he takes me on a little tour through the village. He smiles when I tell him that I am a carpenter and love the Nuristani wood traditions, especially the geometric carving.

He takes me around the old house and tells me that it is more than 150 years old. The façade is elaborately carved with abstract carvings that withstood the seasons for 150 years! The wood is from the Deodara, the Himalayan Cedar trees. They can grow for over 1,000 years, and he tells me how Nuristan is plagued by the illegal logging and trade over the border to Pakistan. The old trees are all gone; the oldest trees you can find now, are maybe just four hundred years old.

He shows me how every piece of wood has been shaped by human hands, the pegs in the roof, the columns that tie in with the façade, each piece is carved with a flower or a geometric shape, representing an element or season, or sun or moon.

The sap wood between the grain is eroded and gives all the decorations fine lines and a subtle relief. The Nuristanis are famous for their wood-carving talent and their gentle love for anything related to wood and trees, the essence of their life. I am weirdly familiar with that through the stories my dad once told me.

He tells me that the traditions in Nuristan, when it was still Kafiristan, a wooden statue was cut for the person who passed, the statue had the deceased's likeness and height. The villagers danced seven nights and seven days with the wooden statue tied on their backs. A year after their death, they made another statue in honor of the deceased and placed it in the village. Sometimes these statues were places where offerings were made.

The ideas of the Nuristanis were peculiar, their philosophies that people originated as biological community beings from a tree. The tree was female, the mother of the community and it was no coincidence that Disani, the mother of all gods, was their main goddess. Nuristanis are born from a tree. So am I.

Chapter 26

DON'T MOAN, JUST DO IT

Gary calls me while I am having tea with Gul in my office in Jalalabad. His voice sounds alarmed as he summons me to Kabul. "Get in the car now Babs, you need to be here by tonight." He does not explain what and how and why, but the tone of his voice makes me feel at great unease. The last few months have become progressively more tense with IRD tightening their reporting on the quality of the schools we are building in Nuristan. Their reports are lying, and false information was passed on to USAID, targeting to fail my project. Gary knew the reports lied, but I felt his hesitancy to fully back me up because that would put him in the position of turning against USAID, who funds many of the UNOPS projects.

Shortly after I arrive in Kabul, I get a phone call from a guy who does not identify himself, but he summons me to the U.S. Embassy and urges that I do not share my visit with anybody. I feel heavy, like a dark force has control over me. I am separated from my staff and am not allowed to speak or otherwise communicate with any of them, pending the ongoing investigation they are doing into my "corrupt activities".

They send a car to pick me up.

In the whole project I am building 167 buildings, mostly schools and clinics. All construction sites are well progressing or already completed, but the schools in Nuristan are a whole different story, by the sheer nature of my project design, to make it possible to build schools in Nuristan at all.

Having nineteen schools and clinics under construction in a remote province where no NGO has been able to build any structure over the past decades is remarkable. But as the work in Nuristan has progressed, I learn more about the about the political agenda of the project. As the veils are lifting, there are hidden agendas. Initially, there were just nine schools on the list, all budgeted to be built to American standards, concrete buildings. In Nuristan the slopes of the mountains are no less than 55 degrees steep, and traditional buildings are from wood for a few sensible reasons. Plus, no local person knows how to build with concrete.

Building massive concrete structures on steep slopes with people who are not familiar with the science of concrete, would be an atrocious idea and dangerous at best, so that is not going to happen on my watch. Under the requirements of USAID funding, I am only allowed to use direct contracting. In Nuristan there are, of course, no contractors who are certified, so I need to find a way around it.

At the start of the project, USAID insinuated to me that I should contract Louis Berger, an American construction company, but I had refused. Local men need jobs, and their children need schools. So, bringing in an American contractor takes away the job opportunities for local men, which pisses off the locals, so it becomes unsafe, and then security people are needed to keep the project "safe", and a massive security budget is part of the project budget. Just as an *fyi*, an American security guard is paid USD$40K/month at this stage of my project. I refuse to go in the field with them because I deeply believe that traveling with armored cars and weapons with helmets and body vests actually "makes" you a target.

What Nuristan needs is employment for the men and schools for children, it is really that simple. So, I talk a lot with my staff, and we design a structure that might do just that. Knowing that this is an opposite approach than what the project is supposed to be, an effective tool to funnel government funds in the pockets of private contractors, I realize there are risks.

Our ultimate goal is to build locally appropriate structures, built by Nuristani men. In order to be able to build with Nuristanis, I come up with "the Nuristan consortium". It is as much as a structure to certify Nuristani men to be registered contractors, so I can contract them directly, which defies donor requirements.

My engineers make floorplans and construction drawings for each building and prepare the bill of quantities with all the required materials and volumes, so we know the total construction cost per site, including labor.

We send word to Nuristan that we'll have a consortium meeting to kick off the project. All the Nuristanis show up in our office, and I see them arrive through our gate, wearing white pakols, the woolen flat hats, which Nuristanis wear in a very specific way, different than anybody else. They have the head bands rolled out, so the flat part stands higher on their heads. Some are wearing the gorgeous, typical Nuristani white woolen jackets with colorful embroidery. This moment is so special! Nuristan has long been this difficult region, not letting outsiders in. As they all enter, I feel their anticipation. I also feel a wave of pride. We are making this possible.

Everybody sits down, and Gul serves the tea and cookies. I initiate a quick round of introductions, so everybody knows who's who, and from which village in Nuristan. Traditional mountain people, who trust me enough to make their way to my office. Me, a white European woman doing a construction project. I have to hold down tears because I feel this moment, the significance of this gathering.

Once we all say our names and our roles or village, we kick off the two-day workshop. In order to become a registered contractor with UNOPS, they need to learn what it means to be a contractor, how to run a project so we can report on it properly.

We break in smaller groups, each with one of my engineers, to go in-depth over the floorplans, to become familiar with the drawings, translate it to the way they build and understand, explain the structural improvements we have added, understand the details and sections. Each group has large pieces of paper in front of them, and they are busy sketching and drawing as they learn. Their eagerness is palpable! Each contractor has the package of drawings for the building in their village.

Most important is the bill of quantities (BOQ), listing all the materials, quantity per material or item, and the price per unit. The BOQ is the spine of the project, the tool that allows us to monitor the implementation, and report properly on the progress. The BOQ is used to monitor quantities and make change orders if the site engineer agrees that the quantity needs to change. The BOQ also lists the labor hours, transport of materials, water, tea and basic food for the workers, everything involved in building a remote school. The line-item material times the quantity; times the unit price is the total dollar amount for each line item. Add all the line-items up and you have the total project cost.

In the weeks prior, my engineers had prepared all the packages for the buildings. Based on the prices in the market, they priced them out including transport and the labor it would take to build them, then I added 10% profit. With this, we can now build structures that are locally appropriate to the earthquake zoning and steep mountain slopes, the local construction knowledge and accessibility of the building materials, while employing Afghan men to build the schools for their own children. One and one is two. My grandma taught me that one and one is two and that when someone says differently, making it more complicated, watch out, because someone is making money, don't trust them. With the budget of the nine "American standard" concrete schools on my initial list, we can now actually build nineteen schools and clinics. The result is ten more schools and clinics for the same budget, an economic injection into the local communities for construction labor. Plus, we do not need security forces or weapons. One and one is two.

My project approach illustrates that without weapons while using local labor, you can do more and actually build the schools and be safe and work with the generous people of these communities. According to the donors' requirements, I should announce that we are building schools, then bring in international contractors, consequentially piss off the locals so they become hostile to the intruders who take away their opportunities for work, and the subsequent need for armed security forces to control the area. Then use that whole trail to justify that the schools cannot be built. In the meantime, the American donor funds are paid to American contractors.

The result is that I am obviously proving something that USAID does not want to have proven, so they aim to put the project in a bad light. All the false reports and intimidations over the last months all lead up to this, being summoned to the embassy.

When I arrive at the heavily barricaded American embassy, I feel sick to my stomach. At the gate, while driving through all the barbed wired roadblocks that prevent suicide bombers to drive straight in, I am asked to identify myself, show my passport and state who I have an appointment with, while guards check the bottom of the car for improvised bombs with upside down mirrors on long sticks. I receive a visitor badge and am escorted inside.

Once inside, a couple of massive armed American soldiers are appointed to me. They walk behind me and shout commands. Take a right, walk on, stop at elevator, get in, dead silence in the elevator box. I can feel my heart pounding. This is not good. Out the elevator, turn left, turn right, with these two armed guys right behind me. One steps forward and opens a door, his hand on my shoulder kind of pushing me inside. Three guys are sitting at the end of the table, the light in the room rather and unexpectedly dim. I am seated at this end of the table, the two soldiers with their machine guns pointed in my direction on either side of me. I'm intimidated, genuinely scared.

I recognize the guy in the middle from one of the initial meetings where we signed the contract for the project. He starts with stating all the lies about the project and me, his tone far from friendly or welcoming. He drones on about the quality of the construction of my schools being substandard, that my project is corrupt, that I am being scammed by the local people, that the locals are clearly taking advantage of me being a woman in this role, stealing from the project.

Then, without asking any questions, the tone darkens and takes me by surprise. He states that my links with Al Qaeda are clear and that engagement with the Taliban is against USAID policy. His tone is progressively more intimidating. The guys behind me take a step closer to me, their weapons now directly held up against me.

He points at all the reports about the schools while grinding in. "You created this, and I will get to the bottom of it here and today, you are not getting away with any of it. You will tell us about all your contacts, your link with Al Qaeda and where the money is going. We will not rest until you have told us everything."

My mind races. How can I ever defend myself against all these lies? It is all a set-up, but they have this room. While he calls for some water to be brought in, there is a silence, a pause, a chance for me to gather my thoughts and to develop a fast strategy. *Okay Alink, stay calm, only answer what you know, do not go against them, you have nothing to defend, so no need to defend yourself.* I start playing chess in my mind and feel my father's presence. I breathe and become calm inside.

The questioning slowly turns into an interrogation that lasts a couple of hours, while I just keep answering, "not to my knowledge", or "that is not correct" and continue playing chess—my father prepared me for this. How did he know? He tries to change his tone a few times from harsh and attacking, to understanding and friendly in an attempt to get me to say more. There isn't more though. I'm steady.

A few hours later, without any apparent closure, I am released and shown to the exit. The car that had picked me up is not there. I feel assaulted and exhausted. I walk out to the street and wave a local taxi down. A friendly face, kindly asking "Where to?" I could have hugged him. In the back of the taxi, in safe company of a friendly Afghan, I break down. The driver passes a box of tissues back to me and nods kindly via his rear-view mirror.

A few days later, I am watching the news with Gary in his 'Oscar I' house in Shar-I-Naw, Kabul, recovering from the huge Christmas party he had organized with his wife, Susan, for all the internationals who had not gone home to be with their families, those who made it possible for the others to be home with their families for Christmas. About 120 guests arrived, all eating a full dinner and all receiving full stockings. Stockings Gary and I had filled the night before, with little gifts that he and Susan had collected during the year for this purpose. While we were placing the stockings under the tree, Gary had an idea. He needed condoms, he had thought of a joke and every stocking needed a condom too. He asked who wanted to come with him and I said yes.

Chicken Street and Flower Street, the busy streets of Kabul, were banned to UN cars in those days for security reasons. So, Gary and I, in his rather conspicuous turbo UN Land Cruiser with the roof rack that extended over the bonnet, drove straight to Flower Street. He stopped in the middle of the street. Told me he'd leave the engine running while I bought the condoms. *You swine*, I thought, grinned at him, and asked the Dari word for *condom.*

I walked into a shop and asked for a pack of 100 condoms, the guy probably thought I was a guy anyway. I never wore a head scarf; I had learned during my first months in Afghanistan that it was more confusing to people than respectful. Without changing his facial expression, the man took a wholesale box of condoms from behind him. I paid and went back to the car. We laughed and sped off. Gary always had things popping up in his head that he needed to act on, everything was possible, nothing was too weird. I can't really remember the joke with the condoms in the stockings. It was something about how you were fucked if you worked with UNOPS.

I don't really care about Christmas, but that party with Gary, that Christmas in Kabul that truly was about being together. Being in an Islamic country, Christmas days were no holidays, so because we were there and continued to work, our other colleagues were able to be with their families at home. That Christmas will stay with me forever.

Eight of my colleagues live with Gary and Susan. Susan asks me to stay over for Christmas too and I happily accept. On Boxing Day, Gary and I are sitting in the TV room and see the first images of the tsunami. In the next hours, we see with horror how the victim figures increase from 4,000 to 20,000 and then to 100,000…ultimately, 225,000 people across eight countries.

"Send me to Aceh," I say to Gary.

"We have no business to be there," he says sternly.

He is responsible for the Middle East region with extensions to Sudan, Liberia and Haiti. Afghanistan is his center for which he is the UNOPS country director. His UNOPS has grown from three internationals with a $1 million portfolio, to the largest UN operation in Afghanistan, employing 600 internationals during elections for which he oversees the logistics. We have 70,000 Afghans on the payroll and a budget of $750 million for the reconstruction projects and the procurement / logistics for the elections.

Gary is an incredible boss to work for. He is motivated by all the right stuff, and deeply cares for Afghans and Afghanistan. His father used to be the U.S. ambassador to Afghanistan, and during his teens, Gary grew up in Kabul. Gary's motto: "We don't moan, we just do it." He is exhausted by the bureaucracy and believes in looking for solutions instead of explaining why something is not possible. "That's what we're here for," he says. "This is Afghanistan, nobody told you it would be easy here or that you can arrange your projects from behind your desk and become rich in your sleep. If you work with us here, you will get your hands dirty and you can be proud of what we achieve here together."

The group of colleagues who are the core of UNOPS in Afghanistan feels like a family, all special people, with a special enthusiasm and crazy enough to put up with Gary's madness— just because he believes that we are here for the Afghans and his motivation is never one of personal profit. We work ludicrous, long hours, seven days a week. Only on Friday, the holy day, do we sleep a bit longer and often share a meal in Gary's garden.

These colleagues see the exaggerated bureaucracy of the UN as an obstacle, a bureaucracy that can be minimized if you only dare to be creative—often too threatening for the settled UN bureaucrats in New York. Gary has either people who do everything for the projects, or people who cannot stand him. Nothing in between. People either love him or loathe him, and the latter tries to destroy him.

"We have no business being there," he says again, referring to the area of the regional UNOPS office in Bangkok, an office full of people who see Gary as a threat to their status quo. UNOPS in Afghanistan does not remain unnoticed in the world of this work; many eyes are fixed on what Gary is doing in Afghanistan and if you want something done, he is your man. Therefore, it does not take long for UNICEF Sri Lanka and Jakarta to reach out to him instead of asking the UNOPS guys in Bangkok. They request Gary to send his best staff to set up projects there.

I had managed the UNICEF schools project through which I earned a bit of a reputation for getting stuff done while the USAID project is again, being held up by the investigations and allegations against me.

On the 9th of January, Gary calls me and says: "I don't want you to breathe your last breath here in Afghanistan. I am sending you to Sri Lanka. Just for two weeks, and then you come back." Two weeks to Sri Lanka to do the initial field survey for UNICEF to map out the actual damage and make an inventory of what needs reconstruction. But I want to go to Aceh, not Sri Lanka. "Two weeks Sri Lanka," he repeats firmly. "Then you come back here. I need you here." That sentence about my last breath stays with me. Before Gary hangs up, he says, "Come to my house now, I'll drive you to the airport in the morning."

I only take a small pack with some clothing for the next few weeks and ask a driver to drop me off at Guesthouse Kilo Oscar. I do not realize the gravity of the situation that prompted Gary to shove me on a flight out of Afghanistan within twelve hours, but no sooner than I walk into their kitchen, his face shows heightened alarm. He says, "Here, eat something. Word is that the Taliban has put a price on your head. We need to get you out of the country ASAP."

We sit down and as I try to stomach a few bites, Gary informs me that the Turkish journalist had disappeared and I would be next. Months ago, an Afghan staff member of USAID had asked me if we had the capacity to take on more provinces. Apparently, there was an agency that did not perform well, and they wanted me to take it over. I passed the request to Gary, and he said, "Go take a break, and when you come back, we'll take it on." Before my short R&R, none of the school sites in those two regions had even been tendered, yet when I returned to the IRD office a couple of weeks later, reports on the walls showed that all these school constructions were now 60% completed.

Before I left, the Afghan USAID man had handed me the list of all the sites that we were asked to add to our project. The Turkish journalist was the boyfriend of one of my colleagues, and I handed him the list for all the sites that now showed 60% completed but were not even tendered a couple of weeks prior, so I knew the reports were fake and there was more to this story. He was going to find things out on the ground. The evening before he disappeared, he sent an email with what he had found out. The "not so well performing agency" turned out to be Five Stones, an American agency directly related to to the U.S. vice president. He also found out that Five Stones had paid the Ministries of Education and Health each a million dollars to shut up about the fact that their schools and clinics were never going to be built.

It's pitch dark and cold. Gary and I get in his car, and we drive out the gate. The guards have a look of wonder on their faces due to the early hour and a curfew in place. Automatically I place my right hand on my heart, smile and nod at them. They smile as well. Gary speeds through the sleeping city, ignoring all the stop signs. He is tense and does not talk. We pass a few check points without any problems— everybody knows Gary. We arrive at the airport.

Gary had booked me on the 6:00 a.m. flight, it's 4:00 now. He wants to ensure I make it safely to the airport before getting trapped in Kabul's early mad traffic. The imminent threat that hangs over my head is palpable. Gary says, "Call me when you board, so I can relax, knowing you made it out and call me when you arrive in Colombo." We fully understood that the Taliban was in fact, the Americans paying Afghans to target particular people. Now, I am a target. He gives me a big hug.

Chapter 27
AFTER THE TSUNAMI

I fly via Dubai where our central UNOPS operational support unit is based. I'm given a set of Thuraya satellite phones to communicate along the destroyed coasts of Sri Lanka where the phone network is out of order, $10,000 to cover our first week's expenses and a letter stating that I have the money and the phones in my luggage on behalf of the UN for the tsunami response activities in Sri Lanka.

I land in Colombo at 5:20 a.m., early morning. I do not sleep a wink all night. The passengers are a mix of white people with predominantly khaki or army green-colored clothing with laptop briefcases and sunglasses, and Sri Lankans returning to their home country after the tsunami to look for their families or support them. The Sri Lankans are restless in anticipation of what they are about to find out. Who knows what they've lost, which family members are missing. The pilot announces: "In the shadow of the recent events here in Sri Lanka, I still wish to welcome you in paradise." It all feels strange. It feels like I'm part of a flock of vultures swooping down on prey, now when hundreds of millions are pledged to the affected areas. It was only two weeks ago that the unprecedented earthquake just off the coast of Sumatra had sent massive tsunami waves to bordering continents.

Palm trees look like black silhouettes against the pale morning sky. The smell in the air is so different from the dry cold air of Kabul always filled with a mix of freshly baked nan bread, woodfires and open sewerage. Sri Lanka, in contrast, reminds me a bit of Thailand, humid and warm with scents of thick tuk-tuk exhaust blended with sweet curry aromas from the food stalls on the streets.

People are very friendly; they smile at me and greet me when they walk past. I see women with bare midriffs, men with only a sarong and bare torsos. In my sleepy state, it all looks a bit obscene, all that naked flesh. I am so accustomed to Afghanistan where you are not allowed to show any skin at all, except your arms. I am surprised how I consider that normal and now react to nudity like this. It takes me a while to realize that it is normal here, this is another country. The timeframe in which Gary had called me to his guesthouse and landing in Colombo has been less than two days. The transition is not easy at first, but then I slowly realize that I can dress differently too, loose T-shirts and no more long blouses to hide the zip of my trousers, a welcome allowance in this hot weather. I also notice how easy it is to go through the city, no restrictions, simply get in a tuk-tuk, a little noisy three-wheeler and buzz around. I really enjoy that, the freedom to move.

What should have been a two-week assessment turns into two months of nonstop exhausting work with my UNOPS colleague, Rainer. He had left Afghanistan a few days after the tsunami to do some explorations on the ground and I met him in our hotel when I arrived in Colombo.

The International agency's attention is predominantly on Galle down the south-east coast of Sri Lanka, the place where tourists were affected by the tsunami, and that seized the international media attention. We decide to go the opposite direction, then descend along the west coast to do damage assessments at our own pace. North Sri Lanka is Tamil Tiger territory and is a complicated place to gain access and establish projects because every move is controlled by the Tigers. This gives us grounding, purpose, as not many agencies aim to venture out there. It feels ridiculous to even mention, but there is competition among agencies to scoop up as many as possible projects, confirm sites and claim project activity for the media, often overlooking the long-term impact or needs, or disregarding how social or governmental structures work.

Rainer and I are not so interested in taking part in the race. We go to the UNICEF office to meet Ted, the country director, and Jasmin, the head of education, who invited us. I instantly like them, and we kick the collaboration off with an aligned vision of what the UNICEF projects need to be. It is clear what we need to do in the next few weeks.

Rainer and I board a flight to Jaffna in the North of Sri Lanka and have literally just some basic clothing and a laptop with us. As soon as we land, we hit the ground running into eighteen-hour days, barely eating or sleeping. My body is still adjusting from a Kabul winter to the Sri Lankan hot humidity. I must be pushing myself on adrenaline because I am physically and emotionally exhausted from what I had been through in Afghanistan. What weighs heaviest on me is that, after USAID separated me from my staff, I had been unable to see them again before I left. I often cry, thinking of Qader Bibi, afraid I will never see her again because of her poor health.

We travel along the destroyed coast, meet with community representatives, talk to locals who lost their houses or family members. We visit and document destroyed schools. The second stop is Kilinochchi. We arrange a meeting at the headquarters of the notorious Tamil Tigers. We are welcomed, very officially, and escorted to a large room with a projection screen and other equipment. Everything is very well-organized and presented.

I am impressed by how organized they are. They hand us a list with the assessment data of all the schools they have already surveyed and prioritized. In just two weeks! They are so overly organized, like with military precision, that it is creepy, and we leave a few hours later, feeling rather unsettled. We have conversations between us about what the implications are. What happens if our assessment comes up with higher needs for different schools? Are we in a position to make changes to the list if our findings point in that direction? We are quite convinced that the list is not according to our priorities for rebuilding but based on favoritism, politics and family alliances. We agree we will follow the list but stay in line with our damage assessment criteria.

As we travel to Mullaitivu, sure enough, most of the schools on the list are not even on the coast, but inland where there is no impact of the tsunami. Rainer meets with the community leaders while I map out each building, draw floorplan sketches, to mark the damage, list all the materials used, especially paying attention to all the asbestos roofing that was damaged and then dangerous. I take detailed photos and write elaborate descriptions of each situation, including data about the number of children, type of school, number of classrooms, presence of toilets on the premises. Some schools are a total write-off, and I indicate the layout of the destroyed school where new construction is essential. In the evening, I organize all the photos in folders with each school location and make a report per school, with current situation and reconstruction requirements.

Where new construction is needed, UNICEF asks me to develop a child-friendly school concept, with playgrounds, number of classrooms based on maximum thirty children per class, proper toilet facilities, water supply, rainwater collection systems, yards with fruit trees and boundaries around the school so the children could be safe. And in case of refurbishing, I have to design the upgrade of the school to meet the child-friendly school standards.

After surveying Jaffna to Mullaitivu, Trincomalee, Batticaloa, then around the south coast to Galle and all the way southeast coast to Hambantota, we return to Colombo. I work with UNICEF to develop the standards for the child-friendly school design to be approved by the Ministry of Education as the new building standards, as per UNICEF requirements for implementation. During my surveys, I was shocked to find asbestos roof sheets on every school. If we wanted to build child-friendly schools, then the new building standards had to include a ban on the use of asbestos. That could be tricky because the local economy was thriving with the asbestos factories doing overtime to meet the enormous demand for rebuilding materials.

Rainer and I work night and day and every day of the week. We rarely take any time to relax, but when we do, we go to the old colonial-style Galle Face Hotel where internationals hang out and enjoy the lavish expat life.

Rainer and I sit on the patio with a beer to cool down and catch a breath, and a casually dressed guy, ripped jeans and short-sleeved, unassuming T-shirt, walks towards us to sit down on the table next to us. I've seen him before, know him quite well, but for the life of me cannot remember in which country we have worked together. In disaster relief work, people follow the disasters and over the years, you see familiar faces in every new country, so I am trying to remember, but nothing. After a while, it bugs me so much that I turn around and say, "I know you, but cannot remember from where." He looks at me rather amused and with a beautifully kind smile, says, "I'm Sting, I'm here because my girlfriend is the ambassador for the tsunami relief." Sting is amused, me slightly embarrassed, then we laugh so hard and have another beer. Isn't it funny that when we meet people out of their typical context, we cannot remember who they are?

By the time I leave Sri Lanka on 7 March 2005, we established an agreed first-ever official ban on the use of asbestos for all schools and clinics, agreed directives for the design of child-friendly schools, a selection list with renovation and new to be built schools, a selection list for the clinics to be built, an office with cars, and twenty-four Sri Lankan staff members we've interviewed and trained.

We receive the news that a plane crashed in Afghanistan, a KAM airplane got lost in the snowstorm above Kabul and crashed. We learn that Andrea was on that plane, a dear colleague, an Italian architect and just a beautiful man. The news devastates me. I also feel that weird sense of envy that I often have when people pass. He is free now, and I am still here. I might have these thoughts when I am beyond exhausted and do not have the resources to incur any more emotional stress. Andrea left a wife and a nine-year-old daughter. I want to write to his daughter, tell her about her father. I want her to know that I lost my father too when I was her age. I get entangled and overwhelmed in my own emotions and just never send the mail.

The last months in Afghanistan had left me empty, I felt kicked in the teeth and ribs from every side. Adding the loneliness through exhaustion here in Sri Lanka, topped with the loss of Andrea, the absence of goodbyes to my friends in Afghanistan; I am fucking depleted. I am an empty battery with broken cells, the acid leaking out. When attempting to charge, all my wires frizzle.

Chapter 28

EARTHQUAKES AND MADNESS

I still want to go to Aceh because it is my opportunity to go to the country where my father had lived for years after the war, the country that we had wayang dolls from at home, paintings on silk, daggers and krisses. The Indonesian food we used to eat, the sambal my dad put on peanut butter sandwiches and me pretending I liked it, the kroepoek, the atjar tjampoer, the green hard-boiled duck eggs that were so salty they got stuck in my throat when I tried to swallow. He also explained that if you wanted to say a word in plural, you simply said it twice in Bahasa Indonesian. Now I can go there, and I want to trace some of my father's roots.

One of my other colleagues from Afghanistan had been sent to Aceh for a quick assessment, but Joe had family problems. Joe has a family so he either had to find a job where his wife and kids could be with him or stop this work. Banda Aceh is definitely not a family station, with the toxic water, horrible hygiene, lack of health care and education, and the general safety situation after thirty years of civil war and isolation.

Colombo, however, is a family duty station already, so Joe and I swap projects. He moves to Sri Lanka and takes over my job, and I go to Aceh where I can build my own project from scratch. So often I was hired as a project manager with an already described and budgeted project, that was always different than what I think the project should be; in how it would match much better with the needs of the locals. The situation in Aceh is a lot more complicated than in Sri Lanka because Aceh had the consequences of a huge earthquake and the massive tsunami; Sri Lanka "only" had the water damage—destructive but much easier to rebuild.

In Aceh, the whole environment has shifted, affecting the building codes and engineering practices. There are two major fault lines close to each other and along the coastal lines of Indonesia; the upper one is known for the "ring of fire", a long series of volcanos along the fault. The lower one just off the coast. The region has been inactive for the last 200 years, with no major earthquakes rattling the islands. The seismic requirements for reconstruction in Aceh have dramatically changed. The seismic zoning, building standards and structural building requirements now have to be developed to be compatible to the new circumstances.

On 8 March, I arrive in Jakarta, meet Paul and go to the hotel to sleep, sleep, sleep. He does not let me go to Aceh right off, but working from Jakarta seems ridiculous. The internal political tensions in the UNOPS are a lot more tangible in Indonesia. Rainer has managed to keep the Bangkok office out but the man in Jakarta reports to Bangkok to keep them happy there and because he fit better in the Bangkok mentality. Paul, my temporary boss, is on his own in an office in Jakarta and has not even been to Aceh or Nias Island once in the four months as coordinator. Bangkok is not impressed by Gary sending his people from Afghanistan, so from the start, I feel resistance, and I am so not interested in these internal politics. There is work to do!

The devastation is overwhelming. The water is acid, and I get a bad burning rash under my eyes and armpits. The food is bad, oily, and deep fried. I gain weight in no time and my blood pressure is super high, like the stress of the project.

The setting up of projects in Aceh is very complicated by the layering of problems and lack of local capacity, one third of the population died, which is severely negated. There are six different seismic categories. Every category indicates the probability, movement and expected strength of the earthquakes. Category 0 are the regions where the probability of earthquakes is nil, the Netherlands, for example; category 6 are the regions where the heaviest and most destructive earthquakes can be expected. Before the huge earthquake of 26 December, Aceh was classified in zones three and four because the region had been seismically inactive for approximately 200 years, but now that had changed, and they realized that the building regulations were not sufficient anymore for the forces the area was now exposed to.

One year before the big earthquake there already was a big earthquake on Simeulue, an island on the coast of Aceh, the first earthquake after 200 years of silence. When the earthquake of 26 December followed with the destructive tsunami, the area became active continuously.

With the arrival of the international attention and the money for the reconstruction of Aceh, the Ministry of Public Works decided to take the opportunity and adapt the building regulations and seismic classification in view of the expected building activities. The zones were adjusted to zones five and six, the highest categories. Safety calculations belong to every category for the design of a building structure, the calculation of the thickness of the columns, the design of thickness and order of the reinforcement steel, the connections, the strength of the concrete, the thickness of floors and foundations. Everything changed, the regulations, the requirements, the safety standards and all the related calculations.

This had huge consequences, because one could argue that if you took the new regulations seriously, no existing building in Aceh would still meet the standards for safe buildings anymore. The renovation of damaged schools would then actually not be allowed because according to the calculations for zone five and six the structure of the building was unsafe. Renovation would only be allowed if there would be a full retro fitting to reinforce the frame.

The adjusted requirements also meant that no architect or engineer in Aceh knew how to design a building in conformity with the new requirements, and no contractor knew how to build a building in accordance with the new standards. Building is a habit; contractors and designers do what they are used to. Buildings like schools are quite standard, the same dimensions for the classrooms and standard sized corridors, teacher rooms etc. The old habits of the designers and builders had to be changed due to the new building regulations, and changing habits is probably the most difficult process ever.

Two years previously, I had pleaded with the project engineers of the ministry for education in Kabul for another roof edge detail of a traditional sun-dried mud bricks school construction with wooden beams and mud on the roof. This detail would be a lot safer against the horizontal forces that would occur in an earthquake there. I explained the new detail and they understood it perfectly but did not want to sign the building drawings because the new detail was on it. When I asked why they did not approve it they unfailingly said we understand that this detail is safer but that is not the way we do it. This is how we make a roof edge detail, and they made the well-known sketch, and therefore, we cannot sign off the drawings. I again explained elements of the safety and the prevention of the collapse of the roof, but every time, "yes, we understand but this is how we do it". After thinking long and hard and trying various arguments I found what would made them sign. The solution was in how the finished roof edge would look on the outside. When they saw the details of the "cosmetic" finishing and were convinced that the exterior of the building would not change much, they signed off and approved the building plans, but it cost me at least two days of pleading (and messing about with engineers who, of course, enjoyed discussing with me building details and arguing how and what).

Changing habits is most difficult because I must find out what the people's motivations are, to understand why people do what they do. If I do not understand why they do what they do, I cannot change anything, but I actually have to get into their skin to understand how they think, what makes them act. That is my challenge in this work. I want to understand why the people act as they do, then I can build on that and connect to it. The idea is not to change people but to build safer schools for the children, and everything centers on this mission.

Contractors are few and far between in Aceh and are all intertwined with the authorities who commission the contracts. The contracting systems are a different story in themselves and actually mean that there is no contracting based on competition, but various parties receive so-called "taxes" from the contractor who receives the contract. As everybody has been paid already, including the authorities who assign the contract, building inspections are not required either. Quality control of materials or concrete strength does not exist and where there are token laboratories, you can just pay for good results. We have to "adapt" that mentality with our engineers too.

There is a total lack of trained people, and the engineers and architects in place have no applicable knowledge for the task waiting in Aceh. In addition to all these difficulties the use of concrete is hugely unknown. Concrete and its use are a science; you do not just bang together some gravel, sand and cement and cast a pillar, even though that was the way it was used before in Aceh. Standards for zones five and six prescribe concrete disks of at least 25 MPa (megapascals), and that strength is not easy to achieve.

The huge demand for building activities after the destructive earthquake and the tsunami require first training people in material and quality control, and in everything involved in construction, from designs to delivery. A whole group of the population would have to be trained to have the slightest chance of building safe schools. And would it not be a perfect opportunity to arrange this properly from the start with all the money and know-how that arrived in Aceh? But it didn't happen.

The media pressure is probably a big disaster on top of the natural disaster after all that money is donated for the tsunami victims. All that money creates expectations from the authorities, the people who pin their hopes on outside help, and the eyes of the whole world who has pledged billions in the expectation that because so much money is collected, Aceh will be out of the woods quickly. Numerous organizations come to Aceh. There is so much money that everybody can do their own programs. There are no directives. Local authorities are not equipped for this scale of work, and the national authorities in Jakarta try to get a grip at all costs on the big international presence doing everything solo.

After the first phase of the emergency help, it is a completely bizarre situation where people with the best intentions create total chaos: nurses building schools, doctors building hospitals and well-intended volunteers helping to build houses, with everybody convinced they are doing the right thing. The egos of the organizations and individual volunteers create a situation of competition instead of exchange and cooperation. The organizations in the field are exposed to the shortcomings of the given situation with donors breathing down their necks and murderous expectations of the universe for a better world for poor people who had survived the tsunami.

The madness in disasters is that all organizations go to the area "en masse" and plant their flag before the country itself indicates what they want or not and how they want help. Because organizations bring money, the affected country immediately seems to be in a dependent position. Help organizations are no longer at the service of people but primarily at the service of a whole industry that slowly has morphed into a vehicle for donors who want to see their interests met.

Just imagine, hypothetically: the tsunami happens, emergency aid is given, and everybody takes over the place. A coordinating organization makes an inventory with the authorities and creates a plan with priorities for the next five years. Based on the plan, organizations who can handle part of it are invited and monitored by the same coordinating organization that developed the plan. The whole plan includes the present capacity, availability of materials and feasibility. Such a plan would run over ten years and is based on the full construction of the society in all its aspects. The objective is not to build schools against the pressure while there are no materials or capacity but build up capacity to build schools safely and do a lot more than only build schools. Imagine, how much sense would that make?

But okay, I am crazy! I am so crazy that I take on the fight with UNICEF and advise to firstly, not repair the existing schools, and secondly, insist that we not build a single school in the first year after the tsunami, but build capacity by training people. The pressure of the media and the Indonesian authorities who have been promised 500 schools by UNICEF is huge, and maybe they understand my message in private, but to the outside world, they face the pressure and make promises and in turn, put more pressure on me. I create the TSU, the Technical Support Unit, to train architects, engineers, quality controllers and building supervisors. Together, we build a 13 x15 meters-large, new office in the backyard of our office, with coconut trees snapped off by the tsunami and lightweight steel frames. In the central part between the columns, I insert a tennis table.

I need room to move, and the table in the center of the office has an important function. Somebody starts playing in the overflowing work program, to let off steam, and get rid of energy, after being immobile for hours in front of the computer. In the TSU, I work with forty-three colleagues: one Australian and the rest Indonesians, architects and engineers. That team becomes more fun after a while, but it takes an incredible amount of energy to let people notice that building capacity is the only way we can do the program that will ultimately be successful. We need a long time to demonstrate that more investment in training will provide results, but the pressure is too high to build schools immediately and our timespan is not long enough.

People in Aceh are very reserved and do not quickly make contact. I feel no special connection with the Aceh people, I can't read them, I don't get them. I cannot see the difference between someone who just lost her mother or someone who just had a festive meal with friends, and I find that very difficult. I feel nothing around them. In Afghanistan, having been invited daily for a meal in their home, for a wedding, for tea and to meet their wife and children, in my sixteen months in Aceh without any invites, it's a cold contrast. People are distant and seem emotionless. The praying never annoyed me in Afghanistan. I felt a deep respect there for the way people practiced their faith. I joined in prayers in Afghanistan. In Aceh, the praying annoys me because it seems as if they use it at all times to avoid working. It's a display of what good Muslims are. They come to work too late, then need breakfast, at the office, then snacks with coffee, then lunch, then praying again, then again coffee or tea with snacks and praying again at four. They never leave the office later than five.

As consolation, I think about my father often, knowing he had spent time here. My mother and father met in the laboratory of the salt industry in the village of Boekelo. My dad was twenty-eight years old and worked in the lab when my mother, as a young eighteen-year-old girl, was introduced there as the new lab technician and given a guided tour. The moment they saw each other my father thought, *I want to marry that girl*, and my mother thought, *that man*! Because he was so much older, we did not know a lot about his younger years. But we did know that in the years before he married my mother, he went to crashed airplanes at night as a young man to nick their meters and command panels. In 1945, he boarded a ship to Indonesia as a radio engineer, against his mother's wishes.

After three long months on the ship, the war was over when they finally reached Jakarta, then Bavaria. He used to tell great stories about those three months on the ship, that they sailed through the Suez Canal and that when he wanted to eat fish, he had to stand on deck with his plate to catch the flying fish. The flying fish were magical in my imagination, images I could fantasize about. Unreal, but in Aceh, I see them fly out of the water with my own eyes, sailing meters above the water surface before they disappear again. Although they do not fly above the deck of the ship, they are truly magical animals, like I had imagined as a child.

Over time, I create a team that does more than just building schools. The TSU becomes a special team that achieves things and materializes work that attracts other organizations. We are an example of how to approach a project, and other organizations come to us for advice. The involvement so natural in Afghanistan takes months in Aceh to soak in. Afghanistan is my love, and I continue to compare Aceh with Afghanistan.

In early April, after a month in Aceh, I go to Canada for ten days holiday. In Aceh, I had spent my time to visit the destroyed areas, to speak with the people of UNICEF and established contacts with the local authorities. There were still strong aftershocks every day, sometimes more than one a day, sometimes nothing for a day, but always the looming threat of one.

Though it is 40 degrees, I sleep with my clothes on in the suffocating humidity, so when I have to run outside during the night, I am not naked. Wherever I go, I always identify possible escape routes and assess the risks for being locked in if the building were to collapse.

Earthquakes affect your psyche in a strange way. The earthquakes vary from 4 to 6.2 on the Richter scale, and some of 6.9 and one of 7.2. I literally lose the ground from under my feet, and I shake. I start to feel earthquakes when there are none and after a while, I place a glass of water on a cupboard as an external proof of an earthquake if there truly is one. When I feel something, I look at the glass. If the water sways, we have to run. If the water does not move, it is only in my head, which happens more and more often.

Marlene had bought a house in Canada with my money and had not even told me about it. In Canada for a short R&R, I am exhausted, and don't know where to find the strength anymore to express my anger, to do anything. Marlene had put the content of a box of magnet words on the fridge door. I am sitting on the floor in front of the fridge. I move the magnets around, forming French words and weird sentences. I make formations of words and irrational poems. I am so absent-minded I don't even realize that I have been aimlessly messing about with those magnets for hours, until Marlene is so disturbed that she grabs my shoulder. She shakes me and says, "You freak me out. What are you doing?" The door of the fridge looks like a poem by a madwoman and is completely illegible. I stare at the sentences and realize how far away I am. It scares the crap out of me.

I call a psychologist who has experience with people living in two worlds. With a few intense sessions, and a couple of weeks off work, I feel ready to go back to Aceh again. (*Yeah, right!*)

Back in Aceh, I set up field offices, stay in Calang on the west coast for a while, where everything is gone, not one house left. We sleep in tents, recruit staff and strengthen contacts with the authorities. A new project manager arrives from Afghanistan, a very nice man, but clueless about the organization of a large-scale project. He locks himself in his room and lets me do the project. When I encourage him to hold staff meetings, he says he gets lost amongst people, that I have to do that. This situation does not last long. An earthquake in Pakistan occurs, and he is sent there. I continue with the project before the arrival of the next project manager.

By the time the new project manager arrives, the situation in Bangkok becomes so dire that they take over the project from "Gary's people". Everybody is being directly or indirectly removed and Bangkok sends its own team who are friendly with the children's fund, which found good media more important than the actual aim of the projects. By chasing positive media reports, they make one mistake after the other.

Working in Aceh is a life of hard work, long hours and only work. I slowly change into a bitter and twisted person who stands on the side of right but can't do anything about what really should happen. I only see the stupidity around me—idiots who do not see what must be done. I increasingly get caught in achieving less and less because I can no longer cooperate due to frustrations and exhaustion. I create enemies in my head. I no longer have the flexibility or the energy to find ways to make things possible.

Marlene is offered a job at UNICEF in Aceh and finally, an old dream of ours is realized, being together in a place where we both have work. But it comes too late, we are no longer the same. We celebrate Christmas with the orphans just outside Banda Aceh, a Christmas for which we had collected clothes and other useful things for the orphans and widows and distribute them instead of celebrating our own Christmas, but it doesn't help. The feeling is gone. My feeling is gone. The frustrations about shameless politics between and inside the organizations who think personal agendas are more important than building safe schools for the children of Aceh erodes my desire. It's a conflict of interest I no longer can stomach and fight.

The stress is related to Aceh, a place under Sharia law with many local interpretations. Being in a place where public lashings of women are happening as a way of amusement in the middle of the day, the Sharia police function to harass women. Trying to work around the donor requirements adds other stress.

In Aceh, they do not pronounce an "s" if it is the last letter of a word, so my name, "Babs" in Indonesian becomes "Bob", and with all the politeness here, I am always addressed as "Mr. Bob". They know

I am not a mister. I also get a man's status and to my amazement, I even have to turn down marriage proposals in very different countries, not in the least because those marriages would have been with girls.

Site engineers, who just graduated as students with no experience and who I trained for six weeks while paying them salaries, come in with a petition demanding life insurance in their package. The audacity. I fire them all on the spot. If they change their minds, they can come back at 4:00 p.m. They do except for one.

I invent new tendering methods based on what is called their "tax system" that consists of paying other contractors to lower their bid, then get the contract, then build low-quality buildings, with salt water in the concrete, river gravel instead of crushed gravel. My tendering is based on building a proposal with a set price for the specified materials, then add the labor, so we set the minimum price, like I did in Afghanistan to bridge the fact that a contract is in fact, a conflict of interest; the contractor wants the most profit, and I want the best quality. Now, the proposal I need is about their knowledge of quality, standards and capacity, not just the price. We inform them that everyone can have a project so no need for taxes.

Paul and I set up the office in Banda Aceh and hire the first staff. Paul decides to stay in Banda Aceh, while we decide that I should establish an office in Calang, where the need is highest. The community has nothing.

It is hard to set priorities when everything is destroyed, and the tsunami killed a quarter million people. The echo of the deceased is in the many stories that people share about the horrendous noise of the water, coming at them like a huge monster, devouring everything in its path.

The old Russian MI6 UN helicopter flies between Calang and Banda Aceh, but this time, I travel by road from Banda Aceh to

Calang, along the completely destroyed south coast. We are the very first people to drive to Calang, and the trip is treacherous at best.

I feel a weird sense of excitement, of adventure to try and make it to Calang by road. The disaster work has made me excited about dangerous things. I feel alive and energized. At the same time, I am hyper alert that those sentiments live inside of me. I will keep it there. My excitement is not appropriate to the situation, note to self.

As we leave Banda Aceh with two UN pick-ups, we leave the last stretch of houses that are still standing. When we drive around the mountain, a huge ship blocks the road. Surreal display of the power of the waves. Our first obstacle. The road is washed out and we navigate around patches of asphalt that are islands on washed out sand. The wall of water had pushed in a few kilometers inland, and as it retreated, it formed real rivers and sandbanks. Riverbeds perpendicular to the road, making it close to impossible to pass. The whole coastline has changed. Every time we come to an obstacle, there are the locals, building makeshift bridges from the thousands of washed-up coconut trees. We can see extensive fields of snapped off and washed-up coconut trees along the whole coast. It is available and free, but in my mind, I am assessing that it is not the safest material to use for weightbearing structures.

Arriving at a real river where the bridge has washed out, we are directed to drive our cars on floaters of tied together coconut trees, tied up blue jerrycans and metal oil drums along the edges; the floaters are super tippy under the weight of the cars, and the locals are frantically yelling directions at each other to push the floater to the other side and not losing the vehicles.

I am wondering about the rest of the trip. So far, we have only traveled an hour, and the trip to Calang is a minimum of three hours' drive—when the road is intact! We stand on the floater next to the cars. In case something happens, we can at least jump off and swim to the other side. Twelve guys push long poles to the riverbed below to move the floater across.

After a horrendous and exhausting day through sheer devastation, I arrive in Calang, the Ground Zero of the tsunami. There isn't a building or road left; it is 45 degrees C and very humid, the air thick. I wake up in a white tent, on a stretcher. I wake up from a deep sleep, filled with dreams. Breathing is heavy, the tent of thick plasticized canvas, part of the emergency UN camp. I am coming to grips with the sheer devastation around me.

The water rolled in at 15 meters (45 feet) high here in Calang. Over morning coffee in a makeshift wooden shack, I meet some locals. Acehnese people are generally quite reserved, but after their traumatic experiences, they share how they escaped, had seen their children wash away, how they had to let go of the hand of their mother to save themselves. The guilt, the agony of the memories. Their faces are telling.

In the camp are mostly guys, white guys, former U.S. Marines or military in emergency operation mode. I have gained weight during the first months in Banda Aceh. Deep fried food, toxic water, no fresh vegetables, and stress.

My shirts span my breasts and in the humid heat, the confinement and pressure on my breasts is a constant sense of repulsion about them. I have vivid dreams of taking a large knife and cutting them open, emptying them link a melon, and sewing them back up. I wonder so often if I can't just do that, it can't be that hard? In detail I explore all the possible consequences if I were to actually do that. It could go wrong and then I would end up in hospital, where they would treat me, but then already flat, it would be okay in the end. *Flat!* The biggest deterrent is that I would probably pass out before I got them emptied, and then I would wake up in a hospital where they would fix them back. Endless scenarios of what can happen, what technique I would use to cut, where to cut. I explore every little detail under my skin to understand, contemplate what needs to happen to my chest to become flat, gloriously flat.

My health is suffering badly. The life of internationals in Banda Aceh is terrible, drowning in lots of alcohol and bad behavior. It is a hard place to be, adding to my stress.

Chapter 29

BACK TO HAPPY
FOR A COST

After an intense three-month mission in Darfur as one of twenty-three specialists for the UN Joint Assessment Mission to work on the early recovery plans in case peace would break out, I arrive in Vancouver. There is nothing left of my marriage. We are strangers, and all I can think of is going back to Afghanistan.

I receive an email from Vilja. As I read her words, a knot forms in my stomach with years of uncried tears. "Sadly, this is not just a chatty mail. But I must tell you something you won't like to hear. Babs, I am ill. Seriously ill. I have an untreatable cancer of the liver. Unfortunately, it has spread all over. So, no chemo, radiation, or liver transplant for me. Your old miss will not become dramatically bald, or shuffle around in the hospital with a drip on a stick. I have two to twelve months to go according to the consultant."

I immediately fly to the Netherlands. It will not happen to me that she makes her exit without me seeing her. We talk and she makes us a sandwich. She still smokes caballeros without filter tips and although I stopped smoking eight years ago, I light up with her. Vilja is not afraid of death. "I simply know something more than you know, Babs. We know we will die, I just have a deadline, which you haven't, you might even die before I do," she jokes.

She says like a teacher to a pupil, "Babs, know that you have become someone who young people look up to, like you used to look up to me. Now I'm passing you the torch, I am so proud of you."

We say goodbye at the front door. I walk out and turn around to hug her. She stands in the door opening, in the light. Inside was quite dark because light hurt her eyes. Standing in the light, I suddenly see that the white of her eyes is bright yellow. I stare the illness that is destroying her right in the eyes. I well up, kiss her soft cheeks, give her a big hug and say, "I love you." I get in the car, wave at her and drive away.

I burst out in tears; I crank up Mercedes Sosa's "Gracias A La Vida". (Thanks to life.) On the highway between Odijk, Utrecht and Amsterdam, I find a slow truck I stay behind at 70km/h. I cry my eyes out; I am still crying as I reach Amsterdam.

When the crying finally stops, I feel stripped naked and new.

Back in Canada again, I search for jobs to get me back to Afghanistan and apply for one in Jalalabad. Within days, I score an invite for an interview and soon after the interview, I get the job offer. It is a management position to oversee basic infrastructure projects in Jalalabad for an American agency. The irony! Two years prior, I was traumatized by a forced departure with a window of twelve hours to get on the plane from Afghanistan to Sri Lanka, to escape the Americans; and now, two years later, I am on a contract with the State Department implementing for USAID.

I have many internal heated conversations with myself, ranging from "Are you nuts, Alink?" to excitement of going back to see my Afghan friends again, to "What the fuck? How am I going to manage all the insane restrictions that Americans put on their staff, which in fact, makes the work impossible?" I mull over what this means and feel into all the things I feel, the inner conflicts, a sense of fear, the wonder whether this is smart.

But I figure that it is easy to complain about a system from the outside, where now I can possibly be inside, in the role of a wolf in sheep's clothing perhaps but making sure that my projects actually benefit the Afghans, instead of being an instrument to whitewash government funding into the hands of private contractors. So, be it with a heavy heart yet filled with anxious anticipation of returning to Afghanistan, all confused with the contract with an American organization, I notify Marlene that I am going to leave.

I sign the contract, which reads that my salary is $20,000 per month, tax-free and on top of that, they pay for my flights, guesthouse, medical, R&R and danger pay. The contract is initially for six months, extendable. *Deep breaths, Alink.* Yes, it shows exactly what these organizations do: funnel government funding back to private contractors and internationals. It is big business. But maybe it is better that I get the money and can make sure that it goes to Afghans and local people and projects I can support, than going to an expat banking all the cash back in America.

I leave the apartment block with a deep sense of relief; it is over, and it is all good. I am going back to Afghanistan, but with a stopover in the Netherlands, Vilja is deteriorating fast since I saw her just a couple of weeks ago.

Vilja is on a bed in the living room. Her hair looks disheveled, and her arms are covered with scabs and scratch wounds. She lays on her side, her belly distended like she is pregnant with triplets. Her face shows agony, the yellow has spread from her eyes to her whole skin. Her whole body being poisoned. The curtains are closed, the light dim. Vanya, her daughter, is there, and I sit down on a little stool, next to her bed, stroking her over her face, talking sweet words to her. Vilja tells me that it is organized. On Monday, the doctor will perform euthanasia. Two days from now.

Suddenly she looks at me, her eyes clearing up a bit like she has a sudden insight. "You are here now, now all is good," she says. "I can go now." She sounds determined in contrast to her close to passed out state, just before. I reach for Vanya's hand. She's only a teenager, and we carefully hold Vilja's hands, stroke her gently. I bend over to her and kiss her on her forehead and cheeks. "It is okay, Vilja, you can go, it is okay, we are here, we're okay." She closes her eyes, and she lets go.

The departure from Afghanistan two years ago was so rough, and still feels like a deep flesh wound. After two intense months in Sri Lanka, eighteen months in Aceh, the three-month stint in Darfur and now, here I am, on my way to a new job in Jalalabad. I have longed to go back to Afghanistan since that day I involuntarily left, but all the while, Gary had strongly advised against it. It is still too dangerous. "They still have a price on your head," he says matter-of-factly. Two years later, it should be okay to go.

This job with this American agency is very political, I am well-aware of that. Deep down, I know that this is not the right job for me, but my wounds and longing to be back with my staff, my Afghan family, is stronger than reasoning.

I am not a stranger to facing resistance with donors in projects motivated by the hidden agendas of the donor. I have experienced that with the Nuristani schools, where my objective to the project was to employ Afghan men to build the schools for their children, which was not quite the aim of the donor, hence the interrogation just two years ago, after which I had to leave the country.

It is a challenge to work as a "wolf in sheep's clothing" to make a difference for the benefit of the Afghans who I am there for, but it is the only way to stay true to my own values.

When I was five, my iconic grandma, who was raised in poverty, grabbed my shirt and pulled me in her face, and said with determination in her voice to get through to me: "You…you have to go into politics, and then never forget where you come from." When I built the Nuristani schools, I realized, that is exactly what I was doing. I am working for poor people; I have not forgotten where I come from. The Nuristani schools project taught me something that most people

254

haven't got a clue about. Building schools or any reconstruction projects in Afghanistan is hyper-political.

International agencies tend to toot their horns about how their projects help poor people, bring democracy, support women's rights, build water and sanitation system, schools, clinics, and roads, and so on, that they work for the benefit of the Afghans. Most people on the ground have good intentions and mean well, but over the years, I have seen so much of the donor requirements ultimately bending people and projects in directions that did not serve the local people, as the narrative implies.

Returning after two years is emotional enough as it is, and now, I just signed a contract with an organization that embodied all that caused me to leave Afghanistan two years prior.

Couple of days later

I am driving from Kabul to Jalalabad, completely raw from losing Vilja, the images of her yellow eyes staring at me as we said our last goodbye, her largely extended belly and the terror of her body being slowly poisoned, causing horrendous itching that she uncontrollably scratched until bloody, imprinted in my memories.

This return to Afghanistan also marks the definite ending of my marriage, a marriage that was breached long before I found out that Marlene had been dating a male doctor at her work, in pursuing her wish for children. I did not know these facts then, but I felt it, and she felt so distant and unsafe. I chose where my heart was guiding me, back to my beloved Afghanistan, healing one heart while the other was shredded.

Tears are flowing over my cheeks and my dear friend and loyal driver, Gul Mohiuddin (brother of "my" Gul in Jalalabad), who picked me up from Kabul airport, kindly nods at me, hands me some tissues in the familiar kindness I have missed so dearly in these last two years.

He knows what returning to Afghanistan means to me after that forced departure in 2004.

The road I love so much between Kabul and Jalalabad has been surfaced, tarmacked during my absence. The road used to be dusty sand and gravel, covered with eaten out craters that exceeded the name, *pothole*. We used to drive very slowly to avoid them. The road winds through the high passes in the mountains; ascending through barren hills, entering the plateau where the remnants of war are everywhere. A tank turned landmark, destroyed villages, desolate outposts, mine fields marked with white and red rocks, indicating what has been cleared from mines and what not. Coming from Kabul, stunning purple mountains rise on other side of a lake well below the road; minerals color the rock with surreal hues.

This drive allows me to heal my way into landing back where my heart and soul are home. Mohiuddin looks at me, smiles with his gorgeously kind face, and nods. I can just be; he sees me, feels me. After two years, I can finally relax.

Steep ravines as we descend. Around the corner and across on the other side of the ravine, the ominous yellow dust track of the serpentine mine shows up. We drive through the series of narrow tunnels through the pass, the tunnels that are often obstructed by jingle trucks getting stuck against the arched ceiling.

It is winter and there are no Kuchis. Towards the winter and summer, caravans of Kuchis take up the sides of the road. They are the iconic nomadic people who migrate between Kabul and Jalalabad to escape the blistering summer heat of Jalalabad and avoid the harsh winters of Kabul. Huge caravans with massive camels, donkeys, children high up top of the dark brown canvas of the tents and sticks, all tied up around the sides of the camels. Women in bright red and green dresses, with metal decorations elaborately embroidered. The camels' heads are brightly decorated with yellow, red and green pompoms and extravagant jingle belts with tassels around their necks.

I always feel like we are time traveling when passing the Kuchis. They look at us, we look at them, and it is like we are in different times, witnessing, snatching a glimpse into a parallel universe.

Then the road starts winding and the parallel river flowing more rapidly, high waves rolling up against the banks that are barely reinforced. Halfway, we descend into the village of Sarobi, a dangerous bottleneck on this trip. A village where thousands of trucks from Pakistan, packed with building materials and food, pass through. A place where it is tempting to take a break, but with a risk of being robbed, so generally we pass through as fast as possible. Two years ago, it took five to six hours to make it from Kabul to Jalalabad. Now with the new tarmac, we pass through Sarobi after an hour and enter the barren, warm side of the end of the Hindu Kush Mountain range. Sarobi marks the halfway point, also the barrier between tropical Jalalabad and the land climate of Kabul.

It becomes glaringly obvious that the tarmac is not only positive, but it also poses a great danger. People drive like maniacs, and we witness many mangled cars on the side of the road, and experience a few near escapes from what could have killed us.

Half an hour after Sarobi, I see the Canadian toilets on the left side. It sounds weird, but it is a toilet block, built with Canadian funding, a total lifesaver halfway on a six-hour trip.

The toilet block is maintained by the sweetest old man, with a huge beard, barely any teeth left, the kindest guy. He makes sure that the toilets are clean, and he hands out toilet paper when you enter. I can't wait to see him again, and he is there! He recognizes me. I jump out the car and we hug. Not something any woman can do in Afghanistan, but I seem to get away with it. No one is surprised when we hug, and I love this man.

Gul doesn't know where Qader is. Apparently, she has moved away. I go to meet the DAI colleagues, settle in the guesthouse and just feel how it feels to be back in Jalalabad. I am introduced to my colleagues and instantly notice Daud, the QC engineer from IRD who made my life hell during the Nuristan school project. *Holy shit.* My heart races. How do I deal with him?

The following morning, I call him to my office and say, "You know, Daud, I know you are extremely good in quality control issues, and I need a good QC engineer who monitors the projects and our engineers. I am promoting you to be my QC engineer." By his handshake, it's a successful reconciliation.

In the first week, a delegation from Nuristan shows up at the gate, headed up by the governor himself. They set out for Jalalabad when they heard that Ms. Babs was back in Jalalabad. Jonathan, my boss, opens my door and says with a very puzzled face, "There is a whole delegation at the gate here to see you…"

I walk to the gate and ask the guards to please let them in. The governor and I openly hug each other. He puts a hand on my shoulder and says, "Babs, every newborn baby in Nuristan knows who Babs is." The weight of his words touches me deeply—my name now lives on in the stories that Nuristanis share with their children.

Back in the guesthouse Jonathan asks me who these people are and does not understand that the governor came to see me, not him. This creates the first tensions with Jonathan, and he starts obstructing my movements.

Gul calls with a message I'm longing to hear. "Babs jan, I found Qader Bibi, she lives in the outskirts of Samarkhyel." We waste no time in heading out to see her.

Gul and I visit her every two weeks or as often as I can, but every time I do, I am breaching the extra security rules Jonathan has put in place in order to control me. Breaching them further creates tensions. Qader had a stroke and has problems with her right side; she has little control over her hand and walks with difficulty, her leg drags. She looks so frail, yet her eyes have not lost the sparkles.

Floran works with USAID, lives in our guesthouse and her friend comes over one day. Matin Maulawizada, a famous make-up artist who works with celebrities like Angelina Jolie, has his own charity, Afghan Hands, facilitating literacy projects for women who do embroidery for the shawls Matin sells to fund the projects. He left Afghanistan with his parents when he was eighteen, and now lives in New York. Matin and I instantly become friends.

Jonathan is threatened by me, tells me I am scattered and all over the place, even though I exceed all the projections and goals in my project descriptions. Jonathan's dislike of me topped with weird power dynamics between me and my two male colleagues, Phil and Mahe, who are engineers, slowly spawns an impossible work environment. I really need to leave; I am surrounded by restrictive and patronizing men.

I witness a roadside bomb after which excessive shooting breaks out, bullets flying over our heads, we dive behind a mount on the riverbed. Marines kill nineteen of the Afghans, all people we know very well from being on the project side, our workers, women, children. My photos and testimony are later used to expel the Marines in an unusual court case.

The last time I see Qader before I leave Afghanistan we see each other once more. She arrives at my guesthouse because due to the oppressive security restrictions, I am not allowed to go to Samarkhyel that day. Gul picked her up and they arrive at the gate. I feel self-conscious of the situation in the big American guesthouse, a place that does not jive with me while living in Afghanistan. Working with DAI, there is no way I can escape from it.

Outside on the patio with the guards, we drink tea and share laughs and hugs. The guards are clearly taking in what they see. They are not used to seeing any of my colleagues be with Afghans the way I am having tea with Gul and Qader. When Qader is ready to leave, we get up and I put my arms around her. She holds my face with her weathered hands, looking at me with her gorgeous blue eyes. I notice how she is emotional, reflecting in her eyes. She says, "I will not be here when you come back to Afghanistan. I am tired and my body is finished. Khalashu, (enough / finished)," she says with a big gesture and then cracks into her contagious laugh.

I hug her and don't want to let go. I kiss her beautiful face several times, she kisses me and cries. We cry, we laugh, we hold, hold on to let go. Moments later, I watch her walk out onto the street with Gul. That wiggling, little woman, with her long white hair and grown out orange ends under the black head scarf I gave her years ago, which since, she always wore. That image etched in my mind.

I feel so much love, it alters me and barely realize that I am saying a prayer for her, saying the words out loud, as I watch them walk away, "Qader Bibi, source of love. May your soul fly freely as a butterfly, amongst everyone, above everything, released from the suffering of all that your body endured, and may you be welcomed by Allah as a special guest whose soul has never shown a crack. Your love will travel with me for the rest of my life, dera manana (thank you) dear Qader, go in love."

So many things are wrong in my environment that I'm fighting inside to stay in the place that truly defined what I wanted home to feel like. It's not working. It's suffocating. I am done, exhausted, have no fiber in my body left to fight, and I'm torn, heartbroken and empty. I've been empty for some time, and been going on pure adrenaline, often fueled by the fights to do what I needed to do. Had the fights and the need for adrenaline become a way of life? Could I be in a situation where I do not need to fight?

The day before I leave the office, I say goodbye to my staff. Daud knocks on the door and takes a seat as I am packing up. I sit down and look at him. I sense that he is emotional. "Babs, I want you to know that I was wrong then. I did not know." He shares with me that he has cancer and that he will go spend time with his wife, then before he walks out the door, he says, "Babs, you are the best boss I have ever worked for." We hug, leaving me with an intense feeling of closure.

Before I go to Argentina for three months, I stop over in the Netherlands to meet Graciela, a friend who I met in the hospital bed opposite me, when we both had our hysterectomies. She and her husband are relocating back to Argentina, and she invited me to stay with her so I can write. My auntie tells me that my mum is in hospital. She fell off her bike and hit her knee on the curb. After having to wait too long at emergency, the tissue in the swelling had ruptured, and she underwent surgeries and skin transplants. I haven't been in contact with Tonneke for years, but Graciela urges, "Go see her. Why don't you just be kind to her?"

"Well now, there is an idea," I chuckle.

I walk into her hospital room, and she says, "There you are."

"Hi, Tonneke," I say and kiss her on her forehead. Everything that had power in the past has dissipated and we start building a new relationship. I had wanted my mum to change, and what I came to understand is that I was the one who had to change.

While in Posadas, I get an email from Hedvig, the business development officer at Turquoise Mountain Foundation, Kabul. My reputation of working in Nuristan, with its specific traditional woodwork customs, had traveled. In her email she practically offers me a job as senior woodwork advisor. We get on a Skype call and my only question to her is, "How are you funded?"

Hedvig says, "All private funding." I accept the job immediately.

Chapter 30
MAGIC MOUNTAIN

Turquoise Mountain was established in 2006 by His Majesty King Charles III to revive historic areas and traditional crafts, to provide jobs, skills and a renewed sense of pride. In blending heritage buildings, education and enterprise, Turquoise Mountain has created sustainable urban regeneration that hosts the revival of artisan industries. Turquoise Mountain now works in Afghanistan, Myanmar, Saudi Arabia and Amman, having restored over 150 historic buildings, employed and trained thousands of artisans and builders, built fifty small businesses, and supported and generated over $17 million in sales of traditional crafts to international markets.

It is night in Dubai as I land here, I have a long night ahead of me, waiting for the flight to Kabul. The landing is rough, the winds between the mountains always a bit unpredictable. The airport is messy and so familiar. I am so happy to be back here! A driver holds up a sign with "Babs" and we drive to the old mud fort called the Qala No E Burdja, the fort with the nine towers. None of the internationals are here, everybody is still on Christmas holidays, or already in their rooms for the night. I am welcomed by the cook in the kitchen where it is warm.

I am shown to the room opposite the kitchen, one slightly steep staircase up. The fort is like entering a fairy tale, the unpainted mud walls with straw showing in the mix for strength; color-glazed ceramic tiles, marble floors, wooden carved doors, low frames so I have to bend down anywhere I walk through a door frame, reminding me that most people in the world are smaller than Dutch people. Elaborately embroidered dark red curtains, Afghan carpets, it feels like I stepped hundreds of years back in time. I can barely believe I am here; I have that feeling again, that my body is too small to contain this much happiness.

I am exhausted and go to my room to unpack and hopefully sleep. It is minus 28 C and the fort hasn't been heated for two weeks. The cook lights my Bukhari, a locally made stove that is compacted with sawdust. In the center is a fat, round wooden stick. He pulls it slowly out while rotating it, so the vertical hole stays intact. He rolls up a newspaper, lights it and lowers it carefully down the vertical hole the round stick created. As the wood dust smolders down, it gives ambient heat for a prolonged time but is not really the means to heat up a room in this cold. It is also an incomplete combustion system. As the cook puts the lid back on the Bukhari, the room is already filled with thick smoke. The air in the room is heavy and my eyes are prickling, breathing gives a sharp sense in my lungs. I am frozen and keep all my clothes on and get under the blankets. I am cold to my bones. I try to get warm in the thick blankets, but it feels like my butt is freezing to the bed. Luckily, I have the down sleeping bag from my mum with me that I didn't want to bring, but she insisted. I am pulling it out, zip myself in it and roll myself underneath the blankets. It probably saves my life, and I finally fall asleep.

I enter the kitchen through the low doorframe and find some colleagues at the large table. "Good morning, I am Babs."

"We are expecting you, hi I am Rory, welcome to Turquoise Mountain, this is Shoshana, and this is Andrzej, but we call him Pod." Smiles, a warm welcome and coffee. Thank God the kitchen has a very low ceiling and is warm. Rory says, "The others will come back from holidays in the next days. Pod is your colleague in woodwork, and he'll show you around." Rory is a scrawny, young man, hair kind of wild on his head, his accent heavy British, dressed in Afghan clothing and has the presence and stature of a person from a different era, so he is quite well-placed here in the fort.

Pod and I walk out the door, through the garden to the new wood workshop. He lights up a cigarette and offers me one. The smell of wood and workshops has such a historical connection for me. It calls for a smoke. With all the smoke we inhale from the bukharis, I might as well enjoy it. As we inhale the smoke and walk around, Pod shares, "Graham built it with rammed earth, and we are just opening it for the woodwork school." Pod is a Polish guy, perhaps ten years older than me, and we instantly like each other. He is funny and quirky, knows a ton. We don't finish the cigarettes; it is too cold. We enter the workshop, and as we walk through the different levels and spaces. He introduces the students and masters to me.

"There is some tension with one of the masters, but you'll see at the end of the day when we have a week closing," he says. It is Thursday and tomorrow is Jumaat, the holy day. It is mid-afternoon and all the students and masters assemble for the week closing. Pod welcomes me to the meeting and defers to the Masters to give a brief work update for the past week and to share what the plans are for next week.

It is Naseer's turn, a stunningly beautiful, young man, the master carver in classic and floral carving. He does not look very pleased and expresses his complaints about his position, the tensions in the department with the head of school, and ends with, "If this doesn't change, then I will quit."

It sounds like a threat, and I am rather shocked that he expresses this in front of the students. It feels like a management issue. Also, Pod does not respond to which I am surprised. Pod and I walk back to the kitchen and Pod says, "It is a shame we will lose him, he just doesn't gel with the team." I think for a second and ask, "Would you let me have a talk with him? I am new here and it seems there is nothing to lose." Pod seems relieved that I offer.

Saturday morning, everybody is back and with Muhammad Ullah, the translator, we meet with Naseer in a separate room. "A salaam alaykum, Naseer, so nice to meet you."

"Waalaykum salaam, Babs."

He isn't quite sure why he is here, so I start, "I heard you express some concerns in the meeting last Thursday, and I would like to hear more, so I can see how we can find a way to keep you with us here. I hear you are an incredible Master. I am here to listen to your concerns."

Naseer moves forward on his chair and launches in, clearly frustrated by the whole situation and happy to let it out. "Yes, the head of th—" I cut him off.

I lean forward and say with a determined voice, "I am here to listen, but if you ever express your concerns about management in front of the students again, I will fire your ass in a second." He is a bit jarred, shifts on his chair but is focused on what I say. "You and I can work together, and I am here to make sure you can do your work, but what you pulled last Thursday is completely unacceptable." He looks at me, his eyes show an opening. I continue, "I get it, I have lived in Afghanistan for a while, and I understand that you are a Panshiri, yes? I can tell. You encounter problems from the Pashtuns, yes?"

Nail on the head, he sits right up, looks at me and says, "Yes, you understand?"

"Yes," I reply, "but we need to work together. I can be the buffer between you and the head of the school. He is the one putting you down?" That guy, who, frankly, irritated me instantly upon meeting him. He is one of these guys that uses his rank to power over others. Quite arrogant and condescending. I have Naseer's attention full on, and I continue, "What if…you get your own workshop, maybe in that small building in the garden? Separate from the school, you get to manage your own classic carving department?"

266

Naseer smiles. "Babs, that would be so good."

I smile and say, "Anything that comes up, you come to me, you do not directly engage with him or the others, you'll have your own domain."

Pod is so happy, and Rory gives me the go-ahead to arrange what I see fit to make it work. Naseer and I enter the little building in the garden, which is dusty and filled with garbage. The door hangs off its hinges. We take stuff out, clean the space, fix the door, and make some drawings for the work benches that we need there. I take the drawings to the wood school and with the carpenters, we make a cut list to build the benches.

Naseer has a position, his own students, and we develop his curriculum together. There is something really special about Naseer as if I have known him my whole life. He reminds me of my dad. I've only been here a few days, but it feels like months, I feel a deep sense of belonging here.

Mohammad is a big guy for his sixteen years. He has a good heart but is clumsy and a bit unhinged. He does things before he thinks, which is dangerous in a woodshop. I work with him and give him a place where he can learn, feel seen and acknowledged. He is so strong, and I put him in charge of cutting the big logs on the old cast iron band saw outside. The machine is a beast and needs care. He thrives with the responsibilities while working on my side—he is not the dumb guy anymore who they make fun of; now they need to work with him to get their wood supply in the school.

I have a shower after days of frozen pipes. The water from the first rinse of washing my hair is dark grey and I do two more rinses.

Pod and I really get on well, he has the most brilliant ideas to build rocket stoves, with the chimney under the classroom floor, so it heats as it leaves warmth on the floor before it exits the chimney. We build the stoves and smoke together and build work benches, tool boards on the wall, sort the wood stacks outside, source raw timber, build kilns to season the timber, teach classes and start sourcing the machines for the machine room in the wood workshop and I build the curricula.

The old Afghan Masters transfer their skills and knowledge to their students. The Jali Master is well over eighty years old and has an apprentice who has the talent and dedication to become a Master for sure. The Nuristani Master brought his son from Nuristan who, at his young age, is already an exceptional carver, and then there is Naseer, barely thirty, who has trained ten years in Iran and is a world-class carver and designer. It is such a delight to see him handle his tools, work with his students and design and carve the architectural pieces that go into the restoration of Murad Khane, the neighborhood where we work to restore the old caravanserai to become the calligraphy and miniature painting school. Murad Khane is half an hour drive through the heart of Kabul, depending on traffic. There are more Masters in the fort, running their classes, but they are in ceramics, glazing, calligraphy, and miniature painting.

Rory storms in excited. "The Afghan ambassador to Japan is coming today. Ambassador Haroon will be here with his deputy, and they want us to build the complete library for the new Afghan Embassy in Tokyo! Babs, that one is yours, can you give them a tour and go over their ideas for the design?" And he storms out again. *Wow, what?* My colleagues look at me and smile. I love my colleagues; this is such a beautiful environment to work in. Most of them are young, super bright and kind. Pod and I are the oldest, together with the couple of Americans who are engaged with the ceramic section, but I don't have much to do with them, and that feels right.

Haroon is a lovely man, highly distinguished, immaculately dressed and behaved, as is his deputy. I greet them at the door and take them to the kitchen, then on a tour through the woodwork school and finally, the meeting room where we set up for them to share what they imagine this to be. After an hour, he asks, "Babs, can you please design this for us? It is going to be a highly visible piece, and with what Rory told me about you, I want you to design it."

We end up building three cubic meters of walnut, doors, columns, a huge entry door and panels, all elaborately carved and fitted with Jali screens, the intricate lattice work young apprentice Masoud is already so good at. Naseer and I work together on the columns and the massive solid entry doors.

The practice in Afghanistan is to just cut an old walnut tree and let it lay there for ten or more years. Pod and I identify and bring a few of these old logs, completely cracked, because they were not cut in planks to season them properly. It is so sad to see these majestic trees now nearly useless because there is not one big piece of walnut that we can salvage from them. Muhammad and I cut them in long and thin pieces, then stack them in the kiln to stabilize the relative humidity inside the timber. In order to make a 6cm thick walnut door, I design a special way of laminating the door, so we can make two massive walnut doors (each 60x210cm), built from the long, thin pieces we were able to retrieve from the old trees. Naseer carves both sides of the doors while we build the monumental frames to hold the doors.

The air humidity in Kabul is around 15% and in Tokyo around 75%, so we have a massive challenge. Pod and I figure out a way to increase the humidity. We put up a large plastic sheet, completely sealing half of the workshop off, covering the walls with burlap, and we task Zia to boil water three times a day and throw it up the walls, steam up the space. We call it Little Tokyo. All the wood that goes in the commission for Tokyo is stored there. Only when we work on a specific piece, it is taken out of Little Tokyo but put back at night. This way, all the pieces are seasoned and acclimatized for when they'll be installed in Tokyo. It is a mega-complicated project with a lot of risk and excitement. The team is super stoked to work on such a prestigious commission. Woodworkers are not regarded very well, no

269

status as poor people do the woodwork, but working on a commission like this makes them feel that they matter, that their work is respected. They all grow a few centimeters in these months, walk more straight up, engage easier. It is spectacular to witness them grow and take responsibilities and pride in what they do.

Another visitor arrives and Pod gets his project to work on. We are asked to build the Prince's Suite in the Connaught Hotel in London. Guy Oliver arrives. He works for the Prince's Charities, is the interior designer for the royal family and now in charge to pull this commission off. Pod and I organize from start to finish. Naseer designs the headboard for the majestic bed, the wainscotting and the built-in window seat, cabinets, large jali screens in the doors, and spectacular Nuristani carved panels.

In the mornings, Zabi, Anna and Helen go horseback riding behind the old Olympic stadium, notorious for torturing and stoning of women during the Taliban years. Zabi is an Afghan-German and one of the architects in Murad Khane; Anna is one of these super bright, young people who is on a trajectory to be in the White House someday; Helen is French and works with the research team. It is still cold, but I decide to join, see if I still have it, as it's been years since I sat on a horse. The stadium is a grim place, but the stables are on the outside, like nests in the wall. Young Hazara men care for the horses, they sleep with the horses in the stables.

On this nippy morning, the director of the Buzkashi games comes to meet us. He has watched us ride and approaches me. "You, you are tall, you will do Buzkashi," he states. "There is a woman from Badghis who is also tall, her name is Sabera, and she will be here for Now Roz (Afghan New Year), playing for team Badghis, you will play for my team Kabul."

Women do not play Buzkashi, it is rough and wild, but this feels like an honour. He teaches me to flick my left leg behind the saddle, grab the manes with my left hand, pull my right leg up against the belly of

270

the horse, throw my body down the right side of the horse, and while hanging upside down from the horse, grab a sand-filled burlap bag from the ground. It is a sand-filled burlap bag for practice; during a real game, this is a dead calf's torso, beheaded and legs chopped off, which has been put in cold water for a few days, so it is slippery as decay has set in. Hard to pick up and heavy! I join a few times, but the horses are not responsive due to pulling too hard over the years. They are used to rough horsemanship, and that is not my style of being with a horse.

I often go on visits to Jalalabad and see Qader and Gul as often as I can. With Turquois Mountain, there are no crazy travel restrictions.

Charles and Tilo, two of the seven gay men I know in Vancouver, come to visit Kabul. Charles is writing an article for *The Walrus* magazine, and Tilo is a curious photographer. Charles asks me how I figure I will find a girlfriend here. He tells me about superdyke.com, a website for dating and events for lesbians in Vancouver. I look at him, chuckle and say, "Charles, that is nothing for me, I don't do online dating stuff, besides…I am in Afghanistan and working!"

It's late and I am back in my room in the tower. *Oh, what the heck, I can at least look at the site? It is hilarious, superdyke.com?!* I laugh and see that there is a lot more than just dating. I decide to be bold and create a quick profile. The header reads, "dyke, living in Afghanistan." I go to sleep. The next morning, there is a message, sent just two hours after I posted it. It reads, "I live in Richmond, but my parents are from the old country where you are." Thank you, superdyke.com!

I go on a short holiday to Canada and fall in love. Back in Kabul, I stop smoking and drinking, am in love so hard I can barely fathom. I am floating. We speak for hours on Skype, through my nights, as I am halfway around the world. I don't sleep much, as am drunk on love.

271

It is 6:00 a.m., and I am entering the hammam for my morning ritual. It is a beautiful traditional hammam, with an entry room and the domed bathing space behind it. The water is heated in the storage space behind the wall, with a fire under the basin. In the hammam there are two tabs, one with cold and one with the hot water. The room is steamy from the hot basin. I take a bowl and fill it with hot water, throw water on my body with a cup while I sit on the smooth adobe floor. Shoshana has put a rowing machine here for anyone to use. Now that the spring is on its way, it's time. I stopped smoking again, eat healthier and no more alcohol. Instead, I row an hour each morning and take a hot bath.

I walk back to my room and sense something disturbing, people are walking faster, are worried about something clearly. I see Pod. "Pod, what is going on?" Pod's face scares me. He is grey. "There has been an accident. Anna fell of her horse, and it is not good. It's not good, Babs. Helen is with her, but it is bad, Babs." I rush to my room to get dressed and go back into the courtyard.

All the staff is gathered in the courtyard, everyone worried sick. Helen calls and tells Shoshana that Anna tried to cross the road to the field, but her horse bucked when a taxi swirled around her, and she fell off, head down, crushing her head into her ribcage. I am nauseated by the image, knowing the setting at the stadium.

Helen is trying to get her to a hospital. Zabi is on his way from Murad Khane to see how he can help. It is a frantic half hour or so, we don't know much, only that it is bad. Rory receives a call. "Anna has died." He looks defeated. A wave of silence and utter disbelief ripples through the courtyard. People cry, walk while wailing, some fall on their knees, the utter shockwave that crashes down in each of us. A devastating feeling. Everything turns dark. Anna was twenty-four years old and a bright light, with wicked humor and endless love for her work here, for her staff, for this country.

How on earth do you tell parents that their daughter has died?

The evening before Anna died, Thalia, Anna, the other Anna and I sat in the tower room, and sung songs together, did harmonies. Anna loved singing. Her parents are here for the celebration of her life, and to take her body back home with them. It is heartbreaking and gut-wrenching. They want to get to know Anna's colleagues and we all share stories of Anna's life here in the Qala, how loved she was, the jokes she made, and how loud she was as a person. We take them up in the tower room and sing with them, as we share our songs and stories. We plant a tree and hold ceremonies together. This team is able to emit so much love and grace, arms around her parents as we cradle them through the most devastating days of their lives.

I hear rumors that Rory is approached by USAID to accept funding from USAID and CIDA. The ambassadors come to the fort, and Rory asks me to follow them to the wood workshop, so I can give them a tour of what we have established here. I walk behind them and hear the U.S. ambassador say, "Rory, I hope you understand that by accepting our money, you will, when speaking publicly, support our activities here in Afghanistan." It's crushing to hear. I have to leave. Due to the funding changes and the increasingly violent environment in Kabul, I feel forced to quit Turquois Mountain, which breaks my heart. It is a dream job, but I just cannot work with USAID money again.

PART III.
JUST BE

Chapter 31

LOVE OR ADDICTION?

I move to Vancouver, in Canada, a huge leap. I have nothing here except for this woman I am madly in love with, and the awareness that I can simply not fathom going back to the Netherlands after ten years of international work. I left the Netherlands for a reason, and that reason still stands. It is too small and the mindset of people too narrow, judgmental like my mum; it suffocates me.

So here I am in a country I barely know, have no family or friends here except for seven gay men I know from previous visits. We joke that I am like Snow White with the seven gay men, and a real weird Snow White at that! This relationship holds all the promises for settling in Canada, I lay my emotional weight in it. From inception, I make the relationship the reason I am here, I put her under the pressure while she keeps giving me the message that she wants to go slow, build slowly, but in my anxiety of being new here, I force a faster speed. I do not listen to her; I cannot hear her.

I move in with Tilo, one of the seven gay men. He has a basement, which becomes my landing place. I arrange my work permit and find a job as senior installation supervisor, the first step towards my permanent residency. I need a car for the job and buy "Saradja" (1995 Toyota Corolla station wagon).

The aftermath of the last ten years overseas, the stress, bad food, dangerous situations, no sleep, always work under pressure, always in environments where everybody speaks another language, no safety, no security starts surfacing, but I am rather oblivious to it all.

For me, this has all become so normal that I have no idea how sick I really am. The pressure I put on the relationship, the ghosts I live with, my incoherent and incongruent actions and behavior results in her breaking up with me, over and over again, in attempts to get me to hear what she is saying to me. I cannot hear her; I am too consumed by all the cropped-up emotions of the last ten years.

In Saradja, I feel safe, no one hears me, this car is my refuge, a place to cry, scream and sing at the top of my lungs. When she breaks up with me, it breaks my heart like nothing or no one else ever has managed before. I walk out the door of Tilo's basement and walk, tears flowing. I can't catch my breath, my heart hurts, my whole chest is tight as I walk and walk. I have no awareness about where I walk, who can see me and whether they care. I walk hours and hours, day in day out, I don't know what else to do, I feel so lost! The only thing that can save me is if she responds to my texts and agrees to meet again.

2010

I go back to Afghanistan for three months, no job, no agency. I stay with Gul and his family in Jalalabad, and I do my ceremony at Shamsul's house in Kabul to officially become Muslim. I meet Qader for the last time, her body tormented by a series of transient ischemic attacks, she is so skinny now, seems a foot smaller even. I sit next to her on the wooden frame bed, holding her. I love this woman so much, she has taught me what love is. I say, "Qader, I am Muslim now." Gul translates. Her whole face lights up, her brilliant eyes look at me, her toothless mouth opens from joy. I hold her as she says, "Now, I can die without worry, now I know you are safe."

A few months after I am back, I move to a one-bedroom apartment, not too far from Tilo's house, unpack my Afghan carpets, the wood-carved panels I brought from Turquoise Mountain, my bassoon, some tools that arrived from the Netherlands where I had them stored. For the first time in many years, I can create my own space, my home again, am not living out of a suitcase. If I create a home, it may help our relationship too, but it is not the things I do or organize; it is me she objects to because I am messed up. I do not see it.

I get a text from Gul that Qader has passed. She is free, I can feel her.

One night, I sit on the toilet and poop out a long worm. I have the presence of mind to fish it out of the bowl and put it in a plastic container. As soon as I wake up, I am on my way to the tropical section in the hospital, with the container.

The doctor looks at the 8" long worm and is really excited; he's never seen this one before. He asks me where I have lived to contract this. He weighs me and tells me to go do a blood test for deficiencies. I had lost a lot of weight and as it turns out, I am quite malnourished. The medication causes an exodus of impressive proportion.

A few months later, I am on the toilet, and something feels strange, a huge amount of blood comes out with my poop. During the colonoscopy, I watch the camera go through my colon, it feels like a Dr. Who movie. A big polyp shows up, I witness how the instrument removes it, I am fascinated that this happens inside of me. The polyp is sent for biopsy. It's a week later and I get a call, with "sorry for the bad news, but your biopsy shows aggressive cancer." I need to come in because it could have spread to my lymph nodes. My colon looked so beautiful pink and clean, except for the polyp. I am forty-five years old, the exact age of my father when he died of cancer, nice reminder of life. The doctor had forgotten to tattoo the location so he proposes that I have three feet of my colon removed to make sure that no lymph node can be a spreader. It seems like a ridiculous proposition, and I ask, "Would you suggest this for yourself or are you just suggesting it out of liability reasons?"

He says, "I would never have that done."

"Thank you for your honesty," I say, and I leave to never come back.

I am tinkering with pieces of cardboard and metal wire to mockups for the walking aid I envisioned after my mum's comment, "over my dead body I'll ever use one of those." I research what the demographics are, how many people need walking aids and how many are not using something because they are like my mum, "over their dead body", which means they are at the risk of falling. Falls, as I find out, are one of the biggest reasons for injuries and resulting decline, dependency on the medical system and reduced quality of life. I am finding disturbing numbers of 25% of us living with disabilities, 15% of our population with disabilities that relate to mobility. These are massive numbers, yet all the assistive devices seem to be technical solutions for a 'body with a problem' and definitely not designed for the user experience.

I also realize that this is the largest so-called minority in our society. Why don't we hear more about how inaccessible our society is? When I worked at the school for the Deaf in Rongo Kenya in 1999, I noticed a girl behind the door in a house of a friend in town and found out she was deaf with a few more disabilities. She lived behind the door, so the family did not have the shame of the disabled kid. She was slowly dying as no one paid attention to her. You would think that does not happen here, in our so well-educated and developed country. Why are so many people completely isolated at home? My awareness grew about how people with disabilities are not disabled by their bodies but disabled by society. Society disables and labels people. "Give people a label, so you can dehumanize them," said Martin Luther King Jr.

I often think back of the music weeks, where the kids with disabilities were not more or less than the rest; we all made music, sung, danced, and we were our own unique selves. The physical stuff of our bodies did not define us. In these reflections, I become more aware about—and find the language for—how this Western world thrives on dividing us all, and the most effective way to do that is to make our external characteristics to emphasize our differences and divide us. The color of our skin, the gender identifiers, the way we move, all things we *have*, not who we *are* and choose to be. My grandma talked about this often—don't think you are hot shit because you happen to have a white skin in this white privileged world. She shared these sentiments with me in her kitchen or working in the garden; the intergenerational passing of wisdom to prepare me for life. When I decide to be a *kind* person, and be kind to everybody, regardless of their external characteristics, that is who I choose to be. And make no mistake; it is not an easy feat. In this world, it is hard to be kind in all my actions. With every purchase I make, I choose which company I support. In this capitalistic system that only thrives when we buy, when we are consumers, we are ultimately in charge of what is on the shelves of the supermarkets. As long as we buy processed food that poisons us, the companies that produce it are making profits.

The gravity of her words is always with me and has created my view on the world through these lenses, early lessons in systems thinking. My mum often refers to my grandma's wisdoms as "stories from the cold earth".

My menopause is brutal. I feel extreme agitation, personality changes, and I have uncontrollable outbursts of anger. I survey my bank account and realize I do not have enough to pay next month's rent. *Shit, I have to find a job and fast.* I scan Craigslist and see an ad for a senior project manager at a glass studio. I send them an email with my résumé attached, and the text reads: "I attached my résumé for the job of senior manager as advertised on Craigslist. If that piques your interest, please call me." My résumé has grown into a document that reflects a tumultuous professional history. Thankfully, I get a call the same day.

I now work at this glass studio to do a special project, unprecedentedly large for them, hence they hired an outsider to manage the project. The project is to design, produce, quality control, ship and oversee the installation of $17M worth of art glass panels for the sterile corridors and balustrades at the new airport in Doha, Qatar. I am plagued by my menopausal moods and relationship stress, broken heart, madness I do not have any perspective on. I do my own thing in the office. I come in early to catch the contractors in Doha for meetings and tell my colleagues that when I ask them to go away, they should not question it but come back in twenty minutes. I feel so out of control, and the madness of the huge project requirements replacing the hyper focus from the relationship to work.

As a symptom of my hormonal crap from the menopause, my breasts start growing bigger. The left grows faster than the right. I already dislike them, and now I truly start hating them. I have vivid visions of removing them, cutting them off. I hate my whole body, as it is burdened by these two major obstructions that seem to be in my face every moment of the day, adding to the depression I am sliding into.

We are not equipped to deal with the triggers that come with the intensity of the love, the intensity of the violent menopauses we both experience. Apparently after a hysterectomy, the menopause is more violent. They call this a surgical menopause. Why do we never hear about this? My madness and stress levels with added menopause affect the relationship that is turning into being rather abusive. I do not recognize myself but am not leaving. I have convinced myself that this relationship is all I have and that I cannot live without her.

Is it love or an addiction?

A random doctor in the walk-in clinic prescribes anti-depressants but not without my commitment to see a psychologist. After a year, my psychologist says, "You don't see it, hey?" "What?" I ask. He says, "You are addicted." I am stunned, I don't smoke, do drugs, or drink alcohol. "What do you mean?" "You are addicted to adrenaline. Canada, in contrast to the volatile situations you lived in for ten years, is so boring that you need the drama of a dysfunctional relationship to get your fix. Ever heard of PTSD?" What? I did not suffer major trauma! He explains how the accumulation over years of working in intense environments, bombings, dangerous road trips, exposed to very unusual events, stress and incidents, has a toll. A steep price on my wellbeing.

The unwinding from the relationship is excruciating, and it dwindles me deeper into depression and sadness. I find a tiny garden suite in Richmond, only $700 a month, the only thing I can afford. I am isolated and rarely come outside other than to go to the store and get my basics. I turn to more antidepressants and lots of alcohol, and do not even open the blinds.

I sleep in the walk-in cabinet, so I can use the small bedroom as my workshop where I make the first real mockups for the walk-assist I imagine. My mum calls me more than once a day. She senses my miserable decline. She stays on the line, sometimes we talk, sometimes it is just an open line, as I am making coffee, tinkering around, as if she is with me in my room.

I create some mockups from wood and get excited about the mobility concept. In the darkest hours, thank God for creativity. It brews something measurable, generates reasons for being here when I don't feel grounded in anything else.

I need to find someone who can weld! I find Toby who has a three-men workshop where they develop and do small production of adaptive and assistive devices. I need more time to "play" with Toby, so I quit my job. The project is close to completion anyway, they do not need me to finish it up. But I also need more money since my resources are quickly exhausted with the money I pay Toby to design the conceptual prototypes. I need to find investors, but I have no fucking clue what to do, how to start a company…I don't even know what a share in a company is! I go to meet-ups, randomly attending networking events that look interesting, about marketing, social media, incorporating, patents, legal and finance. I meet people and learn copious amounts of what it means to build a company.

I am on my way to the Netherlands to visit my mum for Christmas and New Year's, as she is insistent I come home for the holidays. She has been dead worried about me dying. Well, Prototype 1 is ready just in time to show her what her cheeky words inspired, and I bring it along.

Tom and Barbara, my mum's friends, come around for coffee. Tom wants to try it after I proudly show this first functional prototype. We go outside and he gets on it, flips his cap around and leans forward. He starts running with it and yells, "Ooooh, I have not run for over twenty years." Tom is in his early eighties. I take this scene of my invention in use deeply in. *Shit, if he can run again, then this thing is more than a cool thing that even my mum would use.*

I am becoming a believer of my own creation. I am obsessed with building more conceptual prototypes. We make a total of seven prototypes, all while trying to figure out frame shape, steering, foldability and overall looks. I am adamant that the looks, the cool factor are not to be compromised by the mindset of typical engineers. "It'll be cheaper when you make them straight pipes." I have so many fights and conversations in which I do not budge on my vision that it must look like a sculpture, a piece of art, so that people can be the one on the cool bike rather than being pitied or ignored.

At one of the meetups, I meet a guy who likes what I am trying to do and introduces me to a potential investor, an older gentleman. Alan, who is well beyond retirement age, agrees to function as my mentor. He shares that he wants to invest in something that makes him feel good, a social investment, and he believes in me, invests in me, he likes my views on the world and the vision I have for launching a vehicle for change. He asks me what I see as the next three stages to get to market, and what the related funding requirements are. He helps me to draft subscription agreements and proposes a few of his associates. Together, they are my first investors.

I incorporate the company in 2012. The bike, my invention, now has a name! I call it the Alinker and have a running joke—that the name, "Alink", stops with me and my two brothers because we do not have children. With Alinkers coming to market, there will be a lot of offspring with my dad's name on it. That thought makes me happy, though the Alinker is still far from being a company that has a product in the marketplace.

Toby and I build more prototypes, and the more people I meet who try them, the more I see the impact this Alinker can have. A Japanese exchange student sees me at the Public Market on Granville Island on Prototype 4 and stops me. She asks if she can try it. She is in a wheelchair with muscular dystrophy and has never walked in her adult life. She gets on it and beams, "I feel so tall, I feel so tall!" I have tears in my eyes, understanding the gravity of this moment. She continues to tell me that if she would have had something like this as a kid, she would have not deteriorated so fast—and that more than half of the people who use wheelchairs can still use their legs in some capacity, are ambulatory, but do not have the aid that allows them to keep using them while supported.

In 2015, I am introduced to Willy, the owner of Nijland, a bike manufacturer in the Netherlands who specializes in adaptive and rehab bikes. I am visiting my mum and have Prototype 7 with me. Willy loves the concept and agrees to further engineer it and make it production ready. With me back in Canada and communicating via shared files, drawings and photos, Nijland develops another seven prototypes, the actual pre-production and engineered prototypes to be manufactured.

Willy and I travel to Taiwan, where he introduces me to his manufacturing partners, and Nick and Angela become partners in the Alinker as well. I establish the quality control protocols, and we develop the tooling and moulds for the Alinker's custom parts and frame.

It is kind of ironic that I replace the need for heightened adrenaline in the realm of having PTSD, from the intensity of a dysfunctional relationship, with the intensity of a crazy big project in Doha, and then becoming an entrepreneur. I am gaining the introspectiveness into the damage the ten years international work has done and the need to heal.

As much as the Alinker is a vehicle for change in the context of a sickcare system that predominantly medicates, it becomes a parallel for myself, in need of healing, but I cannot find it in a system that constantly retraumatizes by the constructs of scarcity and fear while trying to build a company.

Potential investors tell me that I might want to consider hiring a real engineer, that I should look for a new CEO, a man who knows the business world. The arrogance, the amount of pushback and resistance, talking over me, telling me what to do, and complete unwillingness to hear what I am actually talking about, teaches me a new level of the constructs of this patriarchal society. I say no to millions in funds that I desperately need, but I cannot engage with the men offering it.

What deep conditioning people in our Western society have been continuously subjected to. I become hyper-aware how different I am, because the conditioning of the typical female, or typical male, never rubbed off on me because it does not apply to me. I had to invent myself. Who am I in this context, in this world? Who do I want to be? A question that I continue to ask myself every day, because it is not a state, a one-time decision. I choose to be a kind person, which means that every decision I make, for every purchase I do, I ask myself, is this a kind action? Is this purchase supporting companies with kind practices? Kind to our mother earth, kind to all living beings?

Through my lens of spending years living and working with the local people in non-Western countries, I have formed a clear perspective on our Western society. I see our world here not as a culture, but as an economic model in which we are conditioned to be consumers. Man-woman-kids-cornerstone of society, now we are the customer profile to market to. A capitalistic system needs consumers to exist. It needs us to be ultra consumers to grow and grow. Growth at the expense of people and environment, growth for the sake of growth and the benefit and greed of a few. In order to sell products to people, they need to know who you are talking to. I must learn this for the Alinker. Who are my customers, and how do I reach them with what I say? What do they want / need to hear?

This is not a culture but a binary construct, a marketing model, the cornerstone of society, the construct to indoctrinate us to be super consumers.

Living in non-Western countries, I learned that only the capitalistic countries have an exclusively binary construct. In all countries I lived in, there were cultural occurrences of gender and role fluidity.

This "cornerstone of society" customer profile seems to work really well. This system is not broken, make no mistake. Over just a few decades, we have all bought into an assumed majority and mainstream idea, which practically makes everybody who moves differently, has a non-white skin color, or is not quite that "perfect" man or woman, feel inferior and unworthy, so we have become perfect slaves to buy all the things that supposedly make us feel better. Sexism, racism and ableism are tools to put everybody who does not fit the mould, in minorities. To the point that we are now so conditioned, that we claim our minority, and self-identify willingly, with the exclusionary language that divides us all. Racism, sexism and ableism are not the problem—these are tools to keep us divided in minorities.

Through living in other countries, I have witnessed and been treated without the confining binary language, often feeling the freedom of not having language at all. The fluidity in Afghanistan, for example, goes far beyond genderfluidity, to the point that I can say that I can live my soul more freely in Afghanistan than in the Western world. These older cultures are not hyper-focused on what separates us, what divides us, but are rooted in the wealth of a community, and values embedded in the collectiveness. When you see these cultures through your own conditioned lens, you might miss the wisdom of the old cultures. Borrow someone's shoes and look again.

Similar are the issues relating the Indigenous peoples of what is now called Canada, here, this land that I am visitor to now. So often, the "problem" or "solution" is seen from a white perspective that is not compatible with a values-based culture where reciprocity, generosity and being one with nature are the foundations.

I have developed an excruciating pain in my back between my shoulder blades. The stress of constantly doing things I don't know, making it up as I go, spending money I do not have, builds up and my body suffers. A friend introduces me to a chiropractor who is also an energy worker. I walk into his office, and he barely looks at me. He says, "Sit down and don't tell me anything." He moves his chair in front of me, closes his eyes and starts moving his hands through space, as if he is trying catch things. He moans, makes other sounds, and then he looks up, right at me. "No wonder you have such a pain in your back, you carry a huge responsibility on your shoulders." I think, *okay, great, so now you can crack me, and problem solved*! Instead, he says, "But it is good. I don't know what you are working on, but I see four people who work through you. Four people who were very close to you, and all passed too young. They were not done yet, and they complete their work through you." I am stunned, but immediately know which four people he talks about. My dad, my granddad, Vilja and Lidy.

He is quiet for a while, as I am waiting for him to direct me to the table to get a treatment. He says thoughtfully, "All you need to do is trust, you need to do the work in this realm, but whatever you do, know that it is guided from the beyond. Just deeply trust that what you are working on wants and needs to be here."

He gets up and thanks me for my visit. I am outside his office utterly confused. I sit down in my car, and breathe deeply in and out, and in and out. I let his words sink in. I feel the presence of these four people who I love so deeply. Guides, my guides! I breathe again and as I breathe out, I feel this peace entering. The pain in my back disappears and to date, has never come back.

I launch Alinker with a presales crowdfunding campaign the Netherlands first. It is a great country to test a new product, not because Dutch people are so progressive, but if you can sell in the Netherlands, you'll be successful everywhere. In 2016, I receive a loan from a local fund of euro200K that allows me to pay for the first container so I can fulfill the orders of the presales campaign. I am approached by a slick business guy who promises me the world but turns out to be useless and damaging. Every time I encounter misalignment with people who want to be involved, I get deeper into the belief that I should do it all by myself. It takes time to find out who I can trust and who is aligned with me. It's exhausting!

In April 2016, we launch a pre-order crowdfunding campaign for North America. I am part of the accelerator program at University of British Columbia for a year, and I feel myself slowly coming out of the dark space, more and more motivated by seeing and envisioning what the impact of the Alinker is. As much as it nearly killed me, it kept me alive.

TEDxEastVan offers me a spot in their next annual event. I do not like public speaking, but this can be a good place to share what I see and why I started calling the Alinker a vehicle for change. I must accept that with being a CEO to a company, I will be a public figure.

Accept, be in service of things bigger than me, and move on. During my talk, I reframe healthcare as our "sickcare" system, and I can hear an *Aha!* moment ripple through the audience. Changing language, investigating words, questioning the words we use, creates awareness and a starting point to decolonize ourselves.

When we question the word healthcare, and call it for what it is, a sickcare system, reactive to sickness, then we can turn around and ask ourselves what health actually is, without staring at the constructs of the "problem." We need a sickcare system, as people do get sick, but calling it *healthcare*, we continue to stare at a problem that is not a problem. Language is powerful and if we don't question it, we are easily persuaded to be conditioned in ways disconnected from what we inherently know is truth or supports the wellbeing of all living beings on this planet.

With some practice under my toolbelt, I am ready to pitch Li Ka Shing in the Sauder School of Business Lecture Theatre. LKS is the wealthiest man in Hong Kong, who owns a lot of land in Vancouver, and keeps his relations through investing in local startups. Every year, they select six companies and miraculously, mine is in the lineup! I have ten minutes. I am the fourth presenter, and I display photos of people before they use their Alinker, and then as users. I talk about the impact it has on their lives but in this investor pitch, I do not talk about money. I am at the end of my ten minutes. I pause and look straight at Solina Chau, president of the LKS Foundation, who I recognize in the crowd, and say: "I have not talked about money, or asked you for money, because I don't even know you, I do not know if we can 'fit through the same door', so to speak." I continue to thank the audience for their attention and close. Solina Chau gets up and starts clapping demonstratively, and because she stands up, the rest of the one hundred or so attendees do, too. I score a standing ovation at an investor pitch!

As I step off stage with my Alinker, an associate of LKS walks towards me and says, "Ms Barbara, would you mind coming with me to a separate room so we can discuss our partnership?" I take a mental picture of this moment and follow her. Solina joins us, asks if we are a certified B Corp, because she treats B Corps as a charity. I am in the process, and we are nearly certified, so yes. Within minutes, she promises a $1M grant to Alinker. No strings attached other than that we should donate Alinkers to partner organizations.

Around the same time as I am at the Sauder School of Business accelerator program, a female investor expresses interest to invest. My finances are a trainwreck, as with most startup entrepreneurs. She introduces me to Tania to clean up the mess. The investment does not happen, but Tania offers to work with me as a fractal CFO. With Tania on my side, everything changes. For the first time in many years, I feel I am not alone—she is shoulder to shoulder with me.

In 2017, Vicki Saunders, the founder of SheEO, a not-for-profit organization that empowers women to achieve their economic potential, calls me on my birthday, and I am still in bed. "Congratulations Babs, you have been selected to be one of the five SheEO ventures this year!" I break out in tears and know this will change my life. From asking white guys in boardrooms for an investment, being told to bootstrap harder, as this is too much risk for them, to now entering a world of thousands of women who selected me, who want me to be successful, who believe in me and say, "What do you need?"

In March 2017, I fly to Toronto for the SheEO retreat. Vicki and I travel the whole year together, and I practically move in with her and her husband, Richard. It saves my life, yet Vicki reflects on this year with, "You moved in, you didn't even ask, and you changed my life."

Finding partner organizations to donate Alinkers to with the LKS grant is a road to discovery that the hidden agendas of charitable organizations around various diseases are a strong parallel with the hidden agendas of the donors I was faced with in Afghanistan and in the reconstruction field in general. I approach the MS Society who mentions that making Alinkers available to their members does not fit in their mandate. How? Why not? I ask what their mandate is then, and they say, "to raise funds for the cure". Once Selma Blair puts the Alinker on the stage for MS, the MS Society and chapters thereof, approach me many times with the request to donate an Alinker to them, so they could auction it off, raising funds for the cure. Not really my mandate, I answer. Isn't it insane that people run to raise for the cure, while eating hotdogs and donuts? The kind of food that inflames the body. The parallel to a food system that is funded by pharma, children's hospital cancer research funded by Coca Cola, etc. I could go on and on about how the systems work, but my focus is always to create a magnet, something that people are attracted to, so they can find a refuge from the systems that rob us from our health and agency.

It is not that long ago that we were all indigenous people. In hindsight, my grandma was a woman who instilled values in me that today, in my awareness of being an uninvited visitor on these lands currently called Canada, are similar values that relate to community, respect for all living beings, not to take more than we need, respect for earth. Inner values make you who you are, not the things you own or have (exterior characteristics). All these deep values that resonate within me are my foundation, passed on through generations.

Amid getting my business in order I need a break from Vancouver, as there is too much emotional heaviness here. Half of my body is stuck in relationship paralysis though the person is long-gone. I get to introduced to Vanessa, a friend of Vicki's. There is attraction and I decide to move to a city where Vanessa and I can be together. Montreal it is!

She calls me "BE" and it strikes me as lightning. Barbara Elisabeth is the name on my passport, but never felt mine. "BE", the initials—it is so logical! Finally, a name that feels as home! I change my name everywhere and start introducing myself as BE. It is weird how much I need to overcome to own my name. Afraid to burden people to change what they are used to. Owning my new name, the name that for the first time in my life feels mine, is a process of a couple of years.

Vanessa has no lived experience as a queer person and does not make efforts to be more fluent. I offer my writings, so she can learn about me when growing up as a queer person, but she never reads it. She claims a lot of my space for her writing though, reads to me, wants my feedback, wants to read it again, while I feel completely dismissed regarding my writing. I feel no interest from her side in getting to know me. The magic I felt in the beginning slowly starts making space for being annoyed with her. I keep hurting myself by not prioritizing what is good for me. At the same time, I enjoy not being single and meeting her family and friends, but it feels fraudulent.

With the profound experience of decades having an inner world where I live, a world without language, and a part that is not in communication with the outside world, I start recognizing that I live a double life. A piece that I share, and a deeper part where I always feel misunderstood. I have no language for how to communicate my inner experiences. The moment I give it words, it gets corrupted by the narratives.

I have had many attempts for relationships in my life; so many that I do not trust my judgment on love anymore. I have always been looking for someone who I could belong with, someone who I can be my whole self with, not understanding myself and what my own wholeness is. I've chased the wrong blueprint—that of my father and mother being utterly in love. Being in the chase of that perfect relationship, I've blamed others for me to not love me for who I am. I created this story in my head that to be loved, I always have to change. An old story, a story of my mum, for who I was always too intense, too emotional, never just good for who I was. But do I know who I am?

When I am in a lesbian relationship, I am a lesbian to my partner, but I am not. When I am with a hetero woman, I am in the role of the man, or the girlfriend like other platonic girlfriends. I lose myself in relationships. I feel there is always only a part of me present, not my whole me. Misalignment is a kind of violence against myself, nonstop self-inflicting blows.

Chapter 32

MOTHER-DAUGHTER HEALING

December 2019

My mum's cancer is back. I fly to the Netherlands to be with her, she needs care. She does not want any treatment, and just wants to "go home". Time with her zooms by, as my attention is divided. It's a critical juncture for Alinker, and in early January, I'm called to be Japan and Taiwan for the Alinker.

I am in Tokyo with my Alinker colleagues, and I want to visit the Afghan Embassy to finally see the library completed. This project had started fifteen years ago. Haroon, who was in charge, has since passed, but his deputy is now the ambassador and gives us the full tour of the library! It is spectacular. I can see only a few tiny cracks in a couple of panels, but with the challenge we had in air humidity, I am ecstatic how perfectly it held up all these years.

After Japan, I continue on to do a photo shoot with actress Selma Blair in Los Angeles. The Alinker is gaining status, and Selma praising the invention accelerates the progress. Seeing our photo on the cover of *SheEO* magazine at their summit feels like a dream. I am weightless on that stage in contrast to the Dark Ages of my breakup and subsequent depression.

After the summit, I fly back to be with my mum. It is the 11th of March; the pandemic is announced and locks down the world. "I am here, Mum, I am here till you are ready to go. I have nowhere to go but to be with you." It feels peaceful.

We talk and drive around, do the things she loves, explore the whole protocol for euthanasia, and step by step, she gets closer. We visit the doctor and start the process. My mum has been talking about euthanasia for a couple of decades and is clear on what she wants and what she definitely does not want. I admire her clarity. Admiration between us never came easy.

As her health deteriorates, I notice that she moves her boundaries, postpones a final decision. I go to my brother, Gijs's place to bring the gravestone of my dad, so their ashes can be joined there in time. Gijs asks what she is waiting for, and we have a conversation. A lot is stirred up and I go home. As I walk in the back door, my mum watches TV and I join her for a cup of tea before bed.

The next morning, we meet in the kitchen as usual, and I ask her, "What are you waiting for? There are two possible dramatic medical events that can happen, the things you want to avoid. You already told me that you do not want me to call an ambulance, so by waiting, you are putting yourself in a position you wanted to avoid, and me in a situation of risk to see my mum bleed out or suffocate to death because I cannot call an ambulance." We talk honestly and realistic. She says she is waiting because she really enjoys having me around and not being alone. The conversation is soft, and we are more connected, we are in this together.

On the 16th of April, she passes, with us there. I am holding her hand, the doctor doing the injections. She is so ready. "I love you all," she says, and it all feels peaceful. When it is time to maybe wash her body, cover her, sing to her, pray with her, be present, mourn, wale, cry, be quiet, I feel awkward, because there is no script. I realize in that moment that the traditions and rituals people in various cultures and religions have are crucial because in this moment, I need the guidance. I long for the ease of rituals now, to know what to do in this moment. In the absence of tradition, I feel clumsy, lost. I feel the poverty of our system that avoids death, stripping all traditions that tend to death, celebrate death and the life of the deceased. The very reason I left the Netherlands so long ago.

Chapter 33
ONE TRUE LOVE

May 2020

I am back in Toronto, in quarantine in Vicki's basement. Vanessa is in our place in Montreal where I simply never return. My breasts have been growing bigger after menopause and have become increasingly more unbearable. The dreams of chopping them off persist. Vanessa is horrified when I talk about them like that. We haven't seen each other for months, and now she wants to be involved in the process, saying, it does not only affect me, but also her in relationship with me. In my soul, I have long parted from the relationship, we just never spoke about it. The pandemic-induced separation is a surreal time in which everything has changed. I retreat more and want to be in my own experience in preparation of starting to organize surgery. I don't want to share the process. It is so personal that I do not want to feel disturbed by having to consider her feelings around it.

It is December 2020, and I enter a walk-in clinic. I enter the walk-in clinic rather apprehensively, knowing that what I am going to share with the doctor is not a usual request. The receptionist calls my name, and I walk into the room she directs me to, mumbling, "The doctor will be with you shortly." I sit down on an uncomfortable chair in a sterile environment with an examination bed and a litany of supplies for medical exams of all kinds.

My mind fabricates different opening sentences, a strategy to tell him what I want and why. I am fiddling with my hands and scanning the room like a wild animal. You know, reading all the labels, sizing up the instruments, nothing useful for what I am here to do!

A few minutes later, a young doctor walks in, mask half-concealing his beard and revealing friendly eyes. He sits down, introduces himself and inquires, "Tell me why you are here." I start uttering sentences I had not prepared in my head, but that is how they come out. I am so ready to share, I have been anticipating this moment for so long yet am so anxious. I'm afraid to be rejected again for a request I know does not fit in the medical requirements for the kind of surgery I dreamt of for decades now.

It's time to appease the dreams of removing my breasts in a healthy way. I've upset so many partners over the years, freely sharing the imagery and practical ideas. But the way I experience them is so different than how a partner wants to appreciate them. And when a partner appreciates them, I feel estranged—they enjoy something I hate.

I start talking to this young doctor. "I want to get rid of my breasts, they have never been mine and they feel as obstructions. I want a double radical mastectomy." I pause and realize how I have no filters in this moment, I don't even care what he thinks, the valve of decades has opened, and it all pours out. In previous efforts to get surgery on the radar, I have always been stopped and rejected by the medical mindset that did not have space or language for someone like me. I continue: "I don't have cancer or want to transition into a different gender, so I am not sure how to approach this. There is no language! I am fine with who I am, just that my breasts feel and have always felt like aliens and obstructions." I get a little more anxious with each sentence that rolls out. My last sentence sounds like a plea: "I just want to get rid of them!"

He has listened to me attentively, with kind eyes. He leans into me and says, "It's been a while, hey?" Tears well up and stream over my face. I am unable to control the crying...I feel seen. His kindness and understanding far beyond what he could ever understand touches me, allows me to let it flow in this moment.

He starts writing and organizing things and shares how it might not be very soon because of the pandemic and essential surgeries prevailing over elective ones. *Elective.* My need does feel crucial, life changing and not as an elective at all! Not like some cosmetic changes. How much of a choice is a surgery when the medical system has descriptions of what is a necessary surgery versus what is elective? Do I have a choice? Did I ever have a choice? These things grew on my body, and frankly, it is a bad design, to hang big things on the front, being in the way of everything! The detriment of not having surgery throughout decades of my life is unmeasurable.

The first plastic surgeon I engage only enlarges breasts. The second plastic surgeon only does radical mastectomies, but I don't have cancer, so he tells me, "I think it is a personal insult to a woman's body to remove them without a reason." I slowly get up and turn around, afraid that if I look at him, I will do some plastic surgery on his face. The arrogance of sexism. I walk out. This failed attempt nearly makes me give up. The walls of having no language for what I want are too high. But then I get an appointment at a hospital in Toronto, with the third plastic surgeon.

I walk in and am not too optimistic after the first two attempts. My name is called, "BE Alink, he is ready for you in room 4." I walk in and sit down. Seconds later, two men walk in, one older, one younger. The doctor has kind eyes and asks me to take off my shirt. He sizes up my breasts and says, "If they are bigger than size D+, we can apply for a breast reduction." I say, "But I don't want a—" He kindly interrupts. "Do you know what size you are?" I don't know. He looks closer and demonstratively says, "Minimum size D+." *This guy wants to work with me!* He continues, "Let's apply for the breast reduction and as soon as you are on my table, I'll do whatever the fuck makes you happy." He sends me to the receptionist to set a date. *Wow.* I'm elated.

This inner process is only visible to me, and it is real in so many moments throughout the day. What meets the eyes is a body with breasts, the external identifiers to determine the female sex, and limiting for that, because it forgoes on my inner experience, the person in the body.

Gender is my experience of who I am, one I had to learn existed first, then explore in the world that only had binary language. In hindsight, I invented myself in the absence of language for what I feel to be me. In our Western society, humans are conditioned to be either woman or man, identified at birth based on the genitalia, with all the attachments on behavior and role in society. The conditioning did not apply to me. I have always felt like an alien in all the available narrative that surrounded me from the moment I could think.

My experience of self is not gendered, it only becomes a requirement to be gendered in the binary construct. Identifying as non-binary would be identifying myself with a title describing what I am not. That feels so ridiculous. Isn't that the actual essence of the binary system?

The BE I invented overrules the sight of the external identifiers. BE is an identity people can experience and feel beyond external identifiers. I've infused my values in my company as well.

The Alinker company has grown, having broken even a year before the pandemic. Doing this business means I am constantly learning from all the people who consider an Alinker or change their lives because they get on one and expand their lives. I am talking with people on regular Zooms we conduct, and our conversations deepen around systemic issues as the pandemic unveils the fragility of supply chains, isolation of people, a collective experience that opens awareness about how community, food and mobility are the foundations for wellbeing and health.

I think back on my participation decades ago in the "music weeks." Disabilities were different than what we see now. The kids had cerebral palsy, spina bifida, spasticity, muscular dystrophy, and one was blind. Nowadays, we have neurological, cardiovascular and autoimmune diseases that might result in disabilities or mobility challenges, but these are rather new. They started multiplying the same time that our food changed; 90% of the chronic illnesses did not exist ninety years ago, which is related to 90% of the goods in supermarkets that did not exist ninety years ago.

The pandemic opens up awareness and willingness to look at ourselves differently. People are more accepting of the wider conversations. I can talk more and more about systemic things, and how we are the systems until we undo them in ourselves. The systems are not outside of us, we perpetuate and are the systems as long as we behave according to how we have been conditioned. We are conditioned to be consumers, so we are willingly eating the stuff that makes us sick, and then willingly do what the doctors tell us, medicating us. I start using language like "the food industry feeds the pharma industry" and it lands. People can hear it as we go through a collective experience that I am familiar with from living in situations where people just went through a war, earthquake or tsunami, collective experiences where people share similar experiences of loss, of grieve, of solidarity, of rebuilding together. Collective experiences work on everybody, whether you want it or not. I am familiar with how that feels from all my years overseas, but I realize that many people here do not see it because they can't recognize it.

We add food and community to mobility and build our narrative around these three components that constitute health. The sickcare system that I mentioned for the first time in my TEDx talk is not motivated to support our health, but since privatization happened, driven by making revenue. We start defining health as mobility, real food and community. Now we can identify that this constitutes health, but when people do not have access to it, we don't reach the people. So, we add the need for access to these factors in and build our company and community on creating access to health by

303

making Alinkers available in different ways, including an integrated platform for crowdfunding campaigns, which has become a huge motor for the community. People not only get an Alinker but also, a community of strangers who showed up when they felt no one cared for them anymore.

My language about systems, and how we are navigating them, becomes bolder during the pandemic. The Alinker becomes a vehicle for change, our community grows and the impact of using the Alinker blossoms into a reflection on what is possible when we are willing to change our narrative from "looking for comfort" to "moving through discomfort" to learn and grow, heal.

I am finding better bridging language to address the process of deconditioning, so people can hear me. We cannot change the world. The food, pharma, fossil fuel and war industries do not want to change, and if we try to change these destructive systems, we perpetuate these very systems, as we are looking at solving problems outside of ourselves. But this world is not a problem to fix. The overwhelm of assumed problems creates numbness and sensory overload, powerlessness, a sense of defeat. That is exactly how these systems thrive.

We have lost our collectiveness, we are divided, we have bought into the language of minorities, and are segmented, fragmented, we all stuck in all the shattered pieces, willingly self-identifying as "minority". But breathe for a second and remember who we are. Like my grandma said, "We are all born as naked, little babies who just want to be happy. Everything that we *have* is what we have been given, is not who we *are*."

I have reframed my language, and my world is one of a vast majority of diverse people, who happen to have different skin colors, different ways of moving and live in a wide spectrum of gender expressions, who just want to be happy. The things we have in common is that we are all mortal creatures, and vulnerable at that, and we share the experience of knowing what it feels like to be dismissed by a system that is not interested in acknowledging and supporting our vast diversity.

What we can do is change ourselves, remembering who we are, be congruent in our actions, stop buying the products from the industries that poison us, and then medicate us, making us collectively sick and dependent. What if we become more curious to who we are, decondition ourselves, decolonize ourselves, in community, become aware of the stories we tell ourselves that are taught behavior—they are not our stories—and decide who we want to be? In community, we can reflect on and support each other, create new stories in which we are worthy and valuable as every unique living being is and in community, we can be a magnet for people to be attracted to, to find refuge in, a place where people can discover themselves beyond the conditioning, and in that kindness, they can change their awareness and practices as well. This is developing and growing in the Alinker community. A woman calls me and apologizes for not having a disability, but can she please be part of our community. *That!*

The essence of my mantra, "I dream of a world where the dismissed people of today become the leaders to tomorrow", starts manifesting in our community. Dismissed people have been confronted with life and have in fact, learned a bit more about life, they had to figure out who they are in a system that likes to discard them because they are "uncomfortable". Like I had to invent myself, so do people who are confronted with a disability and find themselves in a world that no longer works for them. We have more in common than we think when we are willing to go beyond our external characteristics for the minorities we supposedly represent.

The only woman that I have ever felt physically in flow with, regardless of the confrontations, triggers, unprecedented events of violent menopauses mixed with PTSD and denial, living double and hidden lives, I have never fallen out of love with, is the love of my life.

Over the years since we ended the mad relationship in 2012, I have sent occasional texts to her, letting her know I think of her, with love and tenderness. Understanding the ridiculous collision of events, in retrospect, I can see that we never had a flying chance of having a healthy relationship. Too much was colliding, and we had no tools to overcome.

In 2021, I text her again and for the first time in nine years, she responds!

We have a long text exchange that results in a deep relief. I release with a deep cry, from down in my belly.

The day the Taliban retakes Kabul, I meet her in Victoria. I tell her about the upcoming surgery. She is the only one who has never made me feel bad concerning my breasts, never made an issue about them, about me—my body was hers and I never felt any shame or discomfort during our intimacy. We walk and talk and feel an opening, it is kind and gentle. She comes up to my Airbnb and we try to stop ourselves, but the attraction is too great. She wants to enjoy my breasts one more time, and I want her to. Late at night, I walk her halfway to her home. She shares how her mum is sick and dying. We talk about the death of my mum via euthanasia, and what it meant to her to have agency over her own death.

I leave for Toronto to have the surgery on the 14th of September. A week after our reunion, she calls me at 2:00 a.m., crying. Her mum has just passed, and she does not know who else to call. Our talks about being present at my mum's death have helped her to be present with hers in healing, peace, release, love.

It is only a few days till the surgery, having been postponed from May to September due to the pandemic. I start feeling excited, it is really HAPPENING! And as I feel the surgery come closer, I also feel waves of grief well up unexpectedly. Why am I feeling grief when I am excited about the surgery? It feels like I am reliving my life in hindsight, but now with the certainty of the surgery, a way out. I spent decades of longing to get rid of my breasts. I spent many relationships in which I rejected partners, denying them access to my body, pushing their hands away. In relationships I was lost, feeling that I had to change, that I was not loved for who I am, always a whole part of me just present to myself, deep inside. Now I am single again and I feel less lonely than in a relationship.

I stay a month after the surgery in Toronto, after a week the drains are removed. I wake up, slowly. It is dark in my bedroom. I like the dark. I stretch my legs, keep my eyes closed. I pull the thick cotton sheets up a bit, enjoying the warmth and the fact that I do not need to rush to get up. I have built the slow mornings in my days, days filled with more and more me time. I take my time to feel my body wake up. I move my hands over my chest, and I feel my face grow into a deeply content smile. I can feel me, I can finally feel me! My body, the body I always felt was mine, but had obstructions, things that were not mine.

After some weeks of recovery, my hands stroke my chest, follow the scars, still tender. I feel the light swelling around the long scars, like two smileys side by side over my chest. I massage them a bit. Underneath the skin are some lumps that will disappear. I massage them, too, like I am massaging my body to settle into the chest I have always known to be mine. I am now BE flat!

Tania mentions that the basement apartment under her house is vacant after thirteen years, and I blurt out, "Rented!" It's not even a question. I am returning to Vancouver, in my new body and cleansed from past weights.

Tania and I go on daily walks with a coffee and time travel, brainstorm, imagine, dream about what we are in with the Alinker, the world, who we are in this crucial time on earth.

I have Spotify on and suddenly hear a song that grabs me. What is this?! Through this song, "Lost on You", I discover the music, rather the universe, of LP. Soon, I don't play anything else, her androgenous being without using any particular language resonates, her voice is unworldly. The discovery of LP is parallel with growing into my new body. She becomes the voice of this new liberated life. I see that she is on tour and buy tickets to see her in concert in Toronto, by myself. Because the tour was delayed twice due to the pandemic, tickets were in the resale and I accidentally bought a VIP ticket, not knowing what that meant.

I am on my Alinker in the lineup at 5:00 p.m., as an email to all VIP tickets holders had instructed. The people in the lineup are, unlike me, not new to the concept and share with me that we are going to be there at the soundcheck and meet LP. I zip in on my Alinker and get right upfront at the stage. She makes a comment about how she "spotted me zip in on that cool thing."

Teri, one of our Alinker users, has become a friend. She calls me out of the blue. "BE, here is a link, I think this is your cat." A cat? I don't have a life for a cat. She insists, "You deserve love, BE, this is your cat, look at her!" I look at the link and think, *this is not my cat*, then a second voice, *is she*? Teri sends a letter of recommendation to the rescue center, and soon after I get an email with the confirmation, that I can adopt Georgia. Georgia moves in and my level of happiness leaps up from a low level I did not even realize I existed at. She is a divine teacher who opens up my heart again after being shut for so long.

Since I moved to Vancouver, my old love and I have met a couple of times. I introduce her to LP, and she falls in love with her music too. She calls me and says, "I can't believe I missed her North American tour." I say nonchalantly, "Well, she is still touring in Europe, we can go to her concert in Milan." I never expected this to be a real possibility, but a few weeks later, we are flying to Europe, have VIP tickets for her concerts in Milan and Zürich. It is like a dream to travel together after years thinking we would never see each other again.

As the company grows into a vehicle for change, and we advocate for health and wellness, it guides me to be on the path to taking care of myself. I cannot talk about eating healthy and not be congruent with the things I say to others, so I join the first Eat Real to Heal cohort with Alinker users in April 2022 and find my way to caring about myself again. I lose 35 pounds, sleep better, walk straighter, my blood pressure drops from 150/115 to 120/73, my skin clears up and the feeling of being reborn continues and deepens. The more I care for myself, the kinder I show up to the Alinker community and friends. I start feeling happy again after so many years.

For decades, I have said, once I am flat, I will have an Armani jacket. I could only dream! Armani cut is not good with breasts, but now flat.... Just before we leave, I mention to a dear friend that we are going to Milan and she says, "Hey, I can get you in the special warehouse of Armani in Milan." I am flabbergasted.

The day after the LP concert, still in higher atmospheres and ecstatic from the concert, we rent a car and drive outside Milan to the special, somewhat secret warehouse. Admittedly, I buy a few more pieces, but most importantly, as I walk in, I walk straight to the jacket I have always dreamt about. The cut is spectacular, and the cashmere the softest possible. It feels like a second skin. Dreams do come true.

After eight days in which we are also intimate, she is the first (and still) only one who has been intimate with my new chest. It has also become clear that there is no future for us. At least in this life, we are not compatible. But we have healed the past.

She leaves for the airport back to Canada. "I love you."

"I love you too."

The last words we speak to each other.

I travel on to my brother and his wife's little farm in the Netherlands. Twelve years prior to this day, my mum was preparing for her passing, her cremation. She wanted to make sure she was not a burden to us after her death. She spoke with an undertaker about a wish she had. She wanted to be cremated with the remains of my dad, buried forty years prior, and she discussed this with the undertaker, a woman she became close to. The woman says, "It is quite a protocol heavy undertaking (no pun) to dig up someone's remains, and it is not likely that we can organize this at the same time as your passing." She has a proposition for my mum though. "Why don't we organize that now, then you can cremate your husband with your children now they are grownups, and then you can have his ashes at home. By the time you die, your children can then mix his and your ashes together in a place of your choosing." My mum loves the idea and shares the plan with us. We are in, except my older brother, who is fine just not attending this unique ceremony.

My mum organizes the whole event with the undertaker, and a date is set. My mum, my younger brother and I are in the crematorium and stand at the reed woven casket with the remains of my dad in it, forty years after his death. "I want to see his bones," I say out loud, and my brother and mum agree. The undertaker smiles. She has come to know us and knows we are a bit strange maybe, but true to what we feel is right. She leaves us in the room.

My brother and I open the zipper of the white lining in the casket. They had placed the dark yellow bones according to where they are in the body. The bones were dark yellow because the earth at the graveyard was quite wet, so most of the little bones were gone. I hold his jaw and touch his skull. It is so amazing to realize that these bones are the same DNA that I am made of. My mum recites a poem, and we zip the bag closed again, close the lid and call the woman back. For years, the little stone that was on the grave of my dad sat on the terrace behind my mum's house. His ashes in an urn on a shelf in the book cabinet.

After my mum's death, my younger brother had taken both urns of ashes home, so here we are, on the day we set, and surprisingly, my older brother arrives as well. The wife of my younger brother is an artist and made a little grave in their yard. We kneel with the two urns. I sit on my knees with both my hands above the opening in the ground. My brothers each empty an urn above my hands, and my father and mother's ashes are mixed as they fall into the hole in the ground. As they poor the ashes, Willem, my older brother, says, "This makes me think of 'The Big Lebowski'." We laugh. It feels light and good. They are back together after more than fifty years, at peace, healing.

May 2023

I grab the cotton bag in which all my mum's crystals are wrapped up. She had them all hanging next to each other, in her kitchen window. I have no idea why I grab the bag to take with me to this two-week writing retreat in which I will also be held through a plant medicine journey to get me into the writing, feeding me with parallel stories, insights from the other side, blocks I might have not been aware of, to free my creativity. But why am I taking this bag? It's been sitting on my shelf since I came home from her passing. Never unpacked it. Never looked in it, while it was looking at me.

In the medicine: Lisa sits on a chair at my feet. I am sad. I hear myself talk as if there is an inner-me and an outer-me, the outer-me saying things that surprise me, "I am confused, do not know what to trust."

My inner-me responds, "I do trust myself, I trust me, but I have no place here. My mum never truly saw me, why is it so hard to see a rainbow? To be the rainbow, you have to be the rainbow to be seen." I start crying, feel old, deep sadness. "My mum never held me, she never saw me." It starts hailing so hard outside, a horizon-wide, dark cloud with the sun shining from underneath, lighting up all the crystals that fall from the sky, bouncing up from the terrace, and Lisa says, "you've got to see this, you can't make this stuff up." We laugh so hard.

I put my mask back on, back in. I see crystals and rainbows and feel the sadness again. Outer-me: "The people who loved me, all left too young, I had to fend for myself, I had to figure it out." Inner-me, "But that's okay, I know who I am."

Lisa says, "Who left you, who are they?" My inner-me says, "My father, my granddad, Lidy and Vilja. I thought I was done with that, they integrated in me, and I feel close." Yes, I processed the loss of them as a grown-up woman, but I guess what I am feeling now is what the young me felt at the time they left. I cry uncontrollably.

Lisa says, "Can I hold you?" as she comes over to me.

I say, "Yes, *you* can," with emphasis on you. "You know, you see me, you can hold me." I cry while being held. I am being held; I allow myself to be held, no guilt, no feeling that I need to do something in return, I surrender to being held. That is new.

I sleep ten hours and feel light. I work out in the gym as the infrared sauna warms up. I sweat and after thirty minutes, I go back to my room and take a shower. I make some mushroom coffee and sit down, looking at the piles of paper I have printed out to bring with me here for the writing retreat. I put some music on. A random playlist of women and the first song is k.d. lang's "Bird on a Wire", the song my mum asked us to play at her cremation, two years ago this week. I never paid much attention to the lyrics, but right now, I am hearing them so clearly.

If I have been unkind

I hope that you can just let it go by

If I, if I have been untrue

I hope you know it was never to you

Like a bird on a wire

Like a drunk in a midnight choir

I have tried in my way to be free

I feel a flush of forgiveness rushing through my body. Tears in my eyes as I am smiling. Feeling her here, saying, "I love you too mum, you're good, you're free now."

The whole journey there were crystals, light breaking into rainbows. And as I unpack the bag with all the crystals, I realize that in the mornings, when the sun came through the kitchen window, her house was always filled with rainbows, the crystals breaking the light, and showering the whole room with hundreds of little rainbows.

My brother drives me to Schiphol Airport, and I fly on to PEI in eastern Canada for David and Maridel's wedding. David is Vicki's brother. I often stayed with them at the cottage at Stoney Lake after my mum's death. He had joked that if they were to get married, I would be his best man. I arrive at Charlottetown, capital of PEI. It is close to midnight and the taxi driver asks, "Are you sure you want to be here?"

I say, "Yes, of course, my friends are marrying, and I am the best man."

The taxi driver continues, "Well, just so you know, a hurricane is underway."

The wedding is postponed for a day, and overnight, we get smashed and pummeled by Fiona on the north coast of PEI. The damage is insane; only seven of the twenty cottages are still in place, though flooded. The rest is destroyed and swept inland. Hundreds of trees are snapped and uprooted. As the morning light breaks, the devastation is overwhelming. Apparently, we were close from not surviving the night as some of the twenty-eight people there for the wedding had to be saved, David wading through the 4-foot-high waves with 180Km winds. If one window in the big house had broken, it was unlikely that we would have survived.

Among hundreds of fallen trees and debris, no power or water, with the red mud all around us, washed up on the devastated compound, the wedding takes place. In my Armani jacket, I am David's best man. Family beyond bloodlines, and the sacred space of sharing such an intense experience collectively.

I stay a couple of weeks after the wedding, clearing fallen trees, cleaning up the mess, chain sawing, and staying with them so they are not alone with the aftermath. I'm in my element, dealing with a natural disaster!

Back in Vancouver I feel transformed, cleansed and whole. Since entering the world of plant medicine ceremonies, I have added morning and evening meditations to my days, and I just love the rhythm of the daily practices. I rebuild my living room and transform it to a woodwork shop. I am finally creating again, making ceremonial pieces, drums, talking sticks, a spear, an axe, flutes and other instruments. What I create comes to me in dreams, my guides, the bridges between the universes, the various realities, the gateways to our collective consciousness, the realm of abundance, where everything is available to us. *Just close your eyes.*

Creating is further healing and growing deeper in myself. You know, having a company has felt like being on a raging train that I cannot get off. I fought it for a long time, I resented the company for what it forced me to do, but since I am back in Vancouver, and have my flat chest, my daily meditations and Kundalini yoga practices, the sporadic plant medicine ceremonies, eating just plants, nothing processed, no animal products at all, I am clean, healthy and feel better than I ever have; I have embraced my role in this extraordinary company. In this company and the community we built, we are embodying and developing a new model for health, making mobility, real food and community accessible, and it is in fact, exactly the health model I needed to heal myself.

As a kid, I wanted my mum to feel how much it hurt when I hurt my knee and now, after six decades of an intensively lived life, after everything I moved through and grew from, I want you to feel what I feel. I want to share my experiences and insights, share the practices that make me feel connected and anchored in my purpose.

We do not want to change, to let go of what we know; instead, we hold on to what we know, even if it kills us.

It takes courage to set old stories free, old stories we tell ourselves, stories that we have learned, have been taught, have been indoctrinated with, and replace them with messages of love and kindness, to yourself to start with.

I want you to feel what is possible when you move through the darkness, through discomforts, through pain, through grief. I want you to feel the oneness when we close our eyes, the abundance and collectiveness, the infinity of love when we allow ourselves to be in the light.

Once we understand that everything that we anticipate in our future is merely a projection of our past experiences, we can start practicing being present and step in the light. Feelings are just feelings we can be present to. Emotions are feelings with attachments, feelings we attach a thought to, a thought based on past experiences, we create suffering. Detach, be present, feel.

The abundance and infinite love is where we are present, to our heart, to self, to each other, in this moment in time, on this precious planet, and heal.

Close your eyes

and imagine yourself

surrounded by light

close your eyes

and imagine your body

healthy and strong

breathe in deeply

expand into the third eye space

send love to all living beings

hold your breath for a few counts

and be still, feel

breathe out

be empty for a few counts

and feel our oneness

breathe in

slowly and deeply

and feel loved

you are loved

THE COVER OF THIS BOOK

February 2023

During the first plant medicine ceremony, I have my mask still on, as we have been a few hours in the medicine.

Woosh, boom, I've just fallen to the ground. I try to figure out where I am, I am looking at the ground, I sit kneeled, my back arched. I feel that I have massive wings, and I realize I'm a raven. My wings have large feathers that have all the colors of the rainbow.

I look up and there is this gigantic vulva, this enormous vagina opened right above me. It's dripping of blood on me. I've just fallen out of this dripping vulva. I don't know whose vulva it is, but it feels like a tree, a massive totem pole. As I look up, a gorgeous, weathered face high up looks down on me, an old matriarch.

I've fallen out of her vulva onto the ground and I'm noticing I have large wings and a beak. I am a raven. I inspect my wings and they're colorful, all the colors of the rainbows, and I'm sitting kneeled down looking at this dripping blood around me.

I get some words through, like the matriarch's voice talking to me. She says, "Take your mask off and write this down: You are born a raven, you are a rainbow child and you're extremely well-protected."

Fun fact: After we come out of the medicine, I ask Tania to take a picture of me sitting on my knees, arms wide, mimicking the position as I fell out of the vulva during the plant ceremony. I load the photo on my iPad and start adding the raven head and coloured wings. I decide that I want this raven rainbow inked on my chest above my scars. A few months later, the tattoo is done. Tania comments, "You still have your socks on in the photo." I have not erased them for the tattoo. We crack up laughing!

You know, just saying, my socks are important to me. So, I am always prepared to have someone knock me off my socks.

To all the people who feel I have changed their lives, please know that you saved mine through allowing me to get to know you and grow this community in which we can belong and share in kindness and heart—the place I needed to heal myself.

With all my gratitude and love, thank you!

—BE

Visit BE's website for special offers!

See exclusive, behind-the-scenes pics following BE's amazing story!

Milton Keynes UK
Ingram Content Group UK Ltd.
UKHW030624251124
3094UKWH00018B/110/J

9 798991 549820